POLITICAL PATTERNS IN TODAY'S WORLD
SECOND EDITION

POLITICAL PATTERNS IN TODAY'S WORLD

SECOND EDITION

D. W. Brogan
Professor Emeritus, Cambridge University

Douglas V. Verney
York University

HARCOURT, BRACE & WORLD, INC.
New York   Chicago   San Francisco   Atlanta

To Manning Dauer

ISBN 0-15-570711-6

Library of Congress Catalog Card Number: 68-24777

Printed in the United States of America

PREFACE TO
THE SECOND EDITION

This book was written for those who want a brief, comparative introduction to politics and society, and for students of American government who wish to compare that government with other liberal democracies and with communist systems. Until very recently, books on comparative government have had separate sections on the various countries examined. This book treats the liberal democracies—or at least four of them—together in Part One and considers three variations of the communist pattern together in Part Two.

The question of which political systems should be included in our analysis was influenced by two considerations: (1) whether the system has shown a capacity to last and (2) whether it deserves the description of "seminal." Little will be said about the systems of former colonial states, because many of them are unsettled and it is too early to discern the pattern of their development with any confidence. However, to exclude all twentieth-century systems because they have not yet shown a capacity for longevity would mean omitting the part on communism altogether. To confine the study to systems that have lasted more than one generation would mean excluding every variation of communism other than that of the Soviet Union. This would only serve to perpetuate the myth of a monolithic communism. We have therefore compromised: although in Part Two we describe the total communist pattern rather than that of the U.S.S.R. alone, we have drawn on the more limited experience of other communist states mainly for the purpose of indicating what political factors seem to be common to the communist world and what factors are peculiar to the Soviet Union.

The contents of the first edition have been updated and reorganized in this edition. Material has been added where further comparisons seemed desirable, as for example in the discussion of the social and economic policies of the four liberal democracies. Two variations—those of Yugoslavia and China—have been added to the communist pattern. In other places the contents have been streamlined somewhat by the deletion of the section on Gaullist France and by an abbreviated discussion of dictatorships. In particular, references to the Nazi and fascist forms of dictatorship have been pared, for these systems no longer seem relevant to the contemporary political scene.

In general, the substance of the text has been given a new focus in this edition. Instead of treating the two main patterns of government as challenges to each other or as political systems in collision, we have assumed that our readers will wish to consider the merits and variations of each pattern individually so that they may draw their own conclusions. The Introduction stresses the importance of the world's political heritage from Europe, and the Conclusion considers the implications of our analysis for new states.

The term "communist" is used in its broad sense, with the understanding that no Communist party has yet achieved a communist society. "Democracy," on the other hand, being a vague and misleading term, has been qualified as "liberal democracy." There are many countries where plebiscites are held and government is in a sense by the people. The addition of the term "liberal" makes "democracy" explicit, for democratic government must really depend on the consent of the governed. The liberal concepts of rule of law, freedom of speech, and emphasis on the individual are as much a part of the heritage from western Europe as democracy itself—and of course liberalism predates democracy (in the sense of universal suffrage) by many centuries.

We would like to thank Grey Hodnett of York University for his assistance in the revision of Part Two; Erwin C. Hargrove of Brown University for his helpful criticism and suggestions; the information services of France, Britain, and Sweden in New York for providing recent data for Chapter 4; and Miss Marlyn Aitken, Mrs. Helen Allen, Mrs. Diane Goodwin, and Mrs. Joan Stimers for their assistance in typing the manuscript.

D. W. Brogan
Douglas V. Verney

˙CONTENTS

PART TWO
THE COMMUNIST PATTERN
Three Variations: The Soviet Union,
Yugoslavia, China

INTRODUCTION:
The European Heritage

In the past thirty years the political map of the world has changed beyond recognition. When war broke out in Europe in 1939, there were forty-eight members of the League of Nations. In 1967 the United Nations numbered 122 states. Thus a contemporary series of books on what is now called comparative politics has to be very large if it is to do justice to every part of the globe, and it has to be constantly revised. Today there is perhaps an excessive anxiety to be up to date and to be familiar with the latest developments of the political and social situations in, say, eastern Europe or West Africa.

The student of comparative political systems has three choices. He may theorize about systems generally as Gabriel Almond and his colleagues have done;[1] or he may analyze certain features of a large number of polities after the manner of Russett, Banks and

---

[1] See, for example, Gabriel A. Almond and Sidney Verba, *The Civic Culture: Political Attitudes and Democracy in Five Nations* (Princeton: Princeton University Press, 1963); Gabriel A. Almond and James S. Coleman, eds., *The Politics of Developing Areas* (Princeton: Princeton University Press, 1960); and Gabriel A. Almond and G. B. Powell, *Comparative Politics: A Developmental Approach* (Boston: Little, Brown, 1966).

1

Textor, and Duverger;[2] or he may follow our example of asking two questions: (1) which countries have shown a capacity for stable government since the 1930's? and (2) which political systems by virtue of this capacity and their longevity have influenced other nations and justify the description "seminal"?

Five major political systems selected for treatment in this volume—the systems of Great Britain, France, the United States, the Soviet Union, and Sweden—seem to satisfy one or both of these latter criteria. Britain's political arrangements have influenced the United States and the Commonwealth and, to a lesser extent, the continent of Europe, notably Germany and the French Fifth Republic. French political ideas have influenced not only western Europe, South America, and parts of Africa, but even the communist states much more than those states realize. For the modern political world dates not from the Glorious Revolution of 1688 in England or the Declaration of Independence of 1776 but from the French Revolution of 1789.

The political systems of the United States and the Soviet Union were until recently treated by people living outside their boundaries as unique. But increasingly the American style of government, particularly its presidential executive and its separation of powers, is influencing politicians and political scientists alike, while the Soviet system, suitably modified, has been copied throughout the communist sphere of influence.

These first four influential political systems represent all the permanent members of the United Nations Security Council except Nationalist China. But in themselves they present too stark a contrast for a meaningful comparison. A study of them suggests an obvious distinction between the "Anglo-Americans" and the "Continentals." At another level of contrast there seems to be a great difference between the British constitutional monarchy with its long evolutionary tradition and the three republican systems formed after revolutions.

To prevent presenting only an oversimplified contrast, Sweden has been introduced as the fifth system. It meets the criteria both

---

[2] Bruce M. Russett and others, *World Handbook of Political and Social Indicators* (New Haven: Yale University Press, 1964); Arthur S. Banks and Robert B. Textor, eds., *A Cross-polity Survey* (Cambridge, Mass.: M.I.T. Press, 1963); Maurice Duverger, *Political Parties: Their Organization and Activity in the Modern State*, trans. Barbara and Robert North (London: Methuen, 1954).

of longevity and—as a one-time great power—of influence, at least in northern Europe. There are indications that its influence is increasing as more becomes known about its method of operation (for example, the Ombudsman). An understanding of Swedish—and Scandinavian—politics engenders a more subtle appreciation of the differences among the other systems. Sweden has its own unique political heritage, but it has been an ally of France, an admirer of Britain and the United States, and an influential neighbor of both Germany (which Sweden invaded under Gustavus II in the seventeenth century) and Russia (which some say Sweden founded and which it also invaded in the reign of Charles XII). Sweden's system lies somewhere between the "Anglo-American" and the "Continental"; its constitutional monarchy reminds us that the British monarchy is not unique, and its stable multiparty system is Continental, though not in the French style.

No communist system other than that of the Soviet Union has existed more than a couple of decades, and none can be regarded as stable and influential until the revolutionary generation has been successfully replaced. But to compare the four established liberal democracies with the Soviet Union alone does some injustice to the comparative approach, particularly since Yugoslavia and China have both demonstrated a determination to pursue their own paths of national communism. For this reason a discussion of their systems has been included in Part Two to indicate the variety of communist patterns, but their inclusion is qualified with the caution that these variations have yet to show that they can survive the deaths of Tito and Mao Tse-tung.

Some scholars have suggested that there is a new form of government to be found in the new states, or "developing areas"; some go even further and argue that all new states have something in common that distinguishes them from older systems. It is true that students have often found their training in traditional political science with its emphasis on the older democracies inadequate in dealing with the new states.[3] This is largely because they have looked at the established institutions of old societies whereas they have concentrated on the problems confronting new states. Thus they have studied British cabinet government—but only incidentally England's failure for eight hundred years to come to terms

---

[3] Harry Eckstein and David E. Apter, eds., *Comparative Politics: A Reader* (New York: Free Press, 1963), p. 25.

with Ireland; they have studied American state and local government without always recognizing the social implications of racial conflict in the South; they have studied French constitutions without considering *incivisme*[4] as a French mode of life that citizens in other countries may prefer to Anglo-American political involvement. The study of new states has clearly indicated the need to go beyond the traditional political framework and to explore the sociological and psychological attributes of nations.

Some writers have tended to treat political systems (and with them political science generally) as emerging after 1945.[5] Such a method encourages a clear-cut division in kind between established and new polities. Yet new states are in fact only passing through phases of development (and their consequences) such as established states endured in previous decades or centuries. It therefore makes more sense to study the historical context of political systems than to narrow one's focus to the post-1945 period.

The study of political systems has passed through its behavioral phase. There is now a renewed willingness to assess the merits of political systems as well as to quantify their various characteristics.[6] There is also a determination to avoid some of the naiveté that has on occasion characterized the behavioral approach—and a greater readiness to consider empirical data in the context of a nation's history, literature, law, and philosophy.

Despite the many changes in the political map of the world, there are still two main patterns of government. One is the pattern loosely termed liberal democracy, a form of government that was established in Europe and the United States. The other is communism, a pattern much more homogeneous than liberal democracy, found in the East—that is to say, in eastern Europe, the Soviet Union, and China. Liberal democracy is well established; communism is a new political form that began in 1917, when a band of revolutionaries led by Lenin seized power first in Petrograd and then throughout the whole of the decaying tsarist empire. Both creeds claim to satisfy man's deepest needs, and since 1945 the world has been witnessing a contest of wills between the great powers, as each tries to extend its philosophy and its influence over the rest of the world. Thanks to modern means of transportation

---

[4] *Incivisme* means lack of a civic sense rather than a want of patriotism.

[5] For example, Almond and Powell, *Comparative Politics*, Chapter 1.

[6] Robert Dahl, "The Evaluation of Political Systems," paper read to the American Political Science Association, New York City, September 1966.

and communication, from jet planes to Comsat, the world has never been brought closer together, yet owing to the rise of communism never has it been more deeply divided. Liberal democracy, which President Wilson thought had reached its zenith in 1918, is challenged on a worldwide scale.

We shall be concerned in this book with the fundamental patterns of politics as they offer themselves for explanation today. Chiefly we shall consider the gulf between East and West—the nature of liberal democracy and the communist alternative that is being presented to it. But we shall also examine the subdivisions in the democratic and communist worlds. It remains to be seen whether the communist states will continue to support one another. It is equally questionable whether the European liberal democracies will remain separate nation-states, each with its own form of parliamentary government. If Europe unites, it will have to adopt a common form of government, and it is worth considering the main alternatives. Will Europe prefer French or British parliamentary government, the two main and distinctive forms? Or is there a possible compromise presented by Swedish parliamentarism, which has retained certain characteristics of the separation of powers that are so much a part of American politics? It may well be that the American federal system with its strong single executive will prove of interest to nations used to men of the caliber of de Gaulle and Adenauer. All these possibilities make a study of the more stable democratic forms of government of considerable contemporary interest.

Finally, having considered the varieties of democratic government as well as the variations of communism, we shall consider the two main patterns against the background of what is sometimes called the Third World, a world in which a number of nations have to decide whether to follow the example of the liberal democracies or be tempted by the communist way of life.

Today when the Soviet Union challenges the United States in the exploration of space, in economic growth, and in influencing the policies of the now uncommitted nations, it is difficult to realize that until comparatively recently these two nations were on the fringe of the main center of power—which was in Europe. The present situation is very different from that of 1918, when Wilson demanded self-determination for subject peoples, and even more different from that of 1914. It is important to understand the changes that have taken place so that we do not imagine that our own world is any more permanent. For there are more than enough states in a position to upset the calculations of the policymakers in Moscow and Washington, and there is a new Europe that may try to restore the balance of power disturbed twice in this century by what historians may ultimately consider to have been civil wars between the peoples of European stock.

In 1914, then, Europe was the center of the world and London the capital of the greatest empire the world had ever seen—one that encompassed the globe. America and Russia, though powerful states, were under Europe's influence. The Russian nobility spoke French; the tsar's government depended on loans from France. The Americans were closely connected to Britain by ties of language and inheritance, the Revolution and the War of 1812 notwithstanding; they had depended very much on British capital for the development of their country. (For example, when Wall Street panicked in 1907 and John Pierpont Morgan saved the day, the Bank of England sent gold specie at a crucial moment.)

The world in general had become a European province, paying its tribute of food and raw material and receiving European culture and civilization, as well as manufactured goods, in exchange. South Americans spoke Spanish and Portuguese, educated East Indians conversed in English, and those Africans who were literate were absorbing the culture of the colonial powers that had so recently divided the Dark Continent among themselves. Europe, and people of European descent, straddled the world, going west as far as California and the Yukon, south to Argentina and South Africa, and east to Vladivostok, Singapore, and Sydney.

But to speak of Europe as an entity is misleading. It was a continent divided against itself—one in which successive powers vied for supremacy. With the decline of the Holy Roman Empire and Spain in the seventeenth century, a new nation-state, France, had appeared as the dominant power in Europe. But the efforts of men such as Louis XIV and Napoleon between 1660 and 1815 were in vain: France failed to subjugate the continent. By 1914 a new power had emerged—Germany—only recently united as a nation-state but strong enough as early as 1870 to challenge and defeat the French. The first French Empire under Napoleon Bonaparte was defeated by the British and the Prussians at Waterloo in 1815. The second, under Napoleon III, was humiliated at Sedan in 1870 by the Germans alone.

Nowhere was the shift in power from France to Germany more

quickly recognized than in the United States after the Civil War. In the closing years of the nineteenth century, America as a re-united nation was undergoing an industrial revolution. American poets and painters might still stroll the boulevards of Paris, but American chemists and engineers were studying at German universities. For it was in the development of science (including the sciences of history and of society) and technology—and, oddly enough, the social services—that Germany was now preeminent, as it had long been in philosophy, literature, and music. The great influence of Germany on the development of American higher education was reinforced by the migration of intellectuals from Hitler's Reich in the 1930's.

One might go so far as to say that until the emergence of the United States and the Soviet Union as superpowers, the course of events in the twentieth century was determined in general by Europe and in particular by Germany, the most dynamic and the most politically insensitive of the European nations. Twice Germany tried against overwhelming odds to succeed where France failed—to become the master of Europe. Hitler, like Napoleon over a century earlier, was defeated in the sizzling deserts of Egypt by the British and on the frozen steppes of eastern Europe by the Russians. Yet today, when power no longer lies with Germany, the German question remains the most intractable of all.

What caused Germany's turbulence? One explanation is that Germany's unification came too late for her own, or for other people's, comfort. There were no continents to conquer in 1900: eleven years later not even the two poles remained undiscovered. Various European nations, including little Belgium, had laid claim to vast tracts of Africa, which was the last of the continents to be explored. All that was left for the kaiser was a part of East Africa (now part of Tanzania) and South-West Africa (now administered by the Republic of South Africa) and the little enclaves of Cameroon and Togo. James Bryce, one-time British ambassador to the United States, had taken it for granted in 1912 that the European powers "have now portioned out the whole world of savagery, barbarism and semicivilization among themselves."[7] He failed to notice that some resented the fact that they were not allowed their full share of the white man's burden. In revenge the Germans put together the finest army in the world and built a fleet

---

[7] James Bryce, *South America* (London: Macmillan, 1912), p. 452.

to match the Royal Navy. They suggested that their destiny lay in Europe, in what they considered the less civilized portion to the east. Hence the term *Drang nach Osten* ("yearning for the East").

It is extraordinary, in retrospect, to see how the other powers were drawn back into Europe during 1914–18 after their lusty expansion across vast continents during the previous decades. The age of the cowboy, which forever symbolizes for the world the expansion of America westward, lasted but a brief generation; by 1890 the frontier was closed. The last continental states, Arizona and New Mexico, joined the Union in 1912, and shortly afterward massive immigration from Europe came to an end. Canada's prairie provinces were admitted to the Confederation in 1905. As the railroads raced across America to the Pacific, so a generation later they pushed their way eastward across Russia to the western shores of the same ocean. America came into conflict with Spain and won; 1898 saw the end of Spain's empire in the New World. Russia met Japan in the Far East and lost; twelve years later in Russia tsarism was replaced by communism. It was a fascinating period of robber barons, predatory potentates, and intrepid explorers, occasionally, as in the life of Cecil Rhodes, finding their combination in a single man. By a curious historical coincidence the great powers stood together in the opening year of the century in Peking, capital of the oldest and most majestic of the empires of the world. The European and European-influenced powers (including Russia, America, and Japan) were all anxious to carve spheres of influence out of the Chinese body politic and had established missions to further these ends. The Boxer Rebellion of 1900, an abortive military uprising against these foreign elements, was encouraged by the reactionary government of the empress; it was an outbreak of Chinese antipathy toward Western influence. The missions, supported by a few troops, stood firm until they were rescued by a composite force of British, French, Italian, German, Austrian, Russian, American, and Japanese troops. But before China could be disposed of, the powers were drawn back into Europe and war.

History alone can show whether Lenin was right in asserting that the years leading up to 1914 were the Age of Imperialism, an age destined inevitably to end in war between the rival imperialist powers. It is arguable that other forces were at work, not least the apparently eternal rivalry between France and Germany.

But whatever the reasons for the holocaust of the First World War, its course in its essentials followed a familiar pattern. An alliance emerged to defeat the dominant power. Instead of France under Louis XIV or Napoleon attracting a coalition of opponents determined to prevent it from becoming the mistress of Europe, now it was Germany's turn. This time there was one important difference. On previous occasions the European powers, including Russia, had been able to deal with the threat to their security. Now, so powerful was their opponent that victory proved impossible until the New World in the form of the United States came in to restore the balance of the Old. Nothing demonstrated the might of modern Germany more than the size of the coalition necessary to defeat her. And in the process France bled white at Verdun in 1916, the Russians withdrew, battered, from the war in 1917, and the British never recovered their once predominant position in the world. When Wilson spoke of a world being made safe for democracy he was thinking as an American. For most of the other belligerents their world was not safe; it was in ruins.

The Americans, who entered into the fray last and perhaps gained least in terms of territory from the war of all the victors, at least lost less than their allies and survived unscathed to fight, and win, another day. Economic power passed to the United States. Whereas the Bank of England had helped American financiers in 1907, twenty years later the attempt to repay the debt, when Britain got into difficulties in returning to the gold standard, was a contributory cause of the great crash of 1929. This time Europe could not help America, and America could not save herself, still less Europe, alone.

Power, then, passed from Europe after the First World War and the stage was set for a new alignment of forces. But it was not until 1945 that the decline of Europe became readily apparent and the fact that Europe had lost her world supremacy was generally recognized by Europeans. As late as 1938 the leaders of Britain, France, Germany, and Italy met at Munich to settle the affairs of Europe—without the participation of the United States or the Soviet Union. Why was there a failure to grasp the significance of the changing balance of power? Was it simply that the world had become so used to European supremacy that it was taken for granted?

We may put the question another way: why did no one piece together the Europe broken asunder by the First World War? One explanation is that many people seem to have thought that defeating the Germans, the Austrians, and the Turks was all that was necessary to make the world a happier place. There were other reasons. The Russians, defeated even by the Poles in 1920–21, were powerless; the Americans, frustrated and dejected by the peace negotiations, withdrew into isolation and what they were to call "normalcy"; the British pondered on their imperial responsibilities. France was left as the sole European victor, a France alone and afraid and destined to hide behind the Maginot Line, which was constructed as a protection against a further invasion. Instead of tottering empires of eastern Europe there was a string of new and supposedly liberal democratic states, mostly former subject nationalities of the Austrians, Russians, and Turks. France eagerly formed alliances with four of them (Poland, Rumania, Czechoslovakia, and Yugoslavia), but no one knew how it would be able to protect them against a resurgent Germany or Russia; indeed, France appears to have thought of them as its buffer, not as clients it was to protect.

The postwar reconstruction of Europe does not seem to have been handled responsibly by the victorious powers. Peace was supposed to be preserved by the League of Nations, which was led by Britain and France in the absence of the other great powers for much of its existence. (The United States never joined at all.) Until 1939 the British still considered themselves the mistress of the seas and at least the moral custodian of world peace. British liberals blamed the government for failing to keep Japan out of Manchuria in 1931 and out of China in 1937, for being unable to stop Mussolini's conquest of Abyssinia in 1935, and for not assisting the Spanish government against Franco between 1936 and 1939. Most of all, they were incensed over the assimilation of Austria in 1938 and the dismemberment of Czechoslovakia that followed as Hitler staked Germany's claims to be the dominant power in Europe, filling the partial vacuum left by the peace of Versailles. When Hitler went too far and invaded Poland, despite having been warned of the consequences, Britain and France declared war on Germany, and the Second World War began. Once again Europe was the center of hostilities and once again the issue was decided in the end by the powers on the periphery— by the British Commonwealth and above all by the United States and the Soviet Union.

History, it is said, never repeats itself, but it would seem as though the Second World War in one respect is the parallel—or at least Part II—of the First. On each occasion the giant of

Europe, Germany, threatened to engulf its neighbors. Twice it required the combined forces of the other great powers to overwhelm Germany.

Where the parallel breaks down most obviously is between the uneasy peace of Versailles that followed 1918 and the truce (for no peace treaty was signed) that followed 1945. This time there were no European empires, other than the recently acquired German Reich, to break up. It was not only the German army that was defeated in 1945. The Allies made sure that the German people suffered to the full and would have no excuse for saying as they did after 1918 that they lost merely because they were "stabbed in the back" by faint-hearted politicians. If their second defeat did nothing else it demonstrated to the Germans the folly and futility of their dreams of a thousand-year Reich stretching from the Atlantic to the Urals—unless they had strong allies. Germany, like France, had failed to unite Europe on its own.

But the defeat of 1945 did more. It showed that Europe, the old Europe that had virtually conquered the world, was itself defeated. The armies that roamed across the Danube and the Rhine were Russian and American. Not only Germany lay in ruins but much of Europe from the bombed docks of Liverpool to the grim and twisted steel of Stalingrad. Though a French armored division liberated a joyous Paris, France was but a nominal victor. Even Britain, like France allotted a permanent seat in the Security Council, was really a second-class power.

After 1945 the division of Europe, and with it the division of the world, began to harden as the Soviet Union looked with mistrust at American ambitions to liberate eastern Europe in the Wilsonian tradition, while Americans suspected that the Soviet Union retained its ambitions for world domination. Although the great exponents of the Cold War, Dulles and Molotov, have gone, the division remains and the armies of both nations face each other in Germany. Whatever may happen in the Middle and Far East, the Russians have made it clear that this division is still the central political fact of our time.

The division must not be thought to be absolutely clear-cut. There remain a number of interesting anomalies. On the northern flank Finland is still domestically a free country with a Scandinavian type of democracy—but is dependent on the Russians in foreign affairs. The Russians have always treated the Finns better than they have their other neighbors. To the south lies Yugoslavia, which (as Serbia) was a cause of the First World War and which, under its colorful Second World War leader, Marshal Tito, abandoned democracy for communism. But it is a communism of a maverick sort that occasionally irritates the Russians and enables Yugoslavia to receive American aid. In the center there is tiny Austria, a country that after much bargaining by the Russians has been allowed its independence as a liberal democracy, provided that it behaves as a second neutralized Switzerland.

As for the perennial problem of Germany, the Soviet Union has feared that a united nation would not only join the Western camp but would be once again a source of danger. For the Russians remember the capture of Moscow by Napoleon, their defeat by the Germans in 1917, and above all the fact that they won in 1945 only after grievous losses and the occupation of their country east as far as the Volga, south to the Caucasus, and north to the gates of Leningrad itself. Russian policy has aimed at the establishment of a buffer of eastern European states under communist control and the division and disarming of Germany to eliminate the threat to Russian security from central and western Europe. But the Soviet Union has been hampered in its military strategy by its ideological hostility to the "bourgeois" democracies. This has precluded an agreement with the West over Germany. Indeed, Russian hostility to the West sufficiently alarmed the liberal democracies to cause them to take the grave step of encouraging West Germany to rearm, having withdrawn their own military control of the country.

The Soviet Union has therefore, thanks to its Marxist dogma, brought about the very danger that it wished to avoid. For with more finesse the Russians might have won the sympathy and support of those in western Europe who share their fear of a resurgent Germany. Instead, West Germany has been given its independence and already, with a population of fifty-six million, is the largest country in Europe even without the seventeen million people of the eastern zone and West Berlin. Its army promises once again to be the finest in Europe; all it lacks is the bomb. The most troublesome meeting place of East and West is Berlin, which is inside the eastern zone but under joint four-power control. The United States has promised to defend Berlin; West Germany has not renounced East Germany, and neither it nor the United States has agreed to accept the new border between East Germany and Poland—the Oder-Neisse line. Without the powerful presence of the Soviet Union and the United States, Europe could be in a state of unrest once more.

There has been another consequence of the war that has only gradually made itself felt in the world. This is the emergence of new nations that are affecting the balance of power between East and West. The First World War, while it ruined four empires in Europe—the German, Russian, Austro-Hungarian, and Ottoman— left the overseas empires of the victors and neutrals untouched. The Second World War undermined even these. The British Empire, which emerged from the war undefeated and prided itself on its political enlightenment, was one of the first to begin to disintegrate. India, Pakistan, and Burma became independent in 1947 and were followed by numerous colonies elsewhere. The process is now almost complete. Other empires followed suit. The French gave up Syria and Lebanon, Indochina, Tunisia, and even in the end Algeria, formerly considered to be part of metropolitan France and not a colony at all. The Dutch left Indonesia. The Belgians hurriedly departed from the Congo, leaving the United Nations to pick up the pieces and to be more appreciative of the way other nations had prepared their colonies for independence. The old League of Nations had been an organization of Europeans. The new United Nations is increasingly sensitive to the view of the Afro-Asian group of powers.

For a time it seemed as though the French Union and the British Commonwealth might provide a bridge between the Old World and the New and between the white peoples and the colored races, but this has become less certain. Communist propaganda has stressed the exploitation the former colonies have endured and has said nothing about the benefits accruing from European technology and civilization. South Africa has been dropped from the Commonwealth because of its racialist policies, and the Ian Smith government in Rhodesia has been declared illegal. Britain has passed a Commonwealth Immigrants Act that limits immigration for the unqualified (that is, for colored people). Britain's application to join the Common Market has been thought by many in the Commonwealth, white and colored, to threaten its continued existence as a viable organization (though people of British stock in Canada, Australia, and New Zealand will of course retain their links with the mother country). No one can foretell the implications of the new patchwork of nations across the globe, but it looks ominously like an extension of Wilsonian national self-determination with a power vacuum that eventually will be filled.

The emergence of new nations has meant that the Soviet Union and the United States have extended their line of contact from Europe to the rest of the world, where they carry on their struggle by economic means, largely through foreign aid. They have fought everywhere for the minds of men, each being fully aware that in the long run it is here that victory lies.

So far the communists have done better in the world at large than in Europe itself. Western Europe is largely anticommunist, and eastern Europe, so far as one can tell, is still unconverted to the communist creed. The most dramatic of communism's successes was the conquest of China in 1949, a country whose 760 million people already outnumber the populations of the United States, the European Economic Community, and the Soviet Union combined. There is a well-known joke that optimists learn Russian but pessimists learn Chinese. The United States has managed to prevent the excursion of China from the mainland, but, like Germany in an earlier Europe, the new China seems to find the urge to expand irresistible, as the peoples of Southeast Asia have become uneasily aware.

The communists have now established regimes from Berlin to Peking, and they claim that they govern a third of the world's population. They have established beachheads on other continents, notably Guinea in Africa and Cuba in the Americas. There are some observers who think that communism's appeal is mainly to backward nations and that as the world increases in prosperity the attractions of the creed will diminish. It is true that the example of Europe offers some confirmation of this hypothesis. In the 1950's the Russians were compelled to repress risings in both East Germany and Hungary, and faced unrest in Poland. But these countries are still firmly in communist hands. Moreover, there is still a large communist vote (up to 25 percent) in such liberal democracies as France, Italy, and Finland. It is too early to say that communism will not make any headway in the advanced countries.

The pattern of world politics that emerges from this survey is twofold. On the one hand there is a Europe apparently finally defeated, the two great powers dividing it into spheres of influence. On the other there is the spectacle of the non-European world rapidly gaining independence from the European empires of yesterday. It seems more than just fifty-five years since Bryce mused on the division of the world as it appeared in 1912.

But the picture we have drawn has been too simple. Yet certainly as far as the Russians and the Americans are concerned there has been a tendency to hope that the present balance of power will continue. The Soviet Union tries not to think too hard about China, though it has conspicuously failed to provide the Chinese with the bomb. The Americans are pleased that Germany is a friend, but there is no suggestion that Germany should share atomic secrets even with Britain and France. The balance of power has been thought to depend on the balance of terror provided by the euphemistically termed "nuclear deterrent." According to one interpretation, this makes stalemate the only practicable policy and "peaceful coexistence"—that is, economic and ideological competition—the only sane policy for either side.

At this point we must glance into the future without being at all certain what it portends. One thing is clear, however, and it may be as significant for the United States as the emergence of China was for the Soviet Union. We are observing today a movement toward a "United Europe," one which if successful could restore the European peoples to a position similar to their old predominance. Here is taking place the very opposite of the movement toward national self-determination fashionable in the rest of the world. Europe, itself the foster parent of nationalism, is now more interested in what are called supranational institutions. Three have already been set up, the European Coal and Steel Community, Euratom, and the European Economic Community (the Common Market).

Of course not all Europe as yet is involved. So far the European Economic Community consists of France, West Germany, Italy, Belgium, the Netherlands, and Luxembourg. But these six countries, second- and third-class powers separately, are together more populous than either of the two superpowers and may soon be able to compete in productive capacity. If the movement toward economic unity is successful and if some form of political federation follows, as many people hope, then the balance of power in Europe and the world could be affected.

What we are witnessing is an extraordinary about-face on the part of the European nations. Having fought separately for supremacy on the continent over several centuries, accompanying this in modern times by competition abroad in colonial expansion, they now have foregone their colonies and decided to sink their differences in a common cause. France and Germany, each having failed to conquer Europe by force of arms, hope to dominate Europe together, preferably by peaceful means. Great Britain, having been compelled to abandon its traditional policy of keeping Europe divided (the last abortive attempt being the European Free Trade Area of the "Outer Seven") has applied for admission to the European Economic Community and has recognized the political implication of this move.

The Americans, with a certain wisdom, would like the French and the British to give up the bomb. This can be interpreted as self-interest or as an attempt to preserve the postwar dialogue. But they are uneasily aware that if a United Europe emerges of which Germany is a member, perhaps the strongest member, then the nuclear deterrent will be at least partly in German hands. Much therefore hangs on the negotiations for a United Europe in the years ahead, and the peace of Europe depends on the success with which the other liberal democracies prevent a resurgence of German militarism and ensure that any emerging new Europe is founded on liberal democratic principles. Otherwise the wheel may come full circle, much to the dismay of the peripheral powers, as Europe rises again. Britain's devaluation crisis in November 1967 indicated that the Bank of England and the Federal Reserve banks need the backing of bankers on the continent if they are to support the pound and the dollar as leading currencies.

The postwar emphasis on new developments, on the new states rather than on the world's European heritage, has tended to put the patterns of politics out of focus. For the new states are still weak, poor, and divided. They look to the great and formerly great powers for advice and aid. These powers are for the most part European, not necessarily in the sense of being located in western Europe (though some of them are) but in the sense of being of European stock. It is this that distinguishes the United States, Canada, and even the Soviet Union from the new states of Africa and Asia.

These new countries are themselves becoming increasingly Westernized, often to the dismay of their traditional leaders. It is true that they have ancient cultures, many of which are older than European culture and certainly older than American culture. They want respect for their historic achievements. But their *political* culture is for the most part derived directly or indirectly from

Europe, the source of most of the world's political ideas and practices. There has been nothing like the European political innovations of the past three centuries since the days of Greece and Rome, which were themselves the only European civilizations of the ancient world.

In Part One we shall examine the variety of political institutions that have emerged from Europe; in Part Two we shall consider the communist variations. Finally in the Conclusion we shall assess the implications of what is sometimes called the challenge of communism for the new states of the Third World. For many of these states the enormous problems of political modernization and social mobilization have led to experimentation with the single-party state as introduced by Lenin and copied by Mussolini and Hitler. But, as the experience of Yugoslavia shows, industrialization can be accomplished so swiftly that within a generation the age-old problems of liberty and limited government and of equality versus expertise emerge. At this point, the long experience of the liberal democracies and the great tradition of European political thought dating from Plato and Aristotle become relevant once again.

PART ONE

THE
LIBERAL
DEMOCRATIC
PATTERN

Four Variations:
The United States
Great Britain
France
Sweden

1

PRINCIPLES:
Government by Consent

The nations of what is often called the free world can be divided into two types: those that have comparatively recently experimented with liberal democratic government and that have yet to demonstrate long-term stability, and those that have enjoyed democratic institutions for a long time and seem assured of their position in the years ahead. Among the former must be listed countries newly emancipated from dictatorship, such as Italy and Germany, or countries recently given independence, such as Nigeria and India. A new category, which includes Ghana and Indonesia, consists of countries that have achieved independence and have subsequently suffered a period of one-man rule. It is no exaggeration to say that the nations that have long enjoyed stable democratic political systems, a few smaller countries excepted, owe a great deal to the British, as well as to the American, example. The Parliament at Westminster has been called the Mother of Parliaments (though Iceland can claim an even longer tradition), and British common law has spread throughout much of the Commonwealth and the United States. Just as in the American colonies of the 1770's the first successful group of emancipators met in the Continental Congress, so today in Britain's African colonies native political parties emerge to plan the escape to freedom. The British do not seem to have been unduly worried about subversion: it has been an occupational hazard of colonial imperialists for nearly two centuries.

The common tradition for liberal democratic systems can best be summed up in the phrase "government by consent"—a rather nebulous and somewhat negative expression (very different from Lincoln's positive "government of the people, by the people, for the people"). It means that there is a point beyond which government cannot go without antagonizing the people and their representatives. It was summed up by John Locke as long ago as 1689 when, in his search for the source of power, he explained that in a very tolerable sense one could argue that supreme power lay with the executive, but he added that it really lay with the legislature—and with the people. To this day no one can give a precise answer to the question: where *does* power lie in the British political system? It all depends on the particular decision at hand.

Constitutional monarchies such as Great Britain, Sweden, and Canada lack the clarity and precision of political principle that is evident in countries such as France and America. Monarchical constitutions do not claim that all men are equal, still less that sovereignty lies with the people. For it lies with the crown, which once meant the monarch and now means the cabinet. There is a certain fuzziness about British political thought and experience that is puzzling to foreigners but is in fact the secret of the system's success. Locke absorbed the ideas of Richard Hooker, who wrote in the time of Elizabeth I in the 1590's, and Hooker in turn was influenced by the thirteenth-century Thomas Aquinas. Hooker's is a stand very different from that of the tough-minded men of the Renaissance—of Machiavelli and Hobbes—and very different from the eighteenth-century Enlightenment in France and Germany that gave rise to Rousseau, Hegel, and Marx. It is arguable that it is Britain, so long the enemy of Catholic Spain and France, that has been most imbued with Catholic and indeed medieval political thought—which in its turn was much influenced by Aristotle. One may thus trace the tradition of government now practiced in Washington, Ottawa, New Delhi, Lagos, and Dar es Salaam in part—and of course only in part—back through the centuries-old history of political thought. And nowhere has greater emphasis been laid on the transmission of political ideas than in

Britain, to which so many of the leaders of the liberal democracies have looked for inspiration.

French thought about government by consent has been derivative rather than formative. The philosophers of the Enlightenment in France were, like American statesmen, influenced by Locke; but instead of seeing in him the upholder of the Whig oligarchy that helped to depose James II, they saw him as a radical ally in their search for support against the Bourbons. At this point the French, also like the Americans, went much further than the British in their understanding of the implications of government by consent. The French people did not merely check the executive: as the sovereign electorate, they were the source of its authority.

Yet a fair appraisal of all the contemporary examples of democratic systems seems to indicate that it is a combination of their theorizing and experience that has contributed to their present way of life. All of them owe something to Locke and Montesquieu, to Rousseau and Mill, and to Jefferson and Lincoln. It is no exaggeration to say that the British Labour government of 1945 profited by the experience of the New Deal in the United States and the Social Democrats' success in Sweden. By no means have all Europeans recognized their debt to the principles underlying the American political system (for they have paid more attention to the French Revolution and Napoleon than to the American Revolution and Washington). Yet the many novelties of the United States—its written constitution, its republican form of government with its president as a strong head of state and of government, its federalism, separation of powers, judicial review, checks and balances, and limited government—are among the great contributions to political theory that are all too easily ignored by the political philosophers and too much taken for granted by political scientists.

All the liberal democracies glory in their tradition of liberty. The French have their Declaration of the Rights of Man, their *Liberté, Egalité*, and *Fraternité*; the Americans have their Declaration of Independence and Bill of Rights; and the British their Magna Carta and Bill of Rights. The Swedes proudly boast that they never experienced serfdom even in the Middle Ages, and their Freedom of the Press Act, which has very wide implications, dates from 1812. All have opposed absolutism, whether it be the bumbling imposition of Divine Right by the Stuart kings, the centralized mercantilism of the Bourbons, the machinations of George III, or the personal rule of Gustavus III. Each country believes that the executive should depend on the legislature and that its members should enjoy free speech. It is because they practice what they preach that they are able to say their tradition is indeed one of government by consent.

2

POLITICAL PROCESS:
The Politics of Organization

It is customary to distinguish between the operation of government in a country and what is termed its political process. By the latter is meant the political life of the nation as it involves the people generally. Many persons are members of community associations, business organizations, or trade unions that seek to influence the operation of government by bringing pressure to bear on the executive or the legislature. Many people are so concerned with politics that they join political parties, organizations that are interested in taking a positive part in government itself.[1] All of us, if we are good citizens and aware that the success of our democratic system depends on the support of the electorate, believe we should vote in elections. The liberal democracies differ from one another in three important components of the political process: groups, parties, and elections. It is often assumed that there is an Anglo-Saxon and a Continental political process. It will be shown that this is not altogether true and that it is not always possible on this point to compare Britain and the United States on the one hand with France and Sweden on the other. It is always dangerous to make

---

[1] In many countries party membership involves the payment of dues. In the United States membership may simply mean registration with a particular party for voting purposes.

this type of analysis, for political systems are not usually as symmetrical as theorists would like them to be.

Homogeneous and Heterogeneous Societies: The Role of Groups

Of the four liberal democracies, two—Britain and Sweden—appear homogeneous in social composition and two—the United States and France—heterogeneous.

The Politics of Organization: Britain and Sweden

THE "OLD-BOY" NETWORK IN BRITAIN

A favorite remark made by Americans visiting Britain is that it is a homogeneous society. This surprises the British because they are aware of a number of features of their society that the Americans find it convenient to do without and that would seem to make Britain much less homogeneous than the United States. The Tory element, for example, was eliminated from the United States during the Revolution, and what passes for conservatism in America is really old-fashioned liberalism. There is no American nobility, no gentry, no established church, above all no Establishment such as characterizes Britain. At the other end of society in the United States there is no fourth estate of trade unions: that position of political influence, long held by the press, is now shared with other mass media, particularly television.

To an Englishman, conscious of the remnants of what we may call feudalism for want of a more precise term, conscious of the encroachments of socialism, of the bitter fruits of religious conflict, and of the erosions of nationalism in his own country, America would seem to have more of the attributes of a homogeneous society, with its devotion to liberalism and to the cultivation of a broad middle class society. Yet reflection suggests that the American visitors are right in one respect: *politically* at least Britain is a homogeneous society. The dangerous lunatic fringes of right or left, which permanently disfigure the politics of so many countries and which appear from time to time like boils on the face of American politics, seem less significant in Britain.

Indeed, the most insistent element in British society is the acceptance of class superiority. There remains a small upper class that has no counterpart in the United States—a class of fairly ancient lineage that sets the tone of society and is ably backed by an upper-middle class that sends its children to the same schools and identifies itself with those in the social stratum above it. The American politician says, "If you can't beat them, join them." The English aristocrat believes that it is better that you let them join you—in your club, your regiment, your school and college, and your House of Commons. Thus there is perpetuated the "old-boy" network that keeps British politics and society as they are. Those who criticize British social structure can be considered to have a chip on their shoulder: if they had been good enough, they would be "in" by now.

The middle class is less in evidence in Britain than in the United States, largely owing to an educational system that tends to identify state education in many people's minds with inferior education for inferior people. There is a swift descent from the imperturbable and privately educated upper-middle class to the insecure lower-middle class, which is made up of the white-collar workers who supported the Liberal party before 1914. Only since the election of Wilson and Heath to the leadership of the Labour and Conservative parties have representatives of the middle-middle class obtained power.

The largest group of people—the workers—have been the backbone of the Labour party. It is the decline in numbers of this class (reflected in a decline in union membership) during the present technological revolution that has caused Labour leaders concern. The militants in the party still think in terms of working class solidarity; the realists recognize that the ladder of social success is too accessible to be spurned. The term "working class" may soon be as inappropriate in Britain as it is in North America. An important fact of British political life since Disraeli's bid for the workingman's vote in 1867 is that a significant minority of the working class has preferred to be ruled by gentlemen. The Conservatives have been the prime beneficiaries of Britain's deferential society.

Today the ties between party and social class seem much looser than in the past. Thus the two old British parties—Conservative and Liberal—and the traditions they preserved could be roughly defined in terms of the kind of groups they appealed to. However, the traditional English party system was, if not classless, at least not dominated by rigid class lines reflected in automatic political allegiance. Some of the best families produced, generation after generation, rebels and radicals. Some of the most depressed and, possibly, oppressed workers were, at least passively, loyal to the old order. These class deviations may have made politics artificial. But both parties operated on the theory that any English political party should be a microcosm of the country; it should enroll dukes and dustmen in the same ranks.

There was a great deal of fiction in this view of English politics, but the fiction had some utility. It prevented the alienation, evident in both France and Germany, of the working class from national institutions. No one's politics were absolutely determined by birth and class, although birth, class, and income, in most cases, did decide party allegiance.

The decline of first the Liberal and now the Labour party has meant a shift in group allegiance. British government has long depended on consent—but this has meant the consent of the great "interests of the realm," or what Americans term "pressure groups." If the Labour party were to disintegrate, the trade unions would remain as one of these interests—and the unions know it. The trade union leaders may even prefer to have a Conservative government in office because the Conservatives are more willing to meet the unions' demands in order not to lose votes. By giving way to the unions and by maintaining full employment the Conservatives have weakened still further the working class allegiance to the Labour party. Certainly the fire seemed to go out of the working class under Conservative rule from 1951 to 1964.

The chief characteristic of the first half of the present century appears to have been the organization of voters by the Labour party and the trade unions in what both hoped would be a working class and therefore majority party. Before the Labour governments of 1945–51 and 1964 to date, this hope was fulfilled only briefly (in 1924 and 1929–31). The traditional support of the British people has been for their "natural rulers," whether seventeenth-century gentry serving as justices of the peace or twentieth-century Conservative gentlemen serving as members of Parliament. No one can put his finger on their organization. For the success of British Conservatism is intangible and consists of a subtle all-pervading class sentiment that expresses itself most forcefully in its distrust of the self-made man (but not his son—if he has been to the right school). Of the four liberal democracies under consideration, only in Britain does the oil of snobbery that keeps all societies in motion lubricate successfully the wheels of politics.

The traditional picture of Britain, then, as a country divided into three main social classes, an upper Conservative class, a middle Liberal class, and a lower Labour class, does have a grain of historical truth but it is misleading—especially for an understanding of the inner workings of British politics. For the British government today, like other liberal democracies, is one that depends on the allegiance of the various social classes only in a long-term sense. Between elections, government is part of an intricate process whereby pressure is brought to bear by the electorate through a large number of organizations, some of which are very important indeed. Those most in the limelight are the associations that demand economic protection or subvention from the government. They fall into three main categories—business, labor, and professional.

Business (including farming) in Britain is represented by a single powerful organization called the Confederation of British Industry (C.B.I.). The upper classes retain their power in Britain, as any communist textbook on British government explains in detail, less through the House of Lords than through the directorship of important companies, which are usually glad to have a lord on the board. (It is often taken by the public as an indication of probity, for, as everyone knows, a lord must be a gentleman.[2])

Some lords of course have been trade unionists. Although there are nearly six hundred trade unions, two-thirds of the eight and a half million members of the Trades Union Congress (T.U.C.) are members of eighteen unions, and eight unions, the largest being the Transport and General Workers' Union, dominate the organization. Thanks to its affiliation with the Labour party, the T.U.C. is powerful politically as a twentieth-century estate of the realm, but each union is autonomous in its bargaining. British trade unions, like trade unions in other advanced countries, are beginning to decline in membership.

By contrast with their American counterparts the British middle classes are surprisingly well organized. The overwhelming majority of teachers belong to the National Union of Teachers

---

[2] A survey of 3,215 directors of British companies with assets of over one million pounds showed, however, that under 2 percent were peers or baronets. (G. H. Copeman, *Leaders of British Industry* [London: Gee, 1955], p. 84.)

(the remainder being members of other teachers' associations); nearly all local and central government employees are organized in powerful associations and the British Medical Association is as articulate as the American Medical Association. Middle class *associations* such as these are not usually affiliated with the Trades Union Congress, for the term "union" is connected with the Labour party and the working class. The title Medical Practitioners' Union indicates the Labour leanings of its members. In addition, a union tends to be more tough-minded: the National Union of Teachers will, if irked, bring its 230,000 school*teachers* (but not the separately organized secondary school*masters*) out on strike. The political affiliations of the organized middle class are somewhat obscure but may prove crucial in British politics in the years ahead.

These three main groups hardly exhaust the numerous British organizations. There are nearly a thousand cooperative societies with over eleven million members, the Church of England, the Roman Catholic Church, the Free Church, organizations of county and city councils, and voluntary organizations of every conceivable kind that are willing to proceed to Trafalgar Square or to 10 Downing Street at the drop of a hat.

Yet few people in Britain were aware of the ramifications of the "Anonymous Empire" until S. E. Finer wrote his book with that title in 1958 to describe the activities of British lobbyists and pressure groups, and even his figures often lack precision. Partly this is because pressure groups have been taken for granted for so long. In 1790 Burke opposed the French Revolution because it did not represent the great interests of the realm—unlike the British revolution of 1688. Britons to this day think of themselves, unless they are ardent trade unionists, essentially as people caught up in a society of social class. They ask what proportion of the working class vote Conservative rather than try to explore the changing political affiliation of the members of occupational groups. They may be out of date in their attitudes, but elections are determined by what the voters think is the situation, not by the facts of life as these are comprehended at the time by social analysts or understood in retrospect by historians.

"ORGANIZATION SWEDEN"

The Swedes are even more homogeneous than the British. Although there is a monarchy and something resembling an upper class, no titles are now given and there is no caste division in the Swedish educational system. The Reformation was carried out much more thoroughly and the Lutheran Church is part of the state administration. Apart from a few thousand Lapps living in the far north, Sweden is ethnically as purely of one stock as any country in the world.

This social, religious, and ethnic homogeneity has not been purchased without a price. The House of Nobility, unlike the House of Lords, was abolished (in 1866); Sweden's part on the Protestant side in the Thirty Years' War (1618–48) established the country as a great power but stretched it so much that it was unable to sustain this role; the inability of the Swedes to avoid friction with their neighbors, the Norwegians, led to the dissolution of the Kingdom of Norway-Sweden by mutual consent in 1905. Had the Russians not seized Finland from Sweden in 1809, depriving the Swedes of a part of their kingdom where a Swedish minority dominated the more numerous Finns, Sweden might have faced the same problem as England in Ireland, Canada in Quebec, or the United States in the South. It is possible that Sweden now suffers rather than gains from its homogeneity; certainly there are many Swedes, and more foreigners, who complain of the lack of excitement in that country.

The Swedes are also more highly organized than the British *politically* and they sometimes refer to their country as "Organization Sweden." A record 85.6 percent of the electorate voted in the general election of 1960. In 1964, 83.3 percent voted. This high turnout is partly because the Swedes take their civic duty to vote seriously. But partly it is because of the highly organized nature of Swedish society. People belong to trade unions, farmers' cooperatives, and other organizations whose candidates they support.

Another feature of "Organization Sweden" is what may be called the horizontal division of the various groups or classes. Whereas in many countries there is a vertical division of rich and poor, upper and lower classes, Sweden is divided into groups that have much in common with the older sectional divisions in the United States in which the farming, mining, and manufacturing interests were horizontally rather than vertically separated, if only because of the size of the country. Certainly the pressure group politics of both the United States and Sweden assume a certain balance or countervailing power between equals or near-equals.

They preclude the accepted superiority of one organized body over another or of an elite over the masses.

Of course it would be misleading to describe Sweden as a country of groups with equal status, a sort of pluralistic classless society. It is little more than a hundred years since Sweden abolished the four estates of nobles, clergy, burghers, and farmers, and some of the sense of social hierarchy has rubbed off on the descendants of these groups. It took some time before farmers in the new bicameral parliament after 1866 became entitled to the title "Mister" and to this day the newspapers divide the parties into workers' (Social Democrats and Communists) and bourgeois (Conservatives, Liberals, and Center or Farmers). A Swede can often place a fellow countryman in his appropriate estate by his name. Less clannish than the Scots, the Swedes are nevertheless more lineage conscious than all except upper class Englishmen and can trace even peasant families back for generations.

On the other hand, even in the old days the Swedes recognized the existence of a fourth estate and gave the farmers a status and representation that they still lack in many other countries. The estate tradition and the acceptance of the idea that all the important groups had their proper social status made the path of the newer classes such as the white-collar employees and industrial workers easier than it might have been. The Social Democrats preached class war in the 1880's; by 1910 all except the Left Socialists had accepted the parliamentary system.

The situation may be summed up, and perhaps oversimplified, by saying that although the Swedes retain a sense of social class more European than American, they share with the other Scandinavian countries and the United States a traditional refusal to allow *social* superiority to carry much *political* weight. An upper class Swede, like an Adlai Stevenson but unlike an English country squire, must tread softly in politics.

Of the old Swedish estates, only the farmers remain politically organized, though urbanization and the growth of industry in the countryside have diminished their power and influence. Two-thirds are self-employed. In spite of their independence, most of them belong to the Federation of Swedish Farmers' Associations. The majority are also members of a sort of farmers' trade union, the Swedish Farmers' Union. The degree of organization is as great as that of the National Farmers' Union in Britain and very different from the divided farmer groups in the United States, where the main organization, the Farm Bureau, represents mostly the larger farmers.

But what distinguishes Sweden is the emergence of organizations that represent new classes and that are somewhat analogous to the old estates. Of particular interest are those that represent the salaried middle class. Professional people join the Swedish Confederation of Professional Associations whose 75,000 members approximate the products of American graduate schools. There is clearly a lively consciousness in Sweden of the need for the salaried upper-middle class to maintain its standards, status, and salaries. The lower-middle class of white-collar workers is even more tightly organized in the Central Organization of Salaried Employees. In the United States such people are among the least organized, and even in Great Britain the "staff associations" are preferred to trade union activity. There is nothing comparable to the 500,000 Swedish bank clerks, telephonists, policemen, customs officers, noncommissioned officers, and others in the thirty-three associations that make up the Central Organization and that include nearly half of all salaried employees. In Britain, where teachers and policemen, for example, are well organized, there is no sign of any national association of salaried employees as such.

As elsewhere, the most vocal and solidly grouped class is that of the industrial workers. Sweden's thirty-nine trade unions are organized by industry rather than on a craft basis, and their membership of 1.6 million in 1964 comprised over 90 percent of all those eligible. Relative to population, the Swedish Federation of Trade Unions is the largest in the free world, and it is a powerful body. It exercises more control over its constituents than either the A.F.L.-C.I.O. or T.U.C. and is able to prevent wildcat or unofficial strikes. The price of this prerogative is a more serious strike when one occurs (the metal workers' strike in 1945 lost eleven million working days) but these are few and far between. On the whole, as the labor correspondents of the world's newspapers are aware, Swedish collective bargaining is a model for other countries.

Sweden is thus more highly organized than many other countries in that more people belong to interest groups, there is a greater identification of the individual with the group, and the numerous occupational groups, whether of employers, farmers, white-collar employees, or workers, are in their turn highly organized in national groups. Each of these four groups tends to be identified with one of the four main political parties, and so important are the groups that a Swedish scholar has stated that when they "arrive at an agreement on some question the matter is in reality generally decided. The government's function in such cases is hardly more than that of ratification."[3] Such is the legacy of government by four estates—very different from the varied assortment of pressure groups and powerful individuals who hope to make some impact on the United States Congress.

The Politics of Individualism: The United States and France

THE "LONELY CROWD" OF AMERICANS

America has never known the organization of society provided by the estates of medieval Europe. The American colonies were founded when this type of society was breaking up. Britain, whose commercial revolution in the seventeenth century transformed its society, was in the forefront of the trend toward individualism, later summed up by the term "laissez faire." "Allow to do" meant in effect that *individuals* should be allowed to do what they pleased—within reason.

The United States not only escaped the estate tradition but to a very large extent was able to eliminate the class system that replaced it in Britain. Instead of a hereditary upper class there was to be a society in which all men were equal. However much Europeans may smile at the respect given to Rockefellers and Roosevelts there is no doubt that this respect is of a very different order from the adulation bestowed on dukes and dowagers. Instead of an established church there is in the United States an extraordinary willingness to treat all religions as equal. And instead of a working class conscious of the need for some solidarity there have been the wide-open spaces tempting the adventurous laboring man to move nearer the frontier instead of leading his more docile workmates to battle in the class war. The skilled workmen succeeded in resisting the temptations of individualism. The carpenters and the plumbers are organized and well paid, but they have long been unwilling to dilute their ranks by mergers with the semiskilled and unskilled. Organization has come to the main body of America's workers only since the depression and it has been nowhere near a complete success. Only a third of those

---

[3] Nils Andren, *Modern Swedish Government* (Stockholm: Almquist & Wicksell, 1961), p. 2. A new edition of this basic text is on the press.

in nonagricultural employment, eighteen million, were union members in 1958. By 1966 nearly twelve million more people were at work, but there was no increase in union membership between 1958 and 1964.

The very nature of what are called pressure groups in the United States surprises the European student of the American political process. There is a dispersion of effort by the important power blocs. The business community operates at a variety of levels of government, often as individual firms or industries as well as through a number of organizations, such as the United States Chambers of Commerce or the National Association of Manufacturers. There seems to be nothing comparable in weight and influence to the Confederation of British Industry or the Swedish Employers' Confederation. The same is true of the farmers, divided into the Farm Bureau, the Grange, and the Farmers' Union. Compare this breakup with the single all-powerful organization that represents the British farmers. Above all, despite the merger of the A.F.L. and C.I.O., the feuding labor unions in the United States have been unable to speak politically with the single authoritative voice of the British T.U.C. or Swedish Federation of Trade Unions.

In the past it has been wiser to consider the United States as a combination of countries represented by such sections as the East, the South, and the Midwest. But it is doubtful whether the various regions of the United States retain much homogeneity today. Even the South is no longer so solid, and a marked feature of recent presidential elections is that of cross-voting. The willingness of the American voter to switch party allegiance or to vote for the man rather than the party is puzzling to a European who takes party loyalty for granted. Americans seem to vote much more as individuals (and for individuals) than Britons or Swedes.

It has been suggested that American society is that of a "lonely crowd."[4] But America has always been the home of individuals, has always been heterogeneous in its composition rather than homogeneous. Its people have found no need for the comforts of a stratified society where everyone knows his place (unless he wishes to change it for a better one); they have preferred not to select one branch of the Christian church and give it official

---

[4] See David Riesman, *The Lonely Crowd: A Study of the Changing American Character* (New Haven: Yale University Press, 1950).

status; and to this day they show no signs of escaping from their individual isolation by forming the equivalent of trade unions in the middle classes. The teachers and university professors who complain so loudly of the sick society that they must endure would probably be the last people to sacrifice their individual freedom for the sort of organization that the British and the Swedes automatically expect. There *is* a loneliness in American life that a European sometimes finds chilling but that Americans, brought up to rely on their own efforts, presumably do not notice. Yet sociologists (and "hippies") are suggesting that the way of life that has been the glory of the United States for so long has outlived its usefulness.

American individualism displays itself not only in the dispersion of effort by large organizations such as pressure groups but in the behavior of those who do not wish to conform. For example, a Nonconformist in Britain is one who opposes the established church and who is part of an ancient tradition of distrust of the royal court, the upper classes, and the Church of England. For a brief period, when they exercised power in the years 1642–60, the Nonconformists rejected the rule of the upper classes, reformed the Church of England, and put the king to death. Thus a Nonconformist feels part of a minority group but lives secure in the knowledge that he is accepted as part of the intricate tapestry that enriches British history. In the United States, by contrast, a nonconformist is an individualist who disapproves of his conforming neighbors. He may even be dismissed as a tenderhearted, impractical egghead. At all events, here is a very different stereotype from the tough-minded Dissenters who formed Cromwell's New Model Army, who provided some of England's most competent businessmen, and who built the empire. One could produce more examples of the use of similar terms to convey quite different meanings. For example, the American conservative is just as much an individualist as the American liberal and is very different from the conservative in Britain or Sweden, who identifies himself with the glorious traditions of the evolutionary past.

FRANCE, WHERE EVERY MAN THINKS FOR HIMSELF

Although the United States is an amalgam of peoples, in many ways it is less heterogeneous than France, a country with a centuries-old tradition as a single national unit. The heterogeneity of French society has been a matter of concern for the Western liberal democracies because of France's strategic position as a European power and as one of the five permanent members of the Security Council. Why is its national unity constantly endangered by internal divisions?

Perhaps the simplest explanation is historical. The Americans were united by the American Revolution as a people never were before. It spelled the end not only of rule by George III but of monarchy itself; with the demise of the monarchy in America went all titles and all sense of aristocracy. The Americans also went further. They banished the supporters of the old regime—the Tories—from their midst, never to return.[5] In addition, the United States abolished the established church (abolished since in Canada, where the Presbyterians, Catholics, and Nonconformists are numerous) and with it what might be termed an official ideology. Finally, though some people may be inclined to deny this, the American nation has kept the spirit of 1776 firmly under control so that radicalism has never endangered its capitalist society. For many Americans, communism is little more than a conspiracy, socialism is a dirty word, and even the term "liberal," which in Europe is used to connote anyone who thinks reasonably about politics, has a somewhat pink hue. Indeed, it is often a euphemism for "radical," and in the nature of things has to comprise a great number of people, especially intellectuals, who would find a variety of congenial homes in the wider European political spectrum. One may deplore the comparatively narrow range of American political life, with neither conservatism nor socialism really relieving middle-of-the-road Republican and Democratic party politics, but one cannot but be impressed by the firm success with which the main contenders at the time of the Revolution, reactionary conservatism and rebellious radicalism, have been contained. Only thus, it is arguable, has the United States remained a stable, two-party liberal democracy, without a single president who has nurtured Napoleonic ambitions.

How different is France! The guillotine of 1793, unlike the Treaty of Paris between Britain and America in 1783, did not signify the end of monarchy. The Bourbons returned in 1814

---

[5] The descendants of some Tories remain in Canada, loyal to the crown and traditionally distrustful of much that is associated with the American way of life. There exists a tradition of conservatism—and a Conservative party—in Canada that has no counterpart in the United States except in odd pockets in the South.

and again on the defeat of Napoleon at Waterloo a year later. Admittedly they did not last long, but the Orleanist and constitutional "July Monarchy" of Louis-Philippe (1830–48) was still a monarchy, as was the more personal rule of Napoleon's nephew, Emperor Napoleon III (1852–70). France finally became a republic in 1875 simply because the monarchists were divided.

France has not, then, established republican government with the enthusiasm of the American founding fathers. There are still Frenchmen with titles; there is still a cultured French upper class; and there remain châteaux in the Loire valley. There is enough of the *ancien régime* in France for the British aristocracy to feel at home there and to regard the ambassadorship to Paris as the diplomatic post par excellence. De Gaulle is not a "republican" in the French sense, for though he does not wish to be king or even first consul, he radiates much of the monarchical mystique so long latent in France. However much Jacqueline Kennedy may have done to bring culture to the White House, she and her husband were very much native—and very much republican, though Catholic—Americans of post-1789 vintage. A Rockefeller can restore Williamsburg without any suggestion of colonial pretensions: truly American history begins in the 1770's. Frenchmen are still divided into those who believe that modern France dates from 1789 and those who think that, like Britain, it stretches back into earlier centuries. For some, France since 1789 has merely endured an interregnum—as Britain did from 1649 to 1660.

France, unlike the United States, has not seen the end of true conservatism. French conservatism has a flavor very different from British, if only because it wishes to conserve a society that most probably has gone forever, whereas the other remains the staunch upholder of widely respected traditions. The British Conservative stands up to sing "Land of Hope and Glory," leaving his shamefaced Labour opponents with nothing better than "The Red Flag." The French Conservative, by contrast, must meet the challenge of those who sing the "Marseillaise" and who take "liberty, equality, and fraternity" as more than useful slogans when the barricades are built. Even de Gaulle, for all his mystique, is no substitute for a monarch. There is no comparison between the French conservatives and their Swedish counterparts. The latter may be a hapless political minority, but socially they remain significant, and they can at all times feel comforted by the existence of the monarchy.

Nor did 1789 see the end of religious controversy. Indeed it began anew. France, unlike Sweden and Britain, had achieved nationhood without abandoning the Catholic Church. This may have been its undoing, not because it led (in 1685) to the outlawing of the Huguenots (French Protestants), but because the absence of a Christian alternative led skeptics to doubt Christianity altogether. The American Revolution ended the established church, but the French Revolution saw the introduction of a godless state and the abandonment of the Christian calendar. The conflict between Protestant and Catholic has been serious enough in the Anglo-Saxon world (for Canada and Ireland especially), but the animosities between clericals and anticlericals in France have been even worse.

The Americans, fighting with due attention to the articles of war, were able to rid themselves of their revolutionary aggressions against the British. The French belatedly exploded as a nation and under Napoleon seized almost the whole of Europe.

By comparison with its neighbors, France seems to have been a turbulent state for which the Revolution raised a lot of questions but produced few lasting answers. Above all, its heterogeneous character seems to have prevented the emergence of the responsible groups that elsewhere in time of crisis exert such a steadying influence. The individualism of the French Revolution, inspired by Rousseau, seems to have been much greater in its influence than that of Paine in the United States. Whereas pressure groups in Britain have been thought of as interests of the realm and in America have often been considered pathological, or at least signs of a fall from grace, in France they have been considered subversive. Perhaps this explains why in 1958, when the government failed, no one and *no groups* seemed able to pull the country together except de Gaulle. One can hardly imagine a Britain or United States reaching the brink of catastrophe without a number of influential leaders coming together to organize national unity. It is only when one considers France since 1789 that the true measure of America's success since 1787 can be taken. Admittedly, today there is firm rule by General Charles de Gaulle, but this is reminiscent not of Napoleon Bonaparte but of a France prior to the Revolution, when Louis XV and Madame de Pompadour are reported to have said, as de Gaulle might well whisper to himself: *"Après nous le déluge."*

Centripetal and Centrifugal Party Systems

It is a commonplace observation that totalitarian regimes allow only one party, that the Anglo-Saxon democracies favor a two-party system, and that European democracies tend to follow the multiparty system of France. A more useful way of looking at the political process is to examine the forces that encourage some liberal democracies to retain two parties and cause others to have quite a selection. There would seem to be centripetal tendencies at work in Britain and the United States, whereas in France and, to a lesser extent, in Sweden the tendencies are more centrifugal.

Centripetal Tendencies: Britain and the United States

The kind of government that has, on the whole, succeeded in Britain and the United States in the past century has depended for its efficacy on the working not only of a party system but of a *two*-party system, although, obviously, a two-party system maximizes all the logical inconsistencies and the intellectual dishonesties that any party system promotes. For it is inherently unlikely that voters will fall neatly into two groups on every issue of policy or persons.

NATURAL CONSENSUS IN BRITAIN

It is not entirely true to say that Britain enjoys a two-party system of government. Since the Reform Bill of 1832 there have been a number of important third parties such as the Peelites, the Irish Nationalists, and later the Labour party. Today the Liberal party is the third party; it must not be overlooked because it is always there should the voters decide that the two main parties are both unsatisfactory. For a surprisingly high proportion of the last 135 years Britain has been governed by coalition governments. Since 1945 government has been in the hands of either the Labourites or the Conservatives. But one has to go as far back as 1924–29 to find the last single-party majority government before 1945.

However, there is a definite tendency toward a two-party system. The British electors vote largely for a government and not for a number of parties that then decide which of them shall form a government. A most telling argument used against the Liberals is that a vote for them is "a vote wasted."

Britain's natural consensus is reinforced by the realities of political power. A split in the opposition would deprive it of all hope of forming a government. The centripetal tendencies are sometimes unable to prevent catastrophe. Whereas the Democrats in the United States met the Populist challenge in the 1890's by nominating a candidate (Bryan) acceptable to the Populist party, the Liberal party in Britain a decade later made too few concessions to the emerging Labour party and paid the price after 1918.

The Labour Party   In the past the Labour party has depended on an uneasy alliance of militant socialists active in the leadership of local constituencies and the trade unions that provide much of the party's money. In the future, as Britain becomes more middle class, the party may have to attract voters who distrust both militant socialists and union leaders.

The Labour party was founded to be, and has remained basically, the political aspect of the trade union movement. And it has been officially, since 1918, committed to "socialism" as the most effective means of securing the ends of trade union policy. But the party now provides for individual membership and party branches. The unions pay most of the cost of running the party, and as they are represented at the annual party conference according to their affiliation fees, they can outvote the delegates of the constituency parties. But the unions are divided in interests, by their own internal politics, by the rivalry of their leaders.

The constituency parties have one great advantage. Their members are more likely to be politically active than are the union members. The tepid political interest of many union members has increased the resentment of the members of the local parties already irritated by the unions' use of the "bloc vote." This is an equivalent of the American "unit rule." When a union decides on a policy *all* its votes are cast by its delegates for that policy. Consequently, union leaders have the place in British party mythology that the city bosses have in that of America.

There was and is an element of fiction in this picture. In the first place, all of the union leaders have an interest in the well-being of the Labour party, if not quite as deep an interest as in the well-being of the unions. In the second place, the left-wing resolutions of the constituency parties may represent no more than the opinions of a handful of local zealots, less, not more, representative than the union leaders.

In order to understand the power structure of the Labour party, it is useful to remember the distinction between "internal" and "external" parties. An external party is one in which the center of authority is outside the legislature. Its object is to put into effect a program drawn up outside. The most perfect examples of external parties are, of course, the communist parties of western Europe where the communist members of the legislatures are openly under the orders of the party leaders. The British Labour party is in many ways an external party, but power still lies ultimately with the parliamentary party. The leader is appointed by the members of Parliament alone (in contrast to Canada where even Liberal and Conservative leaders are elected by national conventions).

The Conservative Party   On paper, the British Conservative party is very much an internal party. It existed as a loose parliamentary group, long before any of the modern democratic machinery or party control was thought of, even in the United States. It has remained a party in which the center of gravity resides in Parliament—specifically, in the House of Commons. The leader of the Conservative party is the man whom the Conservative members of Parliament recognize as leader. He is, on paper, in a much stronger position than his Labour opposite number. He appoints his "shadow cabinet" if the party is in opposition; the Labour party elects its. He appoints the party whips and all the permanent officers of the "central office," the headquarters of the party machine. The leader has nearly complete control of the party funds. And of course the position of the Conservative leader is even stronger when he is prime minister. A Conservative leader is always in the position that an American president with a big majority in Congress and the prestige of recent victory enjoys for the first hundred days of his first term.

But just as the picture of the parliamentary Labour party as an instrument of policy in theory laid down at the conference and in practice laid down by the unions is too simple, so the picture of a Conservative prime minister as dictator is too simple. For the Conservative party has to appear democratic, if not be democratic. There is now an elaborate system of local party organizations, active in local as well as in national politics. The Conservative party is on the way to being a mass party and has probably as many really active members as has the Labour party. A party conference too obviously crushed, too obviously rigged, would harm the party in the eyes of the final jury, the mass of the voters, most of whom do not belong formally to any party organization. Indeed, the problem of the Conservative party conference is the very opposite of the problem of the Labour party conference. The leaders of the Labour party have to worry about splits, quarrels, revolts, about presenting to the country the image of a party too divided to be fit to rule. The Conservative danger is of presenting to the country the image of a party of "yes men" and even of "yes women." However, wise Conservatives see the danger and are not disappointed if there is a little liveliness. For they know that the Conservative party is fundamentally deferential, that it believes that its leaders know best, and that unity in face of the enemy is the greatest of political virtues.

But there is, in both parties, one political activity that escapes central control. The choice of candidates for each party is in theory, and largely in fact, a matter for local decision. Before the Second World War, it was possible in a good many cases to win a Conservative nomination by promising lavish gifts of money to the local associations. But the Conservatives have stamped out that abuse. A candidate is rigorously limited as to the amount of money he may give to the association that nominates him. Indeed, it is in the Labour party that this abuse survives, as far as it does survive. The Labour party, nationally and locally, is much poorer than the Conservative party and so is under pressure to nominate candidates who not only can pay their own way but can help the general funds of the local party.

There is something to be said for the introduction of the American primary system into British parliamentary politics. A campaign for the nomination would eliminate some of the incompetents of the present system—in both major parties. It would involve in the choice of the candidate many voters who, not necessarily because they are bad citizens, are now reduced to choosing between two candidates they may know nothing about or have no interest in.

Yet it is doubtful whether the plea for primaries will make much headway in Britain until the parties cease to mirror their half of the nation, or until they become corrupt machines, or until the possibility of building up a third party seems an impossibility. As one observer has put it, American elections are held in order to bring the parties together; British elections are held to show that there is some difference between the parties. Natural consensus would seem to be the main characteristic of British party politics.

In a sense, the American party system is even more rigorously two-party than the British. Apart from the temporary phenomenon of Wayne Morse, for a good many years no congressman or senator has been an Independent or the supporter of a third party. Such movements as have occurred in the last fifty years to disrupt the dialogue between the Republicans and Democrats have usually been the product of a temporary dissidence within the main parties; they have not led to the formation of a successful third party. One consequence of the pressure to remain within the major parties is that these have to contain not only a broad range of views but even, in the Democratic party, to combine those who most strongly favor segregation and those who most bitterly oppose it.

To most Europeans the diversity within the American parties is one of the great mysteries of politics. One can best explain it by pointing out that American parties are not nationally organized as elsewhere but are basically *state* parties concerned with state matters. Washington is viewed by many good party men as the place to which representatives are sent to bring home the bacon. It is not surprising that internationally minded Americans are appalled to find that America's posture in the world is determined by men whose prime concern is with domestic and even local issues. The amazing thing is that the president and the State Department have succeeded so well as they have with one hand (and occasionally both hands) tied behind their backs.

America is therefore in a very real sense the land of many parties. France cannot match the hundred or so parties of the United States. These various state organizations are, however, in loose coalition and once every four years are frozen into unity by a brief spell cast by the two national conventions. In a few days of frenzy men of varied views meet and agree not upon a doctrine (the sort of policy discussion that dominates the annual party conference of British parties would lead to fantastic dissension) but upon a man, or rather two men—the candidates for president and vice-president. Having performed this midwifery and hammered out a party platform, the party leaders disperse, hoping that the politician they have selected will not alienate too many of the party's supporters or depart too much from the platform presented to him. It is a great tribute to their horse sense that they so successfully nominate men who accept the heterogeneous nature of the United States and who do not attempt to ride roughshod over any region's sensibilities. Thus from an international standpoint the reluctance to eliminate segregation has been almost disastrous for America's prestige; viewed domestically, by contrast, the careful maneuvering by successive presidents has been a masterly exercise in the art of the possible.

It has already been suggested that elections are held in Britain to indicate that there *are* divisions within the body politic and to suggest that it is worth thinking for a while about their nature. Men search for "an issue." In the United States, on the other hand, elections are held to unite the various factions within the two parties and to create some semblance of consensus. Great efforts are made to hide the disagreements that lie below the surface. There is no common doctrine of the sort that binds European and British parties together: national politics in America are more a marriage, or even a liaison, of convenience. Without presidential elections, indeed without a separate presidency, the American legislature might well disintegrate into the factionalism that has characterized so much of modern French party history. What it is that urges Americans, especially the idealists, into politics is a mystery to Europeans, for they cannot understand how parties can exist unless they are bound together by a set of agreed principles.

Yet if one considers a United Europe and the need for all the political parties in the various countries to work together for the common cause, the implications of Europe's traditional doctrinal politics need to be fully examined. It may well be that American political practices (for example, logrolling and the pork barrel), so long condemned by Europeans, have more relevance for the lubrication of the wheels of politics than the political theories that have been so influential until recently in European party history.

The unifying influence of the American party system, however, was not and is not confined to the election of the president. The party system helps to diminish the inherent tendencies of the federal system to splinter. The fact that there is no American national party system on the British model is not surprising. Not only must one allow for the vastly greater size of the country;

one must allow for the far greater autonomy of the local units. In Britain the national parties of course want to be powerful in local government as well as at Westminster. However, all final powers of decision are in Westminster where Parliament is sovereign. But in the United States, although there is a steady and irreversible trend of power away from the states toward the Union, the states are not mere local government units. It matters more that New York should have a Republican governor while the United States has a Democratic president than that London should have a Conservative chairman of the Greater London Council while there is a Labour prime minister. The national parties, or federations of state parties, act as a buffer between federal and state powers whose clashes might otherwise be more embittered, more dangerous to national unity, and less susceptible to mediation by national political needs and national political personnel.

In the same way, the possibilities of clashes between the Senate (which might represent in its decisions a comparatively small minority of the American people) and the House would be immensely increased were there not the bond of party affiliation between the members in each house. True, the discipline of the congressional parties is slack compared with that of the parties in the British or even in the Canadian House of Commons. Even when the same party controls both houses and the White House, there is often constant bickering and bargaining. But party interests mean something; the competing units of the federal government are thus held together in some kind of uneasy alliance.

The American public is accustomed to a party system that is basically illogical. It accepts a party system in which tradition still plays a great part. The seniority system in Congress ensures that the strategically important chairmanships of committees will go, by mere efflux of time, to members who represent the safest districts or states, the sections of the country that least feel need for change. The attractions of congressional power prevent a "rational" reorganization of parties and have impeded the creation of an effective Republican party in the South. By staying in the Democratic party a southern conservative could take advantage of the party's national predominance without doing anything to further the views of the northern voters who provided the majorities that made him chairman.

It is easy to write off the whole system as a confidence trick and to stress the sense of frustration perhaps felt by a Democratic voter in California or New York when he contemplates the congressional results. But the criticism is overdone. There is much more voting on party lines than is usually realized. "Control of Congress" means a great deal to the White House. A president who does not have control (as Dwight Eisenhower did not have for six of his eight years) cannot be an effective political leader, though he may remain a great national figure. As the constitution intended, the division of power between the White House and the Capitol prevents the unification of all powers of command in few hands or in one pair of hands. The American voter, with his power of choice in the primary, has a more intimate form of contact with his political representative than has the British voter. And no congressman, much less a senator, can afford to be as idle and docile as many a member of Parliament is. The voter may prefer, for traditional reasons, to be represented by a Democrat rather than a Republican, but he wants to be represented, not merely to have an indirect voice in the election of the executive, which is about all he gets in the British system.

Centrifugal Tendencies: France and Sweden

France and Sweden have electoral systems quite unlike those based on single-member districts as in the United States and Britain. In each, attempts have been made to reflect more accurately any minority views by various devices that are often summed up by the term "proportional representation." There is no doubt that there is a connection between electoral systems and the number of political parties, but it is going too far to suggest that the nature of elections determines the number of parties—as a comparison of France and Sweden demonstrates.

INSTABILITY: FRANCE

What makes France so different from other countries is that not only are there more divisions separating the extreme right from the extreme left but there are areas where the normal left-right dichotomy does not apply.

Let us take the six main party divisions first—and it should be emphasized that these are difficult to recognize owing to the juggling of electoral district boundaries. On the right are found the Conservatives and Gaullists, in the center the Progressives (M.R.P.) and Radicals, and on the left the Socialists and Communists. But the members of the right do not form a homogeneous group as in England. Some are Conservatives who have desired a form of fascism; some are merely monarchists who are leftovers from the *ancien régime*; and some are Gaullists—that is to say, they favor a modern France with a strong single executive.

The left in France is also something of an enigma. Up to a quarter of the voters have boldly supported Communist candidates since 1945—yet the country hardly seems ripe for a Communist *coup d'état*. Much of the fire has gone out of French communism. Some observers argue that the Communist votes merely demonstrate many Frenchmen's preference, exercised since the Revolution, for the party most to the left. For just as some of them have not learned to live with the Revolution, so others do not believe that the Revolution is finished. Yet it is dangerous to assume that the expression of extreme opinion in France is merely fanciful: the existence of extremes of both right and left has put parliamentary government in jeopardy.

France, it has long been thought, is really a parliamentary republic, if a little unstable. But whereas the United States imperturbably started its presidential system in 1789, it took France until 1875 before parliamentary government was established. The French parliamentary system has always been a compromise, never the expression of a political principle widely accepted. Under the stress of war in 1940 it collapsed, to be revived as the Fourth Republic in 1946. The strains of the Algerian crisis brought this system to an end, and once again, as with Napoleon I, France called on a great military figure, Charles de Gaulle.

Insofar as any parties have been identified with the parliamentary system they are the center parties. The Radicals in particular were associated with the creation of the Third Republic, and like the British Liberals, they grew more conservative with the passage of time. The equivalent of the Labour party emerged. In France this party was very definitely a socialist party and went by this title. But by 1939 it also had been tainted by the scandals and corruption of the Third Republic and showed some signs of a hardening of the arteries. The Radicals had become the party of the small-town politicians; the Socialists were the party of the lower-middle class.

After the war came the Fourth Republic—and a new party that hoped to replace the anticlerical Radicals and Socialists by a progressive group that nevertheless wished to conserve French

Catholic traditions. The M.R.P. (People's Republican Movement) had been before the Second World War a small group of socially minded Catholic progressives, "liberal" in the American sense of that term. Partly owing to its brilliant role in the resistance, partly owing to the discredit that had befallen conservative groups that had not been active in the resistance (not to speak of those that had collaborated with the Germans), the M.R.P. suddenly in 1945 became a major party. Many normally conservative voters supported the M.R.P. for want of a better hole. So, briefly, it became the most popular party in France. As the natural conservative groups re-formed, these new recruits left and the party was reduced to its nucleus—"liberal" middle class Catholics, a large number of white-collar workers (especially among women), and a fairly large group of manual workers in the east and in the north. In several regions, the M.R.P. became the only effective rival of the Communists in its appeal to manual workers.

If the Third and Fourth Republics merely demonstrated the Frenchman's capacity to distinguish between half a dozen major parties (there have been many others) that claimed his allegiance, politics would be proved difficult enough. But six parties in themselves are not a complete guarantee of instability. It was the inability of French members of Parliament to support any government for a considerable measure of time that was the real source of instability: French individualism was taken to far greater lengths than the individualism of American senators. For in the United States, in spite of all the fuss, votes are taken and decisions are made that enable government to be carried on.

At its best the French political process demonstrates the unwillingness of the Frenchman to compromise with his principles. More serious, unfortunately, is the evidence that in times of crisis French politicians are unable to work together for the good of the nation. In 1958, before de Gaulle was called back as president, it seemed as though the politicians were willing to allow the country to disintegrate, without counting the cost. It appeared as if parliamentary democracy was considered simply a technique of government, which could be discarded without regret.

STABILITY: SWEDEN

Too much attention to French politics has convinced generations of Americans and Englishmen that the only alternative to their two-party system (which they naturally consider the ideal) is the chaotic confusion of a multiparty system in which the various parties often mirror shifting doctrines and, at times, are even the product of temporary electoral alliances. Americans recognize that their own party system is unique, but they are tempted to assume that other countries fall into two groups: those that are homogeneous in social structure, like Great Britain, and have a two-party system, and those, like France, that are composed of heterogeneous elements and require a multiparty system to express their diversity.

It is important to remember that there are a number of countries, among them Norway, Denmark, and Sweden, that are as homogeneous as Great Britain, if not more, and yet apparently prefer several parties to two. Moreover, these parties are as stable and lasting as parties in Britain and the United States. Broadly speaking, the four main social groups in Sweden—the wage earners, salaried employees, farmers, and businessmen—are represented in the legislature by the four main parties—the Social Democrats, Liberals, Center (formerly the Agrarians), and Conservatives. A fifth party, the Communist, polls less than 5 percent of the votes. It is doubtless no accident that a people accustomed for centuries to being divided into four estates of the realm should after a generation or two of social and political transition (1865–1905) find a need for four political parties, each tending to depend on the support of one of the main social groups into which twentieth-century Sweden is divided. The age of individualism and of liberalism was short-lived. Sweden has passed very quickly from a condition of semifeudalism to one of semisocialism.

The largest party is the Social Democratic party, which is identified with the largest of the social groups, the one and a half million wage earners. It usually polls nearly half the votes and owes much of its large membership to the trade union movement. As in Britain, a considerable number of workers (estimated at 30 percent) vote for other parties, and a majority of trade unionists do not pay dues to the party. On the other hand, the Social Democrats attract a certain amount of middle class support. The identification of party and social class must not be taken too far.

Those observers who believe that "the swing of the pendulum" is by no means a law of politics can derive some support for their view from Swedish experience. The Social Democrats have been the largest party since 1914, and since 1933 they have been easily the most powerful political force in the country. Their present leader, Tage Erlander, has been prime minister since 1946. The success of the party is due partly to its pragmatic character. It has long been a party of social reform rather than socialization. In recent years there has been none of the bitter controversy over principle that has characterized the British Labour party. The public sector of Swedish industry is not much larger than it was when the Social Democrats came into power in 1933, and today only 10 percent of the industrial workers are employed by the state, half the proportion so employed in Britain.

Why should the Social Democrats be so much more successful than the Labourites? Both parties are based on the largest and most homogeneous social group in each country—the industrial workers—and both have been able for many years to attract the votes of over 40 percent of the population. The difference lies in the nature of the opposition they face. In Britain there is one main opponent, a Conservative party always willing to make capital out of its opponents' difficulties and able to attract all those who become disillusioned with socialism. By contrast, the Swedish Conservatives have never been able to hold on to the power that they wielded before the reform of the franchise in the early years of this century. Still less have the Swedish Conservatives been able to attract the Liberals and the rural voters as the Conservatives have done in Britain. Consequently there remains a divided opposition of Conservatives, Liberals, and Agrarians (or Center, as they now call themselves), varying in the degree of support they have received. But the total of the votes won by all three parties is usually only equal to those of the Social Democrats alone.

It is at first puzzling to a foreigner that the three "bourgeois" parties, as they are called, cannot unite to face and defeat the Social Democrats. In this sense Sweden is centrifugal rather than centripetal in its politics. There would seem to be less of that passion for office that characterizes so many British politicians, and there is also the recognition that in the Swedish political system a politician is more than a mere backbencher. More than this, the parties are kept separate by important differences of principle and interest. The Liberals share much of the Social Democrats' welfare philosophy, and though their insistence on freedom of enterprise and personal initiative prevents them from cooperating with the Social Democrats, their support of welfare legislation prevents them from joining the other two parties on this issue. The Agrarians, like farmers elsewhere, have been largely concerned with protecting their own interests; this in itself is sufficient to prevent them from merging with either the Liberals or the Conservatives. It has not stopped them from entering into alliances with the Social Democrats on occasion when it has served their purposes, and since 1933, whenever the Social Democrats have been temporarily in a minority, they have usually approached the Agrarians as allies. Thus producers and consumers have been partners, concessions to the farmers in the form of price supports being made in return for support of socialist welfare measures. It is as if the urban Democrats of the United States were to ally themselves with the Midwest farm Republicans—an unlikely but formidable partnership. Like the Liberals, the Agrarians have come to terms with the welfare state and lack the reactionary connotation so often associated with agrarian, center, liberal, and radical parties on the European continent. Indeed, in changing the name of their party to "Center," the Agrarian leaders coolly appraised the gradual decline of the farming population and decided to broaden their appeal.

All these variations have made the task of the Conservatives infinitely more difficult in Sweden than it has been in Britain where the left wing of the party touches the right flank of the Labour party. Between the Conservatives and their main opponents stand two parties willing to temporize with socialism either from conviction or from self-interest. The Swedish Conservatives have suffered the fate of many other European conservative parties. Overwhelmed by the Liberals in 1906 (like the British Conservatives at that time), they were unable to stage more than a brief comeback from 1907 to 1911. The inexorable rise of the Social Democrats (and the refusal of the Agrarians and the Liberals to melt away) made the Conservatives a perpetual minority, the party of the top people and the would-be elite. In some ways the Conservatives, like the Republican Old Guard, have simply reacted against the popular mood. They supported rearmament in the 1920's when the world was pondering the possibility of perpetual peace; they favored economic retrenchment in the 1930's when smart politicians were spending their way out of the depression; and in the 1950's, when Sweden took the last steps toward the welfare state, it was the Conservatives who even went so far toward political suicide as to suggest the withdrawal of certain family allowances. Despite all this they have won the support of certain leading intellectuals such as Gunnar Heckscher and even of a number of the workers.

One explanation sometimes offered for the multiparty character of Swedish politics is the electoral system of proportional representation, but this does not explain how it is that half the population prefers one of the four parties; the success of the Social Democrats in retaining support among the electorate over the years is as interesting as the fourfold division of Swedish politics. Compared to the vicissitudes that the French Socialist party and the British Labour party have undergone, the relentless retention of power by the Swedish Social Democrats is amazing. Somehow they have managed not to alienate the new generation, they have avoided the decline of socialism that many Englishmen think is the inevitable consequence of a changing society and the creation of the "new middle class," and they have skillfully prevented their opponents from seizing an issue on which they could unite. After the manner of innumerable British Conservative prime ministers, they have "kept the political temperature low." And like the British Conservatives they display all the characteristics of a party that regards itself as the ruling group.

Styles of Representation

Individualism or Organism:
The United States Versus the Rest

There is an individualism about American elections that would seem to have no counterpart in parliamentary liberal democracies. In the United States the candidate fights alone: he determines to enter party primaries; if successful, he goes on to the election proper. At all times, unless he is a presidential candidate, he confines his attention to his own bailiwick, whether this be a congressional district or a state, and by law he is required to be a resident of the state in which he is competing. It is only *after* a man reaches Washington that he is co-opted into the inner circles of congressional politics. At the start all representatives, or nearly all, come alone to Washington as the delegates of their states. This is as true today as it was when the Constitutional Convention met at Philadelphia, and it is taken for granted in the United States. It is because most Europeans have no understanding of the very different style of representation in the United States that they are puzzled by the Washington merry-go-round.

A good example of this individualism is the way in which many candidates run for office. They raise their own money, often by direct appeal to powerful backers but sometimes through their own family or personal fortune. (Of course it often happens that powerful interests with money search for a candidate, and occasionally a hopeful candidate and moneyed interests meet to the mutual satisfaction of each. In so doing they create their own machine, which may be separate from the regular party machine in a number of cities and counties; it is a commonplace in the United States for candidates to circumvent the local machine.)

Nowhere is this individualism more apparent than at the presidential level. Nowadays there seems to be an increasing tendency for hopeful candidates to trust their luck in the primaries in the hope, not entirely ill-founded, that when the interests finally meet at the national convention they will jump onto the popular bandwagon. In this way John Kennedy clinched the nomination in 1960 and Barry Goldwater in 1964. Everyone recalls the efficient way in which these candidates' political machines operated. How many foreigners realize the extent to which presidential campaigns depend on the candidates' individual initiative and the voters' personal regard for the candidates, rather than on the party loyalties that operate so strongly in a parliamentary system?

The president of the United States, senators, and even congressmen are therefore individualists in the proud American tradition. Alone as they are in the political world (for in Washington itself they move in a political society cut off from the more normal social life of the great cities of the United States) it is hardly surprising that they are open to temptations of all sorts and to pressures from which members of parliamentary systems are to some extent sheltered. Yet if asked, each one of them would probably prefer the independence that this system gives him to the disciplined party conformity expected in the House of Commons. Cross-voting is taken for granted in Congress, and no whip has the power, as he has in Britain, to withdraw the whip and thereby label a member an Independent who must fight the next election alone—possibly against a regular party candidate. In Britain to lose party backing is to receive the kiss of death.

British elections tend to be fought by teams of politicians; in France and Sweden too the party would seem more like an organism than an association of discrete individuals. A budding British politician joins the party as a young man, makes a reputation in the local constituency, speaks to a motion at the annual party conference, and is noted by his elders as a promising candidate. His future does not depend on the longevity of the constituency's incumbent. The party's regional organizer or even head office will arrange for him to fight his first election elsewhere—in some constituency where he has not the ghost of a chance of winning. But this campaign gives him experience, and by degrees he is given more of a sporting chance, if he is worth it. He may never return to his home constituency again. The party, not the candidate, usually finds the necessary funds.

If this pattern of nomination by co-option were dominant in Britain, it would reduce the role of local party organizations to one of impotence, and this is certainly not the case. There are numerous instances of associations considering very seriously whom *they* will nominate, and among the contenders are usually a number of American-style individualists. In every cabinet there are a number of ministers who started their political lives this way at the grass roots.

When an important American election campaign gets under way, a number of British newspaper correspondents tour the United States. Many of them observe with surprise that the citizens of this great democracy appear to know little about the election campaigns in states other than their own. However, the correspondents do not stop to think of the great number of candidates whose names must be known by voters just in their own states. Their British counterparts are concerned simply with their own constituency and its neighbors and with the leading ministers of the parties. Many vote in reality for the party leader and his team. It is alleged that the personality of the average candidate counts for very little—though few would go so far as the rabid Labour supporter who announced to an interviewer that he would vote for a pig if his party thought fit to nominate one. By and large the English electorate is more interested in the policies of the parties than in particular people.

By contrast, in the United States the voters appear to study politicians rather as Englishmen study horses. They know something about the two presidential and two vice-presidential candidates (and have spent some time studying the form of various other potential presidential candidates within each party in the months before nomination). They are supposed to know who are the two senatorial candidates in their state and to recall names of others who contended in the primaries. They may or may not remember the name of the senator not up for election—and his opponents two or four years ago. With luck they will also know something about the people who appear every even year in the hope of being elected to Congress. It is not surprising that few Americans keep abreast of what is going on elsewhere in elections of national interest, though the more politically interested very often do. On top of this every American is expected to have ideas as to who should be governor of his state, his state senator, and state representative. And all this has nothing to do with local elections, in which once again the choice is far wider in the United States than in Britain, where only one councillor has to be elected. Europeans, and many Americans, make fun of the long lists of local officials who must run for office. How often do they stop to think of the extraordinary capacity of Americans to cope with the variety of individuals who present themselves as candidates for president, senator, congressman, governor, and state legislator—all of whom are far more important than local officials?

Since the British have only one M.P. to elect (and one councillor in local elections), it is only natural that they should have a wider perspective in some ways than Americans have on national politics. And the very individualism of American representation helps to make what goes on elsewhere of much less interest. The British parliamentary parties are organisms in a very real sense, so much so that it is they, not the voters, that select their leaders and thus prime ministers, and they may, and do, replace prime ministers in office without thinking it necessary to call an election. Harold Macmillan governed for over two years before the British people were asked to pronounce on his capacity as prime minister.

To describe this difference as purely British versus American would be absurd. On the whole, the individualist style is an American, or at least federal and presidential, characteristic. It is in smaller countries, governed according to parliamentary and unitary principles, that there is much more of an organism. French parties differ in the degree to which the organism permits a man to rise to influence; the Radicals revived after 1945 because they permitted good young men to rise to the top more quickly than in slow-moving bureaucratic organizations such as the Socialist party. The organic nature of French politics has long intrigued foreign observers, who have noted the camaraderie in the legislature. Thus it has been said that deputies of different parties have more in common than a deputy and a voter of the same party. (It is odd that French deputies should nevertheless have found it so difficult to work together in providing stable government, but this raises a different question from that of parties and representation.)

Unfortunately, very little investigation of this issue has been made in Sweden, but the signs are that political representation is quite unlike the American pattern, even though there is a locality rule in Sweden. Partly this is because the constituencies are large, but chiefly it is because Swedish society, like British, is more closely knit than American, and everyone, certainly within a party, appears to know the other candidates. Here, too, the party is an organism—one that seems to change much more slowly than parties in the other three liberal democracies.

Simple or Complicated Electoral Arrangements: The United States and Britain Versus Sweden and France

The United States may have a large number of elections, but at least the arrangements are simple. Two candidates compete and the one who obtains more votes wins. The same simple arrangements are to be found in Britain and much of the Commonwealth. Two candidates from two parties, Conservative and Labour, run or stand for office in single-member constituencies. The arrangement is hard on third parties trying to establish themselves, particularly in the United States where a party must either show a capacity to win a presidential election or go under, but at least it preserves the system from constant harassment by new movements.

Elsewhere some form of proportional representation or list of candidates is common. A glance at Sweden and France shows that these countries not only have several political parties, but that they have been persuaded to adopt more complicated electoral arrangements. It would seem that countries tend to choose between single-member constituencies and simple majority elections, on the one hand, and the pursuit of abstract democratic principles, on the other. But because two things happen together it does not follow that they are necessarily related, still less that A must cause B and not B cause A. Neither Sweden nor France has always enjoyed (or suffered) proportional representation, yet they have never had a two-party system even when they used the Anglo-American electoral system. It is more plausible to presume that complicated electoral arrangements are adopted where there are divergencies of opinion that do not express themselves in a two-party system than to argue that these arrangements have been devised to satisfy some abstract principle at the expense of good government.

That the argument of "principle" has been used to support proportional representation is undeniable. It would seem reasonable to suggest that in an election where 70,000 out of 100,000 electors vote, and where four candidates receive 20,000, 18,000, 17,000, and 15,000 votes respectively, the first has hardly received a mandate from the people, and that such a system makes a mockery of the term "sovereignty of the people." For even if the 30,000 nonvoters are neglected as irresponsible (which may or may not be a justifiable inference), it is difficult to ignore the 50,000 who voted *against* the successful candidate (as it may well be argued that they did).

At this point electors, parties, and legislators have found themselves faced not simply with the question of principle but with the question of the nature of good government itself. For unless a majority of the people believe that they are adequately represented, democratic government cannot survive. It is all very well to say, as Britons and Americans do, "Compose your differences and adopt a two-party system," but this may not be feasible. The Americans succeed by an extraordinary combination of what is both a two-party and a hundred-party system; the British have reached their present position only after much argument and a decline of the Liberal party that was by no means inevitable. Had the three parties attained and maintained parity in the House of Commons and the country, some alternative form of election would have had to be devised.

Proportional representation and the alternative vote have occasionally been introduced for anything but idealistic reasons—namely, to divide the opposition or to increase the relative strength of the party in power. The diverse French electoral systems, for example, have usually had as their object the production of some *disproportion* between votes and seats. There is little doubt that the Swedish Conservatives who introduced proportional representation in 1907 considered it to be more to their advantage than the single-member constituencies suggested by the Liberal government that they replaced. In this they were right, though events proved that nothing could prevent their gradual decline. It is worth remembering, incidentally, that despite proportional representation the Swedish Social Democrats have often been able to win more seats than all three opposition parties combined.

The French political system has oscillated between two poles since the Revolution. It has from time to time tried to get all sections of opinion in a deeply divided country represented, not necessarily in their full strength, in Parliament, and that has made stable government impossible. The divisions in Parliament and the consequent instability are not caused by the political system; the political system reflects the real divisions of the country. Thanks to an admirable civil service, this unstable system, with frequent falls of government (at least from 1875 to 1958), did not work as badly as British or American observers often thought. Thus France could be a pioneer in the creation of "Europe." But no French government could make really unpopular decisions, such as the one to end the war in Indochina or the one to give independence to Algeria. The old system cracked in 1958 and the French turned to the other pole—that of sacrificing due representation of minorities to governmental stability. This was done both by the concentration of effective executive power in the hands of the president (who, it was known, would be General de Gaulle) and in going back to single-member districts, which meant that minorities would lose most of their seats since their strength was widely spread and not concentrated in enough districts. Thus both Communists and Socialists were badly underrepresented in the new National Assembly elected in 1958, while the Gaullist[6] *Union pour la Nouvelle République* (U.N.R.) was absurdly overrepresented. The Assembly had a right to reject de Gaulle's prime minister, but it was soon apparent that the real target of such an action would be the president himself. So when, in 1958, the Assembly finally found the courage to vote him down, de Gaulle retorted by dissolving it, appealing to the country to choose between him and the "parties of yesterday." The public chose

---

[6] General de Gaulle forbade any party to use his name, but this prohibition was evaded. In some districts *every* candidate, except the Communist, professed to be a "Gaullist."

de Gaulle, and, for the first time in modern French history, one party had a majority in Parliament, even if that party was simply the shadow of one man. In 1965 de Gaulle was reelected as president for seven years. In 1967 his party managed (just) to retain control of the Assembly.

But usually when a nation changes to proportional representation it abandons single-member constituencies for good. Perhaps it is the Anglo-Americans who are old-fashioned, clinging to a belief in the traditional two-party dialectic and convinced that in the best political systems there is a political pendulum that swings first one way and then another as "the people" (in reality the marginal voter) choose differently.

For it can be observed from a study of French and Swedish elections that the voting behavior in France and Sweden is not markedly dissimilar from that prevalent in Britain and the United States. There is the same long-term stability of preferences. The fact is that in all four countries the apparent sudden swings of opinion are more apparent than real. Britain, for example, did not go wildly left-wing in 1945 when it returned the Labour party to power with a large majority. The number of electors who voted Labour was 11,985,733. But 13,032,660 voted for other parties, mainly Liberal and Conservative. In the three elections that the Conservatives won, in 1951, 1955, and 1959, they received less than half the ballots cast. This was also true of the Labour party in its 1964 and 1966 victories.

What does all this mean? It would appear that the electoral system of proportional representation cannot be wholly blamed for *causing* multiparty systems but that it is to some extent itself the product of a multiparty division. There is some sense in the old notion that a people gets the government it deserves. Britain and America have escaped some of the ideological divisions common in many countries. (As we noted, Sweden, where for centuries there were four estates, now possesses four parties.) Where the British and Americans have encountered serious trouble they too have resorted to complicated electoral devices. Hence we note the various electoral arrangements proposed for the British African colonies with small white minorities as they emerge into nationhood and the numerous ballots at presidential nominating conventions. There would seem to be some connection between the success of simple electoral arrangements (and a two-party system) and stable government.

Variable or Fixed Election Dates:
Britain Versus the Rest

The British (and certain other Commonwealth countries such as Canada) leave the date of a general election unknown until the prime minister chooses to announce it—and thereby discourage the elaborate voting studies that are carried out at fixed intervals in the United States. The date is not entirely left to the prime minister's discretion, for Parliament has a maximum life of five years—though of course there is nothing to prevent Parliament from repealing this statute when it chooses. Thus during the 1939–45 war there were no general elections in Britain, and the last one prior to the war was in 1935, before Chamberlain became prime minister and before Hitler had started his policy of expansion.

The prime minister (in theory, the crown) determines the date of an election and naturally chooses one to his advantage, preferably when the weather is pleasant, the country prosperous, and the foreign scene tranquil. To ensure this remarkable coincidence he may be tempted to postpone "going to the country" too long and thus be forced in the fifth year to name a date that is not congenial to him and his party. He may even find that public opinion or the march of events compel an early election, as Harold Wilson discovered in 1966 after winning the 1964 election by a small margin. There is thus an element of chance about the system that appeals to the British sporting instinct.

Why the prime minister retains this power is a bit of a mystery. Constitutionally the power of dissolution belongs to the crown as part of the prerogative. This can always be challenged by Parliament, as it was long ago in Sweden when the Riksdag fixed the date of elections in the Parliament Act. An argument often used in Britain to defend the present system is that the prime minister needs the power of dissolution in order to keep party discipline, but this argument is not accepted in Sweden. There would seem to be three different ways of coping with elections: the American presidential system of fixed elections, the British parliamentary method of variable elections, and the Franco-Swedish parliamentary practice, copied elsewhere, of providing for fixed elections but allowing the government to dissolve Parliament under certain conditions. The power to dissolve Parliament is essential in parliamentary politics as the counterpart of Parliament's right to censure and thus force the resignation of the government. But there is no reason why the British variant of parliamentary government should not provide for any fixed elections at all: the system today is merely a relic.

Sovereignty of the People or Sovereignty of the Crown: The United States and France Versus Britain and Sweden

It is no longer customary to distinguish peoples like the Americans and the French who live in republics from others like the British and the Swedes who have kings and queens. The British and the Swedes claim to be as democratic as anyone else and in a very real sense they are right. Of course republicans nurse a secret suspicion that there must be a difference between being a citizen of a republic and being a loyal subject of a queen; yet by no means are all Canadians, for example, convinced that they would gain by adopting the American principles of government.

However, such concessions to the feelings of people brought up in constitutional monarchies (as they were called before they became liberal democracies) should not blind us to a number of important distinctions between monarchies and republics. These were emphasized by Edmund Burke in 1790 when he reflected on the Revolution in France—and Burke is a patron saint of British liberals as well as of all conservatives.[7] In Canada in 1945 the minister of finance, J. L. Ilsley, insisted that the government had authority to act without the express approval of Parliament and added: "The authority of the government is not delegated by the House of Commons; the authority of the government is received from the crown." According to one commentator, this statement "horrified certain ultra-democrats in the house who had apparently been believing that they lived in a republic."[8] Certainly there are many people in constitutional monarchies who are disinclined to believe that there is any real difference in the form of government between monarchies and republics. Consequently many Labour party supporters in Britain were shocked to find the queen selecting a new prime minister in 1957 before the Conservative party had chosen a new leader to succeed Anthony Eden; the queen, in

---

[7] See, for example, Harold Laski, *Political Thought in England, Locke to Bentham* (London: Oxford University Press, 1955), p. 182.
[8] R. M. Dawson, *The Government of Canada*, 4th ed. rev. by Norman Ward (Toronto: University of Toronto Press, 1963), p. 189.

effect, appointed Macmillan as the leader of the party (after appropriate consultation with the party's elder statesmen).

In principle this means that the American and the French constitutions have transferred sovereignty from the crown to the people—whatever that may mean. It is arguable that sovereignty lies in the American constitution, or even with the Supreme Court as its guardian. Ultimately, nonetheless, it is the people in both countries who determine the form of the constitution. Constitutional monarchies, on the other hand, retain the sovereignty of the crown. But much of the power has merely been transferred from the crown in the person of the monarch to the crown in the form of the cabinet: hence the remark of the Canadian minister of finance. Of course, if they wished, the parliaments of Sweden and the Commonwealth could seize all the residual prerogatives of the crown, much as the Continental Congress or the French National Assembly did. The fact remains that they have not chosen to do so. Thus an American can appeal successfully to the Supreme Court for a passport denied to him by the State Department. There is no appeal beyond Her Majesty's Secretary of State for Foreign Affairs should he decide to withhold any British subject's passport. He is exercising the prerogative of the crown. Were he to use this power, however, it is likely that Parliament would pass a statute regulating the issue of passports, and this would diminish the scope of the prerogative. In constitutional monarchies the legislature constantly encroaches on the prerogative in this way, but it does not disappear because the extension of governmental power in the modern world more than compensates for what is removed from its control. It must be conceded that the whole question of the prerogative must remain somewhat mysterious to Americans accustomed to government by a written constitution in which the source of executive power is explained. But an awareness of its existence is essential for an understanding of the difference in style between the two governments.

In practice much of the power has been transferred to the people in Britain and Sweden, for it is they who at election time effectively determine who will become prime minister. Yet the controversy that has gone on during the present century over the rights of the people, in particular the need for the crown in parliament to receive a "mandate from the people," is some indication of the fog that still envelops the electoral process in constitutional monarchies. The situation is complicated in Britain by the notion that Parliament is supreme. For if Parliament has the supreme power, then the people have not. The suspension of elections during wartime indicated that Parliament, if it wished, was supreme; the speed with which elections followed the defeat of Germany in 1945 nevertheless proved that the people could not be ignored. John Locke was right when he hazily observed that in a very tolerable sense, power could be said to lie in Britain with Parliament—and with the people—and even with the executive.

It would be wrong to draw too sharp a distinction between republics and monarchies in this delicate matter, but this is not to say that no distinction can be drawn at all. Perhaps the clearest and simplest way of illustrating the difference between the role of the people and elections in the four countries is to suggest that in the two republics there has been a *positive* insistence on the transfer of power, whereas in the monarchies the crown has yielded to pressure. To take an example: the French people have been asked several times to approve a proposed constitution by referendum. This procedure is unheard of in Britain where the people were not consulted at the time of the Glorious Revolution of 1688 —or when Edward VIII was asked to abdicate in 1936. The great English statesmen from Burke to Churchill have always spoken in the name of the British people and with bland aristocratic assurance have always known the people's views without having to ask. It is too early to speak with assurance about Sweden, as full parliamentary government dates only from 1917. There is the same insistence on the royal prerogative (the constitution stating that the king alone governs the realm[9]), but there seems to be a greater willingness to consult the people through referenda and other means.

To elevate the distinction between the sovereignty of the people and the sovereignty of the crown to a difference in principle might be to grant it altogether too much significance, but to pass over it entirely would be to overlook an interesting divergence of theory. Frenchmen and Americans, heirs of a revolutionary tradition, can without embarrassment plead for a political system based on the principle of one man, one vote. In Britain and Sweden the main electoral reforms were brought about by conservative govern-

---

[9] Article 4.

ments that instead of being swept away by the tide of democracy were able to channel and ultimately to control it.

All this is not to say that either the United States or France lives up to its glorious revolutionary tradition of one man, one vote. The United States Senate overrepresents the rural states, the president is elected by often unrepresentative electoral colleges, and, until recent Supreme Court decisions, congressional districts were gerrymandered on a grand scale. The cardinal fact of the United States political system today is that the people are *not* sovereign: the urban majority is controlled by the representatives of the rural minority. This control is, however, threatened by the 1962 decision of the Supreme Court that voters can sue in federal courts to force states to redistrict, a right that can work only against the rural areas. As for the French, they go even further, blatantly manipulating their electoral system every few years. In 1958 de Gaulle was supported in the Assembly by the U.N.R. party of just over two hundred deputies who far outweighed the fifty Socialists and Communists. But whereas three and a half million people voted for the U.N.R., seven million voted for the Socialists and Communists. If the principle of the sovereignty of the people means that the legislature shall fairly represent the people, then France too is not sovereign. How strange, then, it is to find that gerrymandering is unknown in the two monarchies, and indeed that people are shocked by practices that in the republics are regarded as part of the game of politics.

Conclusion

An examination of the political process therefore shows that there are certain obstacles in the way of any sweeping generalizations about the liberal democracies. The United States is sometimes portrayed as a unique political system (the Canadian example across the border being conveniently ignored). Insofar as this concerns the presidential system the remark is indeed true: the United States system is different from parliamentary systems, as the next chapter indicates. It is also true that Americans, being a vigorous people, not only *run* for office (whereas British candidates *stand* for election) but run as individuals instead of standing pat on a party platform. The apparent gregariousness of Americans often conceals an intense self-reliance.

At other times, when the memory of George III temporarily fades into the background and the grandeur of Winston Churchill pervades their minds, Americans and Englishmen are willing to concede an Anglo-American style of politics (which may be contrasted with a Continental approach). Both the American and British systems are established according to common law, enjoy two-party systems, and prefer simple electoral arrangements. Yet there are many underlying contrasts. One society is heterogeneous, the other homogeneous; one is radical and individual and the other conservative and organic. And added to this there are faint traces of an ancient ideological divide, for the irregular elections of a traditional monarchy coupled with the sovereignty of the crown accord ill with the regular consultation of "We, the People of the United States" and the assumption that all true government is republican.

Instead of a simple division between America and the rest or between the Anglo-Americans and the Continentals there is a more complex relationship, Britain being in some ways more like the Swedish monarchy than like the United States and France having much in common with its sister republic. Above all, each is the product of its own peculiar history as well as being subject to innovations from abroad. The desire to detect patterns of politics must never be allowed to prevent us from noting fundamental differences or cause us to overemphasize superficial similarities.

3

GOVERNMENT

Similarities of Organization

Before the differences between one liberal democratic form of governmental organization and another are examined, we ought perhaps to remind ourselves of what they have in common, for it is this that distinguishes them as a class from other forms of government. One important feature of liberal democracies is their general insistence on the importance of governmental structure. Unlike the communist states, which emphasize the political process, liberal democracies have traditionally regarded parties, groups, and elections—all that is implied by the term "political process"—as the junior partner in the state, not the senior. It is because power really lies with the governmental structure proper that political scientists have rightly been mainly concerned with the organization of government.

Another important feature of all liberal democracies is a recognition of the timeless significance of the principles expounded by Aristotle, Locke, Montesquieu, and others (but nowadays often rejected by the communists as old-fashioned or as a bourgeois device for retaining power) that the powers of government in the broad sense should not be concentrated in the hands of a single institution, still less a single person. It is generally agreed that the responsibility for making laws should rest with an assembly of elected representatives who are in touch with the people and that their execution should be the responsibility of a smaller group of people. The executive branch should in addition be held responsible by the legislature, and there has been some argument in the present century as to whether the executive should be as responsible to the legislature in foreign policy as it is in domestic. Hence the movement in America that led to the proposal of the Bricker amendment, which would have limited the power of the president to make agreements with foreign powers. Similar protests have been made elsewhere; they have met with similar lack of success.

Neither the executive nor the legislature is thought suitable for interpreting the laws of the land, and in each country there is a third branch of government called the judiciary that, though appointed by the executive, is independent of it. Judges are usually appointed for life or a fixed term, and there is a long-established principle that no judge should allow reasons of state to pervert his judgment on what is right and what is wrong according to law. The judiciary is not the creature of the executive. During wartime in Britain the government and Parliament were only able to deal with suspected Nazis by refusing to allow them ordinary legal rights. Had the Nazis been allowed access to the courts they would have been freed because of lack of proof. Rather than try to "persuade" the judges, the government took the grave step, which won popular approval at the time, of summary imprisonment without trial.

The practice of the separation of powers owes much to the English experience admired by Montesquieu in the eighteenth century, a system that seemed so sensible but that was in fact the product of much argument and even war during the turbulent seventeenth century. Americans tend, with some justice, to think that the full expression of the principle—that is, the separation of institutions as well as powers—occurs in only their inimitable constitution. However, the Swedes have long prided themselves on their own indigenous tradition of separated powers exemplified in their constitution of 1809. Only the French seem to have failed to realize its fundamental significance—which may explain why their own organization of government oscillates so much more wildly between the extremes of legislative and executive domination. Yet even the French have paid lip service to the principle and on occasion have attempted to make it the cornerstone of their system.

Separation Versus Fusion of Governmental Institutions

Separation of Powers:
Presidential Government in the United States

Americans have separated their institutions of government in a way quite different from parliamentary liberal democracies. The president does not take his seat in either house; he does not attain his position by co-option through the party ranks in the legislature; he does not usually appoint legislators as cabinet officers; he does not function as chairman of a committee of the House or Senate when he confers with his cabinet. He is alone, the single executive, responsible to the people who elected him and to the constitution to which he swore allegiance when he took office.

The position of president is thus very different from that of prime minister. In the first place, the president need not be a member of the national political leadership group, as a British prime minister must be. He may have had no experience in any executive post or have held no political office filled by popular vote. But the moment he is nominated he becomes the leader of the party in name; if he is elected president, he becomes its leader in fact. He may handle this part of his duties ineptly as, in different ways, Taft and Harding did. But there can be no substitute for the president as leader. The office creates the man, sometimes out of rather poor raw materials. Willy-nilly, senior politicians have to accept him as their leader; his party is committed to his success.

Compared with a British prime minister, the president in his executive capacity has advantages and disadvantages. He can fill not only the cabinet but a great many important administrative posts with his personal choices and draw on a much wider range of knowledge and ability than a British prime minister can. Immovably in power for his four-year term and usually certain of renomination for a second term, he can ignore coalitions and conspiracies against him with more confidence than a British prime minister can.

But he has handicaps as well. His responsibility will not be dispersed over the cabinet as it is in Britain. If one of his nominees makes a fool of himself, the public criticism will fall at least as much on the man who appointed the blunderer as on the blunderer.

The president also suffers a more serious disadvantage. He has not the same command of Congress as a prime minister has of the House of Commons. The chairmen of the great committees are there because they have been in Congress a long time, before the president came, and they will be there, unless death intervenes or they lose an election, after he is gone. They are independent powers. A president, even a newly elected and widely popular president, must negotiate, not order. It is in his skill in dealing with Congress that his political competence is tested.

What weapons does the president have in his dealings with congressional leaders? One weapon, still of some use but blunted as compared with its past efficacy, is patronage. The amount of patronage today is exaggerated. It is limited by a more and more effective civil service system, by the built-in privileges of veterans' preference, by the competition of the business world that makes federal jobs less attractive to the able and ambitious. And there is still truth in the old jibe that giving a job means making nine enemies and one ingrate. Moreover, the fact that the Senate must ratify the nominations to all really important jobs, and to many that are only formally so, means that powerful senators can blackmail the president by threatening to turn down his nominees. Again the president must negotiate, not simply order.

But a competent president has other weapons. He can go before Congress and use it as a sounding board. He can reveal news as well as make news. And since the time of F. D. Roosevelt, the presidential press conference has become a quasiconstitutional institution.[1] The advantages, from the presidential point of view, are manifold. If a president is quick on his feet he can give the public an impression of energy and competence that more formal appearances may not make possible. He can ensure that if he wants to make a point, at least one questioner will let him make it. He can actually influence the press corps in his favor if he is adroit and apparently candid, as F. D. Roosevelt was, or charmingly

---

[1] The regular press conference was invented by Woodrow Wilson, but he practically abandoned it after the United States entered the First World War and never developed its full potentiality—nor did any of his successors until Roosevelt.

indiscreet, as Harry Truman often was. And through the press he can influence and educate the public. The press conference has often been compared with question time in the House of Commons. There are resemblances—and important differences. At a press conference the correspondents from the press (and television and radio) are the president's guests. He can refuse to answer; he can retort; he can evade. In the House of Commons, the minister, even the prime minister, is formally on equal terms with other members of the House. A president can hold as many or as few press conferences as he likes and run them as he likes, but question time in the Commons is a highly esteemed *right* of the members. A president can set the stage for a press conference as a prime minister cannot set the stage for question time. He can, in effect, dictate the main theme although he may be harassed by irrelevant and trivial questions; he can use his time to make real points. In spite of its real defects, the press conference is an instrument of presidential power. So is the television address; the president can always command time on the air, displace even the most popular programs, and suggest, if not impose, his own sense of priorities on the public. Ever since the time of the second Roosevelt, radio and then television have added to presidential power.

Other forces have also added to this power. More and more, the main themes of American politics have been foreign and military policy; this adds to presidential power. Diplomatic negotiation is "executive entirely," as Jefferson insisted. A wise president will take important congressional leaders into part of his confidence, but the decision whether to negotiate or how to negotiate is his. So is the most secret information. Again, a president may keep the chairman of the Senate Foreign Relations Committee and the chairman of the House Foreign Affairs Committee informed, but information, even complete information, is not power. And the power of the Senate to ratify or not to ratify treaties is not as important as it once was, since so much negotiation today is done not by treaties but by "executive agreements" and private deals with heads of foreign states, friendly or unfriendly. Another factor is the growth of influence of the House of Representatives. In the past, the role of the House committee was minor. But foreign policy today almost always involves large sums of money that the House must vote, so that congressional power over foreign policy is now shared between the House and the Senate.

Then, too, the president is also commander-in-chief. As such he has special powers and special responsibilities that Congress cannot whittle down. He can do things as commander-in-chief that he cannot do simply as president, such as sending troops into battle. Military policy is even more wrapped in secrecy than is foreign policy. Independent bodies such as the Central Intelligence Agency can play an important and possibly dangerous role, subject only to presidential supervision. What the French in the old days used to call the *secret du roi* ("the king's secret") is part of the presidential powers today.

Congress resents this. It is safe to say that even at the beginning of an administration in which the president and the congressional majority are of the same party, the White House and the Capitol see each other as rivals as well as partners. No president who does not abdicate his functions can avoid differences, quarrels, possibly open war with Congress. But the lesson of history seems clear. All the trend of American history has been to concentrate the final power in the hands of the president. Congress may deny him money; the Supreme Court may deny him legal authority; but the American people, *if* they want leadership, look always—and more than ever today—to the president for it. For he alone can say, as Truman complained, "The buck stops here." He is the embodiment of the people of the United States and all efforts to cut the presidency down to size are vain. In quiet times Congress may nibble at the executive power, but there are no quiet times today.

A president can make of his office pretty much what his capacity suggests to him. But whatever he does, his is an august, overwhelmingly powerful—and lonely—office.

Fusion of Institutions: Cabinet Government in Britain

Government in Britain has moved down a different path of development. The struggle of the seventeenth century was between the House of Commons and the king. More recently the House of Commons has fought the Lords, and in both battles the Commons was triumphant. Or at least it appeared to be. It is apparent today that much of the power has in fact been transferred not to the Commons but to the cabinet.

Indeed, the tendency of British politics has been steadily to transfer power not only from the House of Commons to the cabinet but within the cabinet to a small group and from that small group to one man, the prime minister. There are and were good reasons for this change. For one thing, great prestige was given to the office of prime minister by the two great rivals, Gladstone and Disraeli, and this was not entirely dissipated by their successors, just as Pierce and Buchanan could not undo all the work of Jackson or Grant all the work of Lincoln.

But more important was the growth of the democratic idea of the "mandate." In the last part of the nineteenth century, British governments "went to the country" with programs not unlike an American platform and that were, indeed, more seriously intended than the average American platform is. The content of this program, the stress put on various issues, depended—finally—on the decision of the prime minister.

This development was greatly accelerated by the course of the First World War. There had to be created a cabinet committee system; there had to be created an inner "war cabinet"; there had to be created a cabinet secretariat; and the cabinet secretary was far more important than any mere private secretary to the prime minister had been. The office of prime minister was now given a recognized, efficient, and expensive organization.

The office and the committee system survived the coming of peace; the way power has of adhering to an institution was proved again. True, an idle prime minister could delegate a great deal of his power if he did not want to use it. Even so drab a prime minister as Neville Chamberlain was able to carry out a highly personal policy, profess to make peace at Munich, and, in fact, later declare war with as much authority as Pitt or Gladstone or Lloyd George.

It is probably unnecessary to say that Chamberlain's successor further extended the powers and exalted the dignity of the prime minister's office. Churchill had held high office in the previous war. In peace, before and after that war, he had also held high office. He had an unparalleled range of experience, an unrivaled knowledge of the higher echelons of military and civilian government, no doubts, no hesitations, and complete confidence in himself.

The new prime minister conferred on himself the office of minister of defense, the equivalent of being commander-in-chief

as well as president in the American system. The cabinet committee system was systematized and the committees and ministers
given real authority, especially in domestic matters.

Needless to say not all of this authority survived the Second
World War. But Churchill's successor, the almost taciturn, un-
emotional, apparently diffident Clement Attlee, showed in a very
different way the powers of his office. The surprise with which the
public learned that the new prime minister was neither dim nor
timid, nor a mere chairman of committees, showed the dangers
of a false public image. People who had known Major Attlee,
literally the last man to leave the blood-soaked peninsula of
Gallipoli after the disastrous campaign of 1915, knew that the
public image had been wrong. So did his colleagues in the war
cabinet. But it is almost certain that as prime minister Attlee drew
on resources that a lesser office would not have called for and that
the office itself gave him a power of action that he had not known
before. As his predecessor was reported to have said: "He has eaten
the royal jelly."

In peace, or so-called peace, Prime Minister Attlee was almost
as powerful as Prime Minister Churchill had been. It was he, as
far as we can discover, who decided to cut the Gordian knot in
India by announcing a date on which the British army and government would leave. The speed and authority with which Attlee
liquidated the old British Indian empire, "the brightest jewel in
the crown," should be compared with the endless chopping and
changing of governments of the French Fourth Republic on the
questions of Indochina and Algeria. Even President de Gaulle has
had to be far more cautious—or timid or evasive—than Prime
Minister Attlee. The prime minister gave a free hand to trusted
aides such as Ernest Bevin in foreign affairs and Stafford Cripps in
economic matters. But the final decision was his. After all, it was
he who had put Bevin in the Foreign Office and Cripps first on
the Board of Trade and then in the Treasury. It was in Attlee's
ministry that Harold Wilson, as a young man, learned the art of
administration. One of the pillars of the authority of the prime
minister is this power, not absolute but fairly untrammeled, of
choosing men for the cabinet and of deciding what offices they
shall hold in the cabinet. In making up his cabinet he is often
choosing a future prime minister, for there is no possible equivalent in the British system of the American "dark horse," the state
politician suddenly put at the top of the federal system or the

senator without any executive experience chosen to be president of the United States. There, in the House of Commons, are all the possible leaders. One or two apparent exceptions to this rule could be noted. Bevin was brought into the House of Commons in 1940 when he joined the Churchill government. But he was already a very important trade union leader who could have entered the House any time he liked. In any case, he was never prime minister or a possible prime minister.

In any House of Commons there are sure to be a number of "ex-future" prime ministers. Luck plays the greatest part in eliminating some and giving the prize to others: luck in being high in the party hierarchy when the time came; luck in keeping a seat in Parliament when rivals were, for the moment, in exile; luck in not having alienated powerful sections in the party. External events may play a decisive role: but for the Second World War, Winston Churchill would never have been prime minister.

But we must not exaggerate these elements. There are no really dark horses in the English political race; at the most there are gray horses. The obscure Stanley Baldwin was only obscure outside the House of Commons; inside it he was a very powerful and influential "private" member of Parliament. And this parliamentary knowledge works in reverse. Some popular and commanding figures outside Parliament have no such weight inside it.

But if the British system works reasonably well in selecting the prime minister, does it work democratically? In a sense, this question is answered by reflecting on the nature of the party system. In the Conservative party it is only negatively that the voter really has a voice. By the kind of man he *won't* stand, by the kind of man he wants more or less warmly, he defines the type that members of Parliament, over a quite long period of years, come to accept as possible or as inevitable. But it is still in the House of Commons that the decision is made. Every attempt to blast a way through to the highest office, whether made by Randolph Churchill (Winston's father) or by Joseph Chamberlain, every attempt to turn the decision of the party "in the House" in a direction it would not otherwise have taken has failed. In that sense, and possibly only in that sense, do the British have "parliamentary government" under a Conservative administration.

And under a Labour government? Here the situation is more complicated since, formally, the ruling group in the Labour party is outside Parliament. Yet the center of gravity in the Labour party still seems to be in the House of Commons. It is possible that a leader might be imposed from the outside, that the real balance of power in the Labour party might after all be as described in the party constitution. The annual conference could come to dominate the parliamentary group by denying authority *in the country* to the man chosen by the party in Parliament.

A prime minister does not have a totally free hand in "bringing young men on." But other things being equal or nearly equal, a prime minister has the chance of giving one young politician a helping hand and of ostentatiously failing to promote the career of another. This fact of life is well known to the young aspirant. He may decide to work his way into office by being useful or by being a nuisance, but for most politicians it is better to be useful. If his foot is to be permitted on the bottom step of the escalator he must have certain qualities. It is not a question of general ability—all the better if he does have that—but he must have political ability. He must be able to talk on his feet ("think" is the word commonly used for this political asset). He must, if possible, have some administrative ability or must show that he can be reasonably expected to learn. He should have shown some power of helping the party outside Parliament. He should be popular or, at any rate, not actively disliked in his own constituency. He must have no publicly bad private habits.

The aspirant at last reaches the edge of the sacred inner circle. He becomes a "minister." Until the First World War, all ministers were cabinet ministers. There were about twenty offices that automatically brought seats in the cabinet, the supreme governing committee. Since the First World War, with the creation of many more departments, only half of the ministers have been cabinet ministers. The others are heads of departments but have no automatic right to a cabinet place and so no automatic right to express their views on all topics at the highest level. They are called on when the business of their department is on the cabinet agenda but not otherwise. They are the rough equivalents of the United States secretaries of war, navy, and air force under the secretary of defense.

The aspirant then is doubly tested, both as an administrator and as a politician. He may get a department that has few problems and creates few problems; but even here a subordinate may commit some intolerable blunder, or some unforeseen accident may make the job suddenly politically dangerous. In allotting jobs, the prime minister is allotting the good and bad tickets in the political lottery.

A leading politician left out in the cold is not, as in America, exiled to the sidelines. He is still in Parliament and may be a nuisance. Only very rarely will a new prime minister discard a really formidable politician. He may exile a few veterans to the House of Lords, and he may drop a few marginal, still climbing aspirants; but he has to "do something" for those who have reached the plateau just below the peak. Of course, since the prime minister is interested in the success of his administration, he may genuinely welcome support from a former rival and be glad of it. He may think that X, in addition to being the runner-up in the race, is admirably fitted in every way for every office in the state—except, of course, the top office.

The distribution of offices is one of the greatest prerogatives of the prime minister. But although Attlee showed how powerful a Labour prime minister could be, a Labour leader who is not prime minister is not in as strong a position as a Conservative leader of the opposition. The Labour leader in opposition does not pick his "shadow cabinet"; it is chosen for him by his party's members of Parliament. He cannot choose the executive of the National Labour party, and in both bodies he may have rivals or open enemies foisted on him. He has, in effect, only one final resource: to threaten to resign and force the party to choose. But the threat may not intimidate and can, in any case, only be used once.

To sum up: under cover of the parliamentary constitution, a system in which there was a balance of power or a tug of war between the executive and Parliament, there has come into existence a system in which the overwhelming balance of power is on the side of the executive and more and more in the hands of the chief of that executive, the prime minister. Elections are between parties, but they are also between the known leaders of the two main parties. The party membership can be seen, if a parallel is wanted, as a permanent National Convention weighing the ability —and the availability—of a comparatively small number of possible candidates for the highest office. And when they have elected the leader he is, in effect, nominated for an office that resembles more that held by a modern president of the United States than that held by a prime minister of the age of Queen Victoria.

The Diffusion of Power: Sweden

The main difference between Sweden and Britain lies in the relation of the ministry to the other organs of government. Whereas in Britain the House of Commons seized all power to itself only to find that much of it went to the cabinet, in Sweden the lower house has not had such an easy time. Instead of the House of Lords there is an elected upper house, and instead of an all-powerful executive there is an administrative structure that traditionally is semiautonomous. Though things are changing, it is more true of Sweden than of most other countries that there is a *diffusion* of power rather than separation as in the United States or fusion as in Britain.

Sweden is one of the few nonfederal countries that has a powerful upper chamber. Indeed this chamber has a say in all legislation equal to that of the lower house and it debates bills simultaneously with the lower house (after the manner of the four estates) to prevent undue pressure from being brought to bear on one or another of them. A plan to abolish the upper house, which would bring Sweden into line with Norway, Denmark, and Finland, has been proposed. A single chamber would more accurately reflect changing opinion and make the quadrennial elections more significant. The proposal to end the upper house was not, it should be observed, based on any experience of obstruction—unlike the opposition to the British House of Lords.

Why has Sweden suffered less from bicameralism than many other countries? It would seem in most part due to the peculiar nature of its parliamentary system, largely inherited from the days of the estates when various devices had to be adopted to ensure a common policy. Having coped with no fewer than four chambers until 1865, the Swedes found two comparatively simple.

Four of the parliamentary arrangements are of interest. First, ministers may be members of *either* house (or of neither), and they may address *both*. There is thus no need, as in Britain, for the appointment of a number of ministers from the upper house. Nor, as in the case of George Curzon in 1932, is a member of the upper chamber denied appointment as prime minister because he belongs to "another place." Secondly, most work is done in committee (as in the United States). There is hardly any opportunity for the general debate that is so popular in Britain. Moreover, the ten standing committees are all joint committees of the two chambers.[2] This unique arrangement helps to eliminate controversy between the chambers. Each house elects ninety-seven members to sit on the committees, which average slightly less than twenty members each. In the third place, on all matters except financial measures the consent of both chambers is required. To prevent the work of government from being seriously hampered, financial measures are put to the joint vote of the chambers if they do not agree. The two houses vote separately on identical proposals and then their votes are combined. The more numerous lower house on these occasions has greater influence. Finally, there is no provision for any vote of censure. Formally at least, the legislature may only challenge the executive by impeachment—as in the United States. In practice Parliament may merely decline to vote for a government bill. Such a demonstration of lack of confidence leads to the resignation of the government in Sweden but not to the departure of the American president. Sweden's experience suggests that two chambers as such present no special problems. Much depends on the political tradition of a country and the willingness to compromise.

It is customary to contrast strong cabinet government (the British preference) with a system in which the center of power is in parliament and the ministry's life is a short one (the French practice before the advent of de Gaulle). Sweden's experience of full parliamentary government dates only from 1917, but Sweden has experienced both strong cabinets and strong parliamentary committees. Before 1917 there was a separation of powers with the king as executive; from 1917 to 1933 there was a succession of minority governments, as in the French Third Republic; since 1933 the Social Democrats have given Sweden what approximates British cabinet government, or as the Swedes call it, majority parliamentarism.

There is now a strong cabinet, at times comparable to the British. Unlike the British Parliament, however, the Riksdag retains certain important powers vis-à-vis the government. Its standing committees are able to alter radically a government bill, and because, like United States congressional committees, they each have special subjects, they are authoritative in their own sphere.

---

[2] See N. C. M. Elder, "The Parliamentary Role of Joint Standing Committees in Sweden," *American Political Science Review*, XLV, No. 2 (June 1951), 464–73.

There is even a special advisory committee on foreign affairs. Although this is but a pale reflection of the Senate Foreign Relations Committee, there is nothing at all similar in Britain or France. In checking the expenditure of the crown, the parliamentary auditors (twelve members of the Riksdag) have wider powers than the British Public Accounts Committee, and individual auditors represent the Riksdag as auditors of the great state monopolies. Two officials—the procurators of civil and military affairs (Ombudsmannen)—are judges appointed by the Riksdag to investigate complaints by the public about the conduct of the civil service and armed forces. In some ways they perform the function of question time in the House of Commons, but their investigations are more far-reaching. The Ombudsman institution has been copied in Great Britain, and some observers think it has a use in all parliamentary countries where government has grown powerful.[3] The boards of certain important financial institutions, such as the Bank of Sweden and the National Debt Office, are traditionally partly or wholly appointed by the Riksdag and not by the government.

Since under majority parliamentarism the government controls the legislative branch through the dominant party, only the institution of Ombudsman retains its traditional importance, but the other institutions—particularly the right of committees to present their own version of a bill to the Riksdag—are not without some significance. They provide some check on excessive government control of affairs, and they are the means whereby, should minority parliamentarism return, government can be carried on by the Riksdag. Like the American political system, the Swedish is designed to operate without the executive necessarily controlling the legislature. Most Englishmen, and some younger Swedes, cannot conceive of a "weak" coalition government. Ticket-splitting Americans are more likely to appreciate the advantages of the diffusion of powers and the need for such checks and balances.

It is a commonplace that by comparison with the separation of the executive, legislative, and judicial powers in American government there is a considerable degree of fusion in parliamentary systems. Not that this should be overestimated: textbooks on British constitutional law very properly stress the importance of

---

[3] See Donald C. Rowat, ed., *The Ombudsman, Citizen's Defender* (Toronto: University of Toronto Press, 1965).

the principle of the separation of powers in British government.[4] As for the Swedes, they have adopted the parliamentary system only in the present century, and so far they have not adopted all the characteristics of parliamentary government. A minister, it is true, may have a seat in the Riksdag, but he does not have that individual responsibility that distinguishes a British minister from an American secretary who is responsible to the president. But unlike the United States, where it is formally the president who is solely responsible for executive policy, in Sweden decisions are made, again formally at least, by the king-in-council. This has meant that the cabinet is overburdened with departmental matters, and it has been proposed that the British system of individual as well as collective responsibility be introduced.

Americans are more likely than most Europeans to comprehend the administrative structure in Sweden. Just as a large number of American agencies (for example, the C.I.A.) are responsible not to one of the twelve departments but to the president himself, so in Sweden agencies (such as the State Railways) are directly responsible to the king-in-council, not to a minister. In fact, whereas in most countries administration is largely carried on *within* departments, making ministerial responsibility both feasible and natural, in Sweden ministers have small departments that merely formulate policy. The great administrative agencies are geographically and legally separate. To introduce ministerial responsibility would mean drastically reorganizing Swedish administration and removing what is quite an interesting variation on the parliamentary theme. The agencies themselves date from the seventeenth century, and they resisted incorporation when ministries were created in 1840.

No doubt there are disadvantages in this peculiar example of the separation of powers, and much of the agencies' autonomy is not very real under majority parliamentarism. But there are also advantages. If it is desirable to separate policy formation and routine administration, this is one way of achieving it. Agencies obey the law, not ministerial directives, and thus conform to the principle of a government of laws, not men. Ministers have greater opportunity to concentrate on policy and to innovate. The head of an agency (the director-general) can concentrate on administra-

---

[4] For example, E. C. S. Wade and G. G. Phillips, *Constitutional Law: An Outline of the Law and Practice of the Constitution* (7th ed. by Wade and Bradley) (Mystic, Conn.: Verry, 1965), Ch. 3.

tion—but where he disagrees with ministerial policy he has access to the cabinet itself. The system offers flexibility. Ministers can be bolder, knowing that agencies can oppose them, publicly if they wish, and a compromise can be worked out. Agencies can obtain informal ministerial backing for projects that may arouse press opposition—but they can act independently if they do not wish a minister to deter them.

Policy-making in Sweden, therefore, has a number of distinctive characteristics that require us to modify the easy generalizations we are tempted to make after a survey of political life in the leading democracies. It would seem, for example, that the existence of two houses with equal status is not a characteristic only of federal systems and that parliamentary government may be divided into minority and majority forms, each with its own problems. The Swedish system is equipped with devices that enable both to be workable. Above all, in these days when the civil service is increasing in size and power everywhere and the bureaucracy and executive are identified, it is worth considering the extension of the principle of the separation of powers long practiced in Sweden—the separation of the public administration from the policy-making executive. This should certainly have appeal to those who believe in government according to law rather than government dependent on the whim of men.

The Dominant Executive: The French Fifth Republic

In the past, the French seem to have taken the question of executive responsibility to the legislature so much to heart that they allowed successive governments under the Third and Fourth Republics hardly any power at all. Ministries fell so frequently that all except the most conscientious observers lost count. Perhaps foreigners took the French system too seriously, applying their own standards to a completely different situation. It should be noted that the Third Republic lasted sixty-five years, including the period of the First World War. Even the Fourth Republic went under only because of external pressures from Indochina and then Algeria, not because of dissatisfaction with unstable government as such. It is true that important decisions were postponed or never made as a result of the changes, but French administration functioned quietly and efficiently behind the parliamentary scenes. The Common Market started with the Schuman Plan in 1950 and continued to develop when the Fourth Republic gave way to the Fifth. In themselves the changes of government have not proved disastrous. What is serious is that they symbolize an underlying instability that has grave long-term implications.

Many explanations have been given for France's governmental weakness. Some have thought that if the power of dissolution could properly be exercised, then France would become disciplined like Britain. Others accuse the electoral system. The plain truth is that so long as Frenchmen preferred to vote for a variety of parties rather than for two or three they had to suffer instability. Until the Swedes showed a distinct preference for the Social Democrats there was a similar period of unstable government in Sweden in the 1920's and the same tendency for parliamentary committees to dominate the government of the day.

Since 1958 the French have experienced government by a strong executive because of the dominant position of President de Gaulle. This was achieved partly through the introduction of a constitution that incorporated features of both the British and American political systems and partly through a new electoral system that deprived the Communists of fair representation until 1967—thus enabling de Gaulle's supporters in the U.N.R. to win a comfortable majority in the 1958 and 1962 elections.

The Gaullists have remained a disciplined party. When, in the 1967 elections, the left and center parties saw their fortunes revive, their limited success was due to a willingness to work together at last. It may be that France, like Germany, is moving toward a two-party system, but unless and until the French people become more politically homogeneous, they will continue to prefer their traditional multiparty system.

In retrospect, de Gaulle's accession to power in 1958 increasingly appears to have been one of the significant events in French history. Commissioned by the Assembly in a formal gesture of power as premier, General de Gaulle set about giving France new institutions. They were not formally his work; they were the work of politicians, lawyers, and administrators. But for the French people the author of the new constitution was General de Gaulle, and, when by an overwhelming majority they endorsed it, they were endorsing not a document that few had read but the leadership of the man who had been right—right in 1940, right in 1946–47. If at this moment General de Gaulle had decided on a presidential government on the American model, with an executive directly elected by the people and formally separated from the legislature, it is possible that other European countries would have seen something to imitate or, at any rate, something worthy of interest. But for reasons that are still obscure, General de Gaulle decided to keep a kind of parliamentary government linked with a presidency that had a good deal more power and prestige than presidents had had under the Third or Fourth Republics. On paper, the premier, who had to have the support of the Assembly to stay in power, was the active head of the executive departments. The president was to be above the battle. He had reserve powers that he could use in great emergencies, but he was, in theory, to be something between a rather idle American president like Coolidge and a constitutional monarch of the British type.

So much was this view of the new constitution held that there were intelligent people in Paris who thought that General de Gaulle would choose to be premier. But he chose to be president and therefore upset the balance, indeed made nonsense, of his own constitution.

President de Gaulle, from the very beginning, made it plain that whatever his constitution said, the general direction of government policy would be determined by the president, who would at best consult the premier, at worst merely inform him. In what has been the most important problem of the regime, the treatment of the Algerian abscess, President de Gaulle soon passed far beyond the boldest proposals of previous governments and defied the principles and passions of his most loyal supporters. He recalled the two Napoleons rather than the republican "constitutional monarchy" of the Third and Fourth Republics. It has been this personal character of the Gaullist regime that has prevented its being a source of political example to other European countries. Just as the Fourth Republic did not inspire imitation because of its weaknesses, the Fifth does not inspire imitation because of its personal character.

Yet it would be wrong to write off the Gaullist experiment as an adventure in dictatorship. Most of the traditional "liberties of the subject" are as safe under President de Gaulle as they were under the Fourth Republic or as they are in Britain or the United States. If until recently there was inadequate criticism of the government in the Assembly, this was in part due to the overwhelming Gaullist membership, for the sweeping triumphs of the referendum on the constitution were followed by equally sweeping triumphs in the 1958 elections to the new National Assembly. Nearly all the old political leaders lost their seats, and a flood of political unknowns entered Parliament. But the elections to local government bodies—to the village and city and county councils—showed that the people were not placing authority at all levels in the hands of one man or of men claiming to represent that one man. The parties claiming to represent General de Gaulle totally failed in their attempt to get control of the local government bodies. The electors insisted on voting for the men they knew (including local Communist leaders), and the stability of French local politics was a guarantee against the dictatorial concentration of power in the hands of one man.

This stability had another result. The Fourth Republic had demoted the Senate of the Third into a mere "Council of the Republic" with hardly more than formal powers. True, the Council began to acquire prestige and a little power, revealed in the way that the members established their right to be called "senators," a title for which there was no legal justification. But the constitution of the Fifth Republic made the upper house (again called the Senate) the equal of the lower and made it an ally that it was worth the while of the executive to conciliate. The Senate was elected by representatives of the local government bodies, which had shown their fundamental conservatism (even when they voted Communist), and as a result it was possible for many political leaders who had lost their seats in the lower house to get back to active politics by entering the upper. Indeed, as far as personal prestige counts, the new French Senate was a more impressive body than the new French Assembly.

But the balance of power between the two houses has, like everything else in the French political system, been upset by the dominating personality of the first president of the Fifth Republic. The Assembly did, from time to time, show signs of anger and discontent; it finally summoned up courage to pass a vote of no confidence and was promptly dissolved. The resulting elections showed a deep cleavage between the politicians and the country. In proposing to alter the system of electing the president by means of a referendum that bypassed the Assembly, President de Gaulle gambled on the degree of trust he had earned and the degree of distrust that, he thought, the Assembly had earned. His gamble worked. If the majority for the new presidential system was not impressive, the majority in the 1962 general election that followed was. For the first time in French history since the fall of the Second Empire, there was a party majority in the lower house. Since that party majority existed only because of the appeal that President de Gaulle was able to make to the country, it was unlikely to rebel and France was guaranteed an Assembly led by the president for five years. De Gaulle's commission has been twice renewed and the next presidential elections are in 1972. The government of France is now plainly presidential.

In such a system, the role of the member of either house of Parliament is unattractive. President de Gaulle has shown, at times, what looks like deliberate contempt for the feelings as well as the ambitions of the members, to a degree that has provoked a protest from so respected a parliamentarian as Robert Schuman, one of the great makers of "Europe." As the constitution of the Fifth Republic has evolved, it has evolved in one direction, away from parliamentary and toward presidential government. For the moment that satisfies the French people.

The new government certainly can take action in both great matters and small with more speed than the governments of the old regime could do. The decision to let the "states" of the stillborn "French Community" go their own way—become independent republics loosely allied with France but not joined by any formal constitutional bonds—was taken rapidly by President de Gaulle on his own initiative, as was the decision to accept the independence of Algeria. A host of minor reforms that had been postponed were put into effect. Plans long gathering dust in official drawers were acted upon. But the drawbacks of one-man rule were also apparent. The president's ministers were specialists; none were politicians of the first rank; most were not politicians at all. The only connecting link was the will and personality of the president. The whole system was under the shadow of one man.

And after that man? President de Gaulle obviously hoped to create a two-party system or at most a three-party system. To judge by the 1967 elections to the National Assembly, he has had some success, for his opponents on the left and in the center cooperated as they had not done for many years. By abandoning the cumbrous system of electing the president by about eighty thousand "grand electors," chosen by a system that grossly over represented the countryside and the small towns, President de Gaulle has created further pressures toward simplification of the party system and has further promoted the Americanization of the French political system. A president elected by many millions of voters is a different official from one chosen by tens of thousands of local councillors. However, the need to organize the millions of voters will (so de Gaulle hopes) still further force a concentration of parties. But (and it is an important "but"), no one really knows how the system will work when the prestigious author is dead or retired. No one will have de Gaulle's charismatic appeal. It is possible that a president other than de Gaulle will not be able to use to the full extent the powers that the amended constitution of 1962 gives him. The premier may recover some of his lost powers. No one knows. The old parliamentary system is not likely to return, but *a* parliamentary system is not impossible, not, indeed, unlikely.

France today is governed under constitutional forms—and with the effective preservation of the fundamental liberties of the liberal tradition—by one man. After his death or retirement, it is as good a guess as any that the Fifth Republic will become more and more like the Fourth. It will be parliamentary. It will probably be more stable than was the governmental system of the Fourth Republic; the various reforms that gave the government effective control of the business of the Assembly and made it necessary to "stand up and be counted" if you wanted to change the government may well survive. Institutions such as the Constitutional Court, which has a limited power of judicial review, may know a life and effectiveness that President de Gaulle has in practice denied them.

The evolution to the new system may be peaceful; it may be the result of violence or the threat of violence. For it is a sad truth that the country that was the exemplar in continental Europe of the principles of liberty, equality, and fraternity has less and less impressed its neighbors with the political institutions in which it has attempted to embody these principles. The solution of the problem of giving France a government of laws and not men, one that is both free and competent, has not yet been found. For all its merits, the governmental system of President de Gaulle is felt to be a temporary halt in a movement forward. Where that forward move will take the French no one knows. There is at least a chance, for the first time in a century, that when de Gaulle passes on, the French will not revert to the dominant legislature pattern of government.

How Important Are Constitutions?

This may seem to be a strange question. Are there not many text-books on constitutional law that are completely devoted to an exposition of the articles of the constitution and its practical workings? Indeed, how would one start to explain American politics without first knowing a great deal about the constitutional framework of American government? The short answer to this question is that some constitutions (notably the American) are more important than others.

Constitutional Monarchies: Appearance and Reality

Least important for an understanding of how government works in liberal democracies are the constitutions of constitutional monarchies. There is no reference in them to the prime minister or the cabinet. Instead there is constant reference to a delightfully old-fashioned world in which power lies with the monarch and his council. It would be very misleading to assume that a reading of the constitutional documents of Sweden or Britain is a reliable guide to the politics of these countries. The legal approach to British politics in particular has serious limitations.

Not that it should be thought that the constitutional documents of these monarchies are totally worthless or designed to deceive the populace. If they were that, some reformist government, for example the Social Democrats in 1932 or the Labour party in 1945, would most certainly have done something about them. The constitutions are kept as they are partly because everybody knows that they are of limited value and that one must read between the lines and partly because in an ever changing world they provide an element of stability and tradition that is a source of inspiration or consolation. But above all, the constitutions remain in force because it has been found possible to adapt the political system to a more democratic age without having to change the symbols. Instead of "king" one may read "crown." The cabinet may not be composed of the king's ministers in the Tudor sense, but it is very much a body of ministers of the crown, as we have already seen. And not only has it proved possible to move from a monarchical to a democratic form of government without changing the letter of the constitution, but no doubt still further changes will be made in the future. To give one example: although the British nation has no single codified document that is called "the constitution," it does possess a number of acts that are sufficiently important to be called constitutional. Among these is the Parliament Act of 1911, which limited the authority of the House of Lords. When it was found by the Labour government that those powers required further diminution, a second Parliament Act was passed in 1949; this too is a constitutional document, as is a more recent act permitting the appointment of life peers. To the question "What *is* a constitutional document by British standards?" no clear answer can be given. It seems to be what a number of informed people think is of constitutional importance, which may seem a peculiar way of determining a country's fundamental law. The British, of course, do not think so. For the most part they tend to think that this is most sensible and that a codified constitution like the American is more trouble than it is worth—not that anyone has ever tried fully to explain the case for and against codification to the British, still less to ask the electorate to vote on the matter.

Perhaps the greatest significance of this willingness to accept the substitution of appearance for reality in politics is that there is no harking back to a Golden Age when founding fathers produced a constitution to which future generations could always look for guidance. The British and Swedish political systems, despite their age-old traditions, seem very much part of the twentieth century; American and French government, despite their republican modernity, have been very much influenced by the spirit of the 1780's—so much so that an Englishman is never so aware of the importance of the eighteenth century as when he visits France or the United States. This is because in Britain there was no comparable ideological break with the past at a particular point in time.

Republics: The Insistence on Reality

By contrast, republics insist on reality. In France, where events have a habit of overtaking constitutions, this results in the need for new constitutions at intervals. As an advertisement once put it: "The Republics pass; X's paint remains." There is a constant and rather pathetic attempt to recapture the spirit of 1789—or

1791 or 1792 or 1800—according to whether the ruling group pre fers parliamentary government, the separation of powers, Assembly control, or autocracy. There is an assumption that somehow one can discover by rational calculation what really are the principles that should govern the politics of the country. Burke was con vinced that the French completely misunderstood what happened in the Glorious Revolution of 1688 and all that Locke was writing about. Generations of Englishmen have taken the same conde scending view of events across the Channel. There are certain things, so the British think, that are best not made explicit.

The Americans have been among the most fortunate of con stitution-makers, perhaps because they were satisfied with a short and not too explicit document and perhaps because they were part of this British tradition. The notion that the fountain of political wisdom is to be found in this document and the common assump tion that politics in America since 1787 has consisted alternately of a fall from grace or an attempt to rise up to the principles it enunciates seem strange to many people in Britain. They forget that they themselves for a long time believed in a Golden Age and that those of their ancestors who opposed the Stuarts in the seven teenth century appealed not to natural rights but to the tradi tional rights of Englishmen. James II was accused of breaking the original contract between king and people and of subverting the constitution.

This contract cannot be found in any document (except pos sibly, by legend and implication, in the Magna Carta) but was firmly believed in by generations of Englishmen. They astutely asked of their monarchs not some form of New Deal but a return to the old ways when mutual confidence was presumed to have reigned between king and people—as indeed it did in Scandinavia whence many of their ancestors came. Americans have replaced this traditional notion of an original contract with a very real and palpable contract between the states and the people—the constitu tion of the United States. If President Kennedy had favored the Roman Catholic Church it would have been construed as sub verting the constitution—exactly in the manner of James II. It i hardly surprising that successive generations of Americans feel an urge to go back to this document for inspiration and encourage ment: it is the very basis of American society, and it has served the country well.

The Civil Servants and Their Role

Nowadays we demand a great deal of our public servants. The ideal is a Dag Hammarskjöld, a man of unimpeachable standards who was able to set the tone for the sprawling worldwide bureaucracy of the United Nations. When a civil servant departs from the accepted standards—as when Sherman Adams as assistant to President Eisenhower accepted gifts that elsewhere in politics and business might be considered petty tributes to a useful aide—his dismissal is summary.

It is easy to forget that until recently there was a widespread view in America that the administrative machinery lay open to the victorious political party at election time rather like an Italian Renaissance city before the advancing *condottiere*. In all the advanced countries there is now a responsible bureaucracy. The main difference between the United States and other countries is that the former is willing to appoint persons who have lived beyond the stage of mature adolescence to positions of authority instead of taking only new graduates of the universities and grooming them for later responsibility. Yet even in Europe there was a time when merit was by no means the only criterion for appointment. Until the early nineteenth century the upper classes did quite well by the civil service when they could find no better means of support. The British Foreign Office, it was long alleged, was a system of outdoor relief for the aristocracy.

Perhaps the most distinctive characteristic of the civil services of the various European countries is that they have never entirely broken with their more aristocratic tradition. Businessmen and politicians would not presume to browbeat senior civil servants: what was an aristocracy is now an elite. The British civil service did not disappear when the Labour government took office; the Swedish colleges and administrative agencies have continued to operate as before 1932 despite over thirty-five years of social democracy, and leading Swedish civil servants are often as conservative in demeanor and political orientation as ever. The French Third and Fourth Republics would have fallen apart long before they did had not a very competent succession of civil servants controlled the administrative machinery. Perhaps the slogan should go down in history as: "The politicians pass: the civil servants remain."

Britain and the United States

As far as Britain and the United States are concerned, there are important historical differences in the way the two central governments have learned to do business. It is since about 1870 that one of the great governmental forces in Britain has been "the higher Civil Service." There had never been a true spoils system in Britain, at any rate not since the passing of the first Reform Act of 1832. But jobs *were* given to political friends and supporters—and just to friends. When an administration changed, these people kept their jobs. But they were increasingly inadequate for the needs of the new booming, industrial society putting out on the dangerous seas of democracy. So, imitating the already famous Indian Civil Service, Gladstone created the Home Civil Service. Entrance at all ranks, except in the case of laborers and craftsmen in the dockyards and kindred workers, was by competitive examination. But the important examination was at the top— the examination for the first division, or, as it is now called, the administrative class. The examination was designed to attract the ablest young men from Oxford and Cambridge (it was naïvely assumed that they would necessarily be the ablest young men in the country). They would pass at once into the governing class. They would from the beginning be well paid and given chances for very rapid promotion. Beneath them would be capable, literate, industrious clerks. But there was next to no promotion from below. This was an aristocratic civil service, a service of officers and enlisted men.

A prime minister or a cabinet minister had at his hand a group of exceptionally able men, who could be relied on to serve ministers of different parties with the same efficient loyalty. A British minister coming into office, however ignorant he might be of his duties, was surrounded from the first by capable advisers who could warn but would always obey. There were no parliamentary committees to lobby. Until 1914, the system worked admirably.

But the First World War expanded the civil service a great deal and extended the functions of the governments. It also introduced new problems for which the higher civil servant, trained in classics or mathematics, had often no answer and sometimes no adequate grasp of the situation. The Second World War magnified the problem. The civil service was now bigger than ever. Many "outsiders" were brought into it—men and women who had not been to Oxford or Cambridge or to any university, who could not be and were not members of the small group (about 1,500 strong) who had made up *the* civil service, as apart from the hundreds of thousands who were merely civil servants.

Two wars and changes in the economy have produced another problem. The number of scientists and technologists has grown immensely, and so has the importance of their work. But they are hard to fit into the old framework. The "specialists" seldom get administrative jobs, although perhaps they do not want them. The old symmetry of the classical civil service structure has been upset. There has arrived on the scene a new, important, and aggressive class that complains that it has to deal with civil servants who do not know what they (the scientists) are talking about and yet have the power to decide between two scientific or technical policies. The creation of a scientific civil service to advise the politician as the old civil service did is thus a matter of urgency.

There is another matter of urgency. It seems evident that the civil service does not any longer automatically attract the brightest young men from Oxford or Cambridge. Civil service salaries have not by any means overtaken the depreciation by inflation that has occurred since 1939; salaries in the nationalized industries are, on the whole, much higher than in the old civil service. They are still higher in private business—and the expense allowances are much more generous. Too, there may be some falling off of interest in public work. The civil service seems dull.

Yet Gladstone's reform still stands. At the center of the British government is a body of competent, incorruptible, intelligent (if somewhat narrow-minded) executants and advisers, without whose services and sagacity the whole governmental system would grind to a halt.

The president of the United States and his high-level advisers have no such instrument at their command. There is, first of all, the obstacle of the federal system. There is also the obstacle of the remnants of the spoils system. Although the spoils system has steadily dwindled since the Pendleton Act of 1882, it is not yet extinct. Some jobs are filled by presidential nominees. This means that the regular civil service sometimes finds itself excluded from the highest administrative posts. This system naturally affects the type who enters the civil service and shuts off from a totally satisfactory career some very able permanent officials who have neither political nor personal pull.

The American federal civil service with its eighteen grades is a complicated structure compared to the simple class division of the British civil service. Instead of a structure of officer, noncommissioned officer, private, there is a delicate shading from bottom to top. Senior American civil servants have not usually had the *esprit de corps*, the prestige, or the power of their British counterparts.

But there are advantages in the American system as well as drawbacks. It is easier to bring in especially competent people who have made their mark in their professions outside government.[5] The top civil service in Britain is mostly composed of men (and women) who entered the service before they were twenty-five, and they may live and often do live a blinkered life. They are admirable in their field, but it is not a wide field.

Yet each country is well served. Each country gets efficient and loyal service and sometimes service beyond the line of duty.

The contrast with the totalitarian systems is revealing. That the Soviet Union and Communist China have many admirably competent and devoted servants is obvious. But all these people work under a system of party control, less extravagant than it was in Stalin's time but rigorous all the same. They must fulfill their "norms"; mistakes easily become treason. This is not good for morale; nor in the long run can it be good for systems that undertake to regulate so much by the action of weak, fallible, if not necessarily traitorous human beings. Of course buck passing, intriguing for promotion, and imputing blame to others are not unknown in Washington or in London. But at worst, Washington and London merely run rat races. Moscow and Peking are "barracuda pools," as a critic has described Madison Avenue.

France

It is impossible to understand the social stability of France under so many changes of regime, invasion, and revolutions if attention is not paid to the enduring framework of French administration. France is governed by a highly competent and honest body of civil servants, chosen by very severe competitive examinations, of which the most famous is that for inspectors of finance. The civil servants are protected from arbitrary dismissal or other

---

[5] This is sometimes done in Britain but not very often.

unfair treatment by an elaborate system of regulations. At the top of the French administrative system stands a very remarkable body, the Council of State. The Council of State not only protects civil servants; it protects private citizens against governmental abuses and offers remedies against governmental abuse of power. It helps both to draft laws and to interpret them.

The civil servants govern France locally as well as in Paris. At the head of each *département* (rather like a big American or British county) stands the prefect. He is appointed by the government in Paris and is responsible to it. Both the Fourth and Fifth Republics have created and preserved a strictly professional body of high-grade administrators. Their first job is to see that the laws and regulations made in Paris are carried out. But they must also do their best to get along with the politicians who serve on the local councils and with *their* civil servants. From the point of view of the implementation of public policy, the French system has great advantages. It is not only that the central government is more willing to use its powers over local bodies than is the British government over local authorities (powers that are out of the question in a federal system such as that of the United States), it is also that the powers are exercised on the spot by a man who knows the area to which the law or regulation is to be applied. The higher civil service in Britain has few of its members working outside of London. They may visit "the provinces," but they don't live there.

There are, of course, drawbacks in the prefectorial system too. It can be argued that the prefectorial system destroys local initiative, although this is much less true than it once was. French cities today often show a good deal of initiative (for example, in public housing). Yet they do not control the local schools and they have insufficient tax revenues. A prefect cannot carry out a policy in flagrant contradiction to that pursued by his neighbors, still less a policy disapproved of by the minister of the interior in Paris. Yet the French central government, more than the British or American, has the means of implementing its policy if only it has a policy to implement and one that it is willing to stick to.

Sweden

The most remarkable characteristic of the Swedish civil service is its separation from the executive as well as the legislature.

Another characteristic is the use of provincial governors appointed by the central government to administer the provinces—a system comparable to the French network of prefects. The more class conscious socialist Swedes resent the fact that the various administrative agencies remain the preserve of the educated elite, some of whose members belong to families who have served the state for generations. As in so many Continental countries, there is a long tradition of public service on the part of a certain class—and of hostility to the "bureaucracy" on the part of others.

In some ways the Swedish administration has more in common with that of new nations than the civil services of Britain, the United States, and France. For a long time Sweden was a relatively backward country where the best careers were to be found in the service of the state. The industrial and commercial development of the past hundred years has altered this, but the attractions of government service remain, for the role of the government in so many aspects of Swedish life has been very considerable. Students from underdeveloped countries who find the independence of business from the civil service such a marked characteristic of the United States and even Britain would gain a great deal from an examination of the interdependence of the two in Swedish life, of the absence of antagonism between businessmen and bureaucrats, and of the loyalty to all governments that has enabled the civil service to serve Conservative and Socialist ministries.

Civil servants have long been taken for granted in the Anglo-American countries. In a world where government is becoming increasingly powerful we are being compelled to examine more closely the servants of government. They can, as in France, compensate for the deficiencies of politicians; they may, as in Nazi Germany, permit atrocities to be committed; but they should, as in all four liberal democracies, dedicate themselves to a great tradition that puts the public interest first.

4
SOCIAL AND ECONOMIC PLANNING

The Fear of "Creeping Socialism": The United States Versus Europe

There is a great deal of confusion over the question of public policy in the areas of economic planning and social welfare. Partly this is the consequence of political propaganda for and against both. To a considerable extent, however, it is because there is a sense that deeply held beliefs about the rights and responsibilities of the individual do not seem to match present-day realities: everywhere large corporations and powerful governments and trade unions seem to be in the ascendant. The confusion has been worsened by the fact that few attempts have been made anywhere to think dispassionately about social problems. This is an area of strong opinions.

It is well to begin by being clear on one point: there is a very considerable difference, as we shall see, between communist planning and that of all Western liberal democracies, including such a social democracy as Sweden, for in the West the electorate has a say. So far the American electors have been uninterested in socialism. In Britain, in 1945, the Labour party was put in power for

97

six years and permitted to nationalize certain basic industries; in 1964 and 1966 it was returned to power, and it renationalized the steel industry. In France, nationalization was a product of postwar enthusiasm among the parties of the left; in Sweden, despite thirty-five years' rule by the Social Democrats, very little socialization has taken place. By contrast, in communist countries the voting population has had no say and the economies have been thoroughly nationalized everywhere. The fundamental difference is between socialism by *choice* and socialism by *compulsion*.

Among the four liberal democracies there are, however, a number of differences between the United States on the one hand and the three European countries on the other. Two differences in particular stand out. In Europe it is taken for granted that many of the utilities such as railroads, telephones, electric power, and airlines are state-owned, a situation very different from that prevailing in the United States, where even telephones and telegraphs are privately operated. (In Canada the Canadian National Railways, Canadian Broadcasting Corporation, and Air Canada are all state-owned.) It should be added that except in Britain much of the public ownership in Europe dates from the period before 1914, and it is difficult to be sure that it is the result of "socialism." A second difference is the commitment of the other liberal democracies to what is loosely termed the welfare state. In each of them a prime object of economic policy is to ensure full employment; each of them has established what Americans call socialized medicine. Thanks to reciprocal arrangements, visitors from one country to another in western Europe are covered by a whole social security network, and this has even been extended (in part) to cover emigrants to countries such as Canada.

The gulf between "liberal" America and "socialist" Europe is not quite as great as some people imagine. It is true that the United States government has not nationalized the New Haven Railroad, the Bell Telephone System, or the Georgia Power Company, but it has increasingly regulated the nation's business—so much so that American antimonopoly legislation became a model for Britain, sixty years after the Sherman Act was passed. It is also true that the federal government has not introduced a complete health service, but Congress has agreed to government-sponsored medical care, starting with the aged. Moreover, there is a vast array of social services in the United States that other countries might well envy. Graduated old-age pensions, recently introduced with much fanfare in Britain and Sweden, have been a feature of the American social security system since 1935.

Yet there does seem to be a difference between the United States and the other liberal democracies. What is it? By and large it would seem to be this: whereas all countries have had to accept increasing state intervention (as a result of industrialization, war, and depression) in their economic and social policies, in the United States a large and vocal minority has *resented* what has been done. For a long time, the old cry "The Tennessee River flows through six states and drains the nation" was heard whenever T.V.A. was discussed. Many conservatives have adopted an individualist philosophy that they find difficult to reconcile with what so many like to call "creeping socialism."

Since this is the distinguishing feature of the United States, it is worth glancing for a few moments at the case against social and economic planning as presented by American conservatives. (These "conservatives," incidentally, are people who in Britain would find the welfare policies of the Conservative party distasteful; they would be dubbed "old-fashioned liberals.") It is a case little understood in Europe and rarely given a sympathetic hearing by American liberals, but it is not without interest if one is to understand the popularity in the Republican party of men such as Barry Goldwater and Ronald Reagan.

In the first place, the conservatives argue, America was built up by men who believed in free enterprise and individual endeavor, whether they were rich Rockefellers or humble homesteaders clearing the western frontier. By their efforts these people created the most powerful, the richest, and in many ways the most exciting society the world has ever seen. Many American conservatives have thought that if only foreigners could be brought to the United States to see the country they would be impressed, as indeed they have been. These conservatives resent the implication that individual self-reliance is not an adequate outlook for present-day Americans, and as for the past they do not poke fun at their forefathers after the manner of Lytton Strachey, who so bitingly revealed the weaknesses of some of the more eminent Victorian Englishmen.

Another reason for American concern about government planning has been given less attention than it deserves. Like other countries, the United States has to decide how to spend its money. In Britain the ceiling for defense expenditure, which was very low after the war, was doubled to over four billion dollars in 1951 with the promise that this was the maximum the country could stand. Since then, an effort has been made to keep defense expenditure down. By contrast, expenditure on social welfare, the nationalized industries, and education has increased enormously.[1] The United States, on the other hand, after a few years of euphoria following 1945, seems to have taken on the burden of defending the whole of the free world and has held the line in social welfare much more than has been possible in Britain. Defense expenditure has for some years been easily the largest item in the federal budget. Guns have been preferred to butter—or, at the very least, missiles to "mothers' aid."

Many Americans are convinced that defense must have priority and that history shows only those countries that adequately defend themselves are secure against attack and conquest. Nothing has happened to change this view; indeed if anything it has been confirmed. It is arguable of course that at least until the Vietnam war the United States could have ensured *both* adequate defense measures and more adequate social welfare, but this is not the main point of the conservatives' argument. They merely assert that no great power should spend money on social welfare at the expense of keeping its armed forces at full strength. While the Europeans (and the British Commonwealth) have been spending money on their welfare states, the United States has carried the overwhelming share of the cost of Western defense—as it has the cost of the United Nations.[2] True, the British have kept abreast of nuclear developments, producing both atom and hydrogen bombs, but this has been at the expense of the regular forces. Britain's fundamental military weakness was illustrated at the time of the Suez crisis in 1956 and even more by the Israel-Arab conflict in 1967. It is difficult to dispute the assertion that the

---

[1] Defense expenditure was $4.2 billion in 1959–60 and $5.9 billion in 1965–66. Expenditure by public authorities on social services and housing rose in the same period from $10.4 billion to $18.2 billion. See *Annual Abstract of Statistics*, No. 103 (London: Her Majesty's Stationery Office, 1966), Tables 37 and 315. Social service expenditure continues to mount.

[2] In 1966 $122 million was appropriated for the United Nations. The Americans contributed 32 percent of this, the Russians 15 percent, and the British 7 percent.

United States underwrote the European welfare states by stationing its forces in Germany.

No doubt some of the conservative hostility to the welfare state is inspired by the fear that Americans are becoming soft suburbanites instead of fighting frontiersmen. People in all countries are rightly aware that the conformity imposed in Nazi Germany, Fascist Italy, and Soviet Russia might establish itself insidiously in their own countries, and the conservatives regard self-reliance as the best antidote.

All things considered, there would seem to be a case in favor of the conservative theory concerning American individualistic self-reliance and free enterprise—that these factors made the country what it is today, that because Europeans "have gone soft on socialism" this is no reason for Americans to do likewise, and that Americans need to spend their money on defense of the free world.

Europe differs from America largely because the middle class liberal tradition there has been challenged by a working class socialist movement and by traditional upper class conservatism. Unlike American individualistic conservatism, this was, and is, in many ways paternalistic. Whereas Goldwater is cheered by American conservatives when he attacks welfare handouts, the upper class British Conservatives contrive to give the impression that they are on the side of the workingman; they have invented the term "Tory democracy."

This traditional paternalistic type of conservatism, some traces of which can be found in the United States (especially in the ante-bellum South), had a powerful hold on Europe for many centuries. It was a philosophy peculiarly suited to a hereditary ruling class that could consider that it had every right to be where it was. The lord of the manor or plantation owner considered that he had some obligation to his servants; he dispensed charity as a voluntary act—hence the term "Lady Bountiful" used for his wife. It was an admirable philosophy for those whom the gods had favored: they could keep their wealth, position, and station in life and at the same time feel a sense of well-being for having attended to their duties. Verily it was more blessed to give than to receive.

This philosophy was hardly attractive to the rising middle class. The stress on equality and individualism was a reaction, especially in America, to traditional European paternalistic society. But the point to remember is this: whereas in the United States (except in parts of the South) the standards of the middle class—puritan, thrifty, hardworking, and self-reliant—were generally accepted in all classes, in Europe they were and are more often associated with a particular class only. The older paternalistic philosophy is still there, offering an alternative to individualism. Traditional conservatism has prepared the way for socialism, and both have been hostile to the liberal spirit of laissez faire. Thus Attlee, former leader of the Labour party, could say that like most Englishmen he felt more at home in the American South than in the North. Conversely, Franklin Roosevelt as a reformer never fully sympathized with either the British Conservatives or their Labour opponents.

Not all Europeans (or all Americans) share the American conservatives' mystique of a Golden Age, of an individualist era lasting almost from the Declaration of Independence to the New Deal. They recall that all that glisters is not gold, and they believe that it was a glistering rather than a truly golden age—an era when the fortunate few amassed great fortunes at the expense of the ill-fed, ill-housed masses. They suspect that when smart entrepreneurs echoed the glorious radical cry of "all men are equal" they added, *sotto voce*, "and all are equally able to look after themselves." This was the voice of Scrooge, the Dickensian character whose response to a Christmas request for alms was to ask whether the prisons and workhouses had been closed. When Charles Darwin suggested a new doctrine of the survival of the fittest in nature, there were those who translated this into a theory of Social Darwinism whereby only the fittest among men did, or even should, survive.

Yet in America and Britain and elsewhere this picture of liberalism was a caricature. The great individualists not only amassed fortunes but disbursed part of them in charitable bequests. The "liberalism" of Woodrow Wilson and Lloyd George was very different from the laissez faire liberalism of a century earlier. There was a sense of social responsibility that arrested the explosive movement that characterized the industrial revolution in other countries.

Nationalization did not suddenly emerge in Britain when the Labour party won its victory in 1945. Commissions of inquiry set up by Conservative governments before the war had recommended the nationalization of Britain's utilities, and when the experience of war was added to the depression, the case for nationalization was generally accepted. Almost no one seriously opposed the nationalization of the coal mines. The Conservatives who were elected in 1951 to "set the people free" sold back to private enterprise only most of the steel industry (the nationalization of which had been controversial) and part of the road haulage industry. The National Health Service introduced in 1948 was merely the culmination of a trend begun by Lloyd George nearly half a century earlier and had been forecast by the report in 1942 of another great liberal, William Beveridge. As for America, it was experience, not dogmatism, that led to the Social Security Act of 1935. Had Chicago and New York experienced bombing in the war and the accompanying evacuation of slum dwellers to suburban homes in Evanston, Illinois, and Westchester County, New York, there might have been a different reception to President Truman's proposals for medical care after the war.

Many Americans, including President Johnson, have considered whether as a rich nation compelled to spend billions of dollars on armaments America should do even more than it does for its own poor. They are appalled at the high cost of medical care and the burden this puts on the poorer section of the population. It has become increasingly apparent that to argue in terms of planning versus free enterprise is to ignore the main issue: the need to solve problems as they arise. The old doctrine of self-help is inadequate today. At one time a man could be expected to provide for himself and his family unless he was reckless or lazy. Today he may be compelled against his wish to retire at sixty-five or be thrown out of work by a decline in steel production or the introduction of automation into his industry. He cannot be accused of irresponsibility if in such circumstances alternative work for him, and thousands like him, is not available.

Laissez faire and individualism have been abandoned in practice because they are outmoded. Yet a return to the older paternalistic philosophy is impossible. The cost of old-age pensions, of unemployment benefits, and of hospitalization is too great for any private organization to bear; charity, however admirable, is inadequate for the job. The state has therefore been compelled to intervene, and the American government, like all others, has accepted its responsibilities to those whose suffering is the result of the complexities of the society in which we live. All countries, including the United States, have thus had to accept a considerable amount of state intervention.[3] To measure its extent and compare the social services of all four countries under discussion would be a formidable task, but since much of the argument over the welfare state turns on the *attitude of mind* of those who support this phenomenon it is simpler and indeed more relevant for our purposes to attempt to explain the main differences between the various liberal democracies in these general terms—to discuss the attitude to the welfare state rather than the amounts paid out in old-age pensions.

The fundamental difference between the United States on the one hand and France, Britain, and Sweden on the other is not between an antiwelfare state and welfare states but between one country, the United States, that has recognized the need to adopt many of the programs found elsewhere but has done so out of expediency rather than on principle and three countries that have willingly accepted the title "welfare state" (and have for the most part adopted its principles). Few Americans would be proud to proclaim the United States as a welfare state even though the country does have an elaborate network of social insurance and social welfare programs—much to the surprise of many Europeans who naïvely believe that once they set foot in the United States they will be well advised to remain in employment, to keep fit, and to die before they reach sixty-five.

For the sake of argument we may distinguish between the *social security state* (the United States) and the *welfare state* (Britain,[4] France, and Sweden).

The American Social Security State Versus The European Welfare State

Despite all the controversy over welfare no one has yet made a serious comparative study of social policy in the United States and

---

[3] In 1966–67 American social welfare expenditures totalled over $100 million. Federal funds accounted for 54 percent of all social welfare expenditures. Of the $100 million, social insurance expenditures amounted to $37 million and education expenditures to $36 million. (Ida C. Merriam, "Social Welfare Expenditures, 1929–67," *Social Security Bulletin*, XXX, No. 12 [December 1967], 3–16.)

[4] The Ministry of Social Security formed in Britain in 1966 merely consolidates the work of the old National Assistance Board and the Ministry of Pensions and National Insurance. There is a separate Ministry of Health, formed in 1919.

Europe. Nor has anyone reached a satisfactory definition of the welfare state. It is arguable that the United States, whether Americans like the term or not, is in reality a welfare state: certainly the federal and state governments pay a great deal of attention to social welfare in all its aspects, and students from all over the world come to study at American schools of social work.

The American Social Security System: The Net

Since 1935 when the Social Security Act was passed there has been an important and expanding federal social security program of old-age pensions in the United States. In addition, there are a number of state-operated programs, the most important of which are public welfare and unemployment insurance. No one can say that the American authorities do not care for the old, the disabled, the dependent children, the unemployed, or the down-and-out. In 1967 aid was provided for no fewer than thirty-one million people below the poverty line. There *is* an attempt to provide social security. Yet the United States is not a welfare state in the European sense. How is this explained?

Two important features of the welfare state as it exists in Europe are missing. One is the absence of a statutory floor that is guaranteed to support all those in need. Instead there is a net that catches most of those who fall but through whose holes a person in need may slip, to be succored, presumably, by private charity. For the statutory American, social services are limited to certain clearly defined groups of people. This means that recipients must fall into one or other of the specified categories in order to be entitled to benefit for assistance. In the Old Age, Survivors, and Disability Insurance program these categories have been extended to cover 95 percent of the population—but the uncovered 5 percent include those most in need. It is true that in theory the states provide a floor for such persons through what is known as "general assistance," but this has languished since the introduction of federally financed programs of categorized public assistance and is in many states quite inadequate for the purpose. To suggest that below the federal net there is a state floor is to take appearance for reality. Consequently, if the definition of a welfare state is that it is one in which the government takes into account the need of all citizens, then the United States is not a welfare state.

The second missing feature is a general program of medical

care. Successive administrations have tried to introduce such a program in the United States, but so far have been successful only in the provision of medical care for the aged. This proposal in itself is interesting in that it illustrates once more the American pattern of social security. Instead of introducing complete coverage the American administration is starting with one category of persons (the aged), and then, presumably, it hopes to extend coverage gradually to others.

There are interesting anomalies in the American social security state. In particular, within it there is a small-scale welfare state already in existence—the Veterans' Administration. Although there was opposition to medical care for the aged there has been no elimination of the elaborate facilities at the disposal of all who have donned uniform. The military are well cared for—throughout their lives. Members of the American Legion, which opposes "creeping socialism" and the welfare state, are of course prime beneficiaries of the munificence of the Veterans' Administration. Few would wish to see the great work that this agency does diminished; indeed it might be used as a model for American social welfare generally.

There is a widely held view in the United States that social welfare makes a country "soft." This is not so. After all, the originator of the social security state was none other than Bismarck, the great German chancellor who transformed Germany into one of the most powerful modern nations. The schemes he introduced in the 1880's were adopted throughout Europe (long before socialists obtained power) in countries as far apart in space and thinking as imperialist Britain and tsarist Russia. Some American states followed suit, and when the depression struck America with appalling severity, the federal government took the lead. In the Social Security Act it went beyond most European countries; there were many in Britain who thought that there was much to be learned from this as well as other parts of the New Deal legislation.

The Swedish Welfare State: The Model Social Democracy

The terms "welfare state" and "social democracy" were once thought to go together. Sweden, like other Scandinavian countries, has long been a social democracy—that is to say, a state where the Social Democrats have long been in power—and it was in many ways the prototype of the British welfare state. The Social Democrats have had more than their share of good fortune, and this may explain their long tenure of office. Whereas the great depression meant the replacement of the British Labour government by a national and largely Conservative administration, in Sweden as in the United States it involved the setting up of a new government determined to introduce many social and economic reforms. The victory of the Swedish Social Democrats in 1932–33 was the counterpart to the New Deal.

But why did the Swedes still return the Social Democrats after the end of the Second World War? Part of the explanation is that during the war Sweden was governed by a national coalition. The Social Democrats were able to formulate new policies toward the end of the war and to appear before the electorate as a separate party with a new program. Moreover, Sweden would have had to go against the general European trend to have voted the Liberals or Conservatives into office.

Thus the Social Democrats could claim to have rescued their country from depression, to have escaped the full rigors of war, and to have been prepared to meet the challenge of the postwar world. It is arguable that the electorate changes a government only when it has good cause to do so, preferring the devil it knows. If this is part of the explanation for the failure of the pendulum to swing against the British Conservatives until 1964, it may equally well serve to explain why Sweden is still a social democracy today.

Sweden, then, is *politically* a social democracy. But the term has often been used to mean more than this. It has implied a different *society* and in particular one where stress is laid on a policy of social welfare. (Of course the reverse is not true, for a country can be a welfare state without being a social democracy.) Nevertheless some of the biggest arguments in Swedish politics in recent years have been over social welfare. Attention today no longer centers on the general principle of welfare, which is accepted, but on what is thought to be an excessive concern for social security. It is the cost of welfare, its extensive nature, and the method of financing welfare programs that are under fire.

There can be little doubt about the extensive nature of the Swedish social services. In 1955 compulsory health insurance was adopted and a national health service inaugurated as Britain had done seven years previously. In 1959 a new pension scheme was enacted by one vote in the Riksdag. This supplemented the ordinary old-age pension with one proportionate to earnings, a scheme that until recently in most European countries (but not in the United States since the 1935 Social Security Act) has been the prerogative largely of the salaried middle class. Contributions are required from everyone in gainful occupations and are paid to the state either by the employer or by the self-employed. Contributions were expected to rise during the first ten years from 3 percent of pensionable earnings in 1960 to 9.5 percent in 1969.

Comparatively minor features of the welfare program in terms of cost—for example, free summer holidays for mothers and young children, day nurseries, marriage and housing loans—have aroused comment abroad. The conception of welfare is clearly much broader than it was in the 1930's when Sweden seemed to be the prototype of the welfare state.

One consequence of the broadening scope of welfare has been the need to tap further sources of finance. In 1939 Sweden spent $70 million on welfare and social security and in 1948 $360 million. The 1956 figure was nearly one billion dollars and in 1963 the sum required was over $2 billion.[5] Family allowances now amount to $180 a child per annum. High school and university students receive study grants from $180 to $315 a year irrespective of their parents' income. Lodging and traveling allowances are paid to those who live away from home. Altogether, welfare spending rose from 10 percent of the national income in 1952 to 17 percent in 1967. Some people think that there are limits to the amount of welfare that even a rich country like Sweden can afford.

A number of arguments are advanced against extensive social welfare coverage. The absence of discrimination on grounds of means often results in prosperous people receiving child allowances or pensions that they do not need. Many wage and salary earners are well-paid and can afford to insure themselves against sickness and old age. However, an examination of the qualifying conditions for receipt of benefits indicates that Swedish welfare is in many instances confined to those who can prove need.[6] And much of the expenditure is financed out of social insurance, not out of general taxation.

Many foreign critics consider Sweden's "Great Society" to be a failure because other social problems such as juvenile delinquency

---

[5] For the latest figures see *Statistisk Årsbok* (Stockholm: Central Bureau of Statistics, annually).

[6] See *Social Benefits in Sweden 1966* (Stockholm: Swedish Institute, 1966).

and venereal disease have not been solved. Some go even further and assume that aid to the sick, the disabled, and the aged somehow *causes* affluent teenagers to lapse into delinquency. Contrary to popular impression, the current illegitimacy rate in Sweden at twelve per one hundred live births is lower than the rate in the period from 1900 to 1940. The divorce rate of five per one thousand marriages is half the American rate. The per capita consumption of alcohol, which rose after rationing ended in 1955, is now back down to the 1955 level and is little more than that of Canada or the United States. The suicide rate is lower than that of seven other countries (twenty per one hundred thousand persons) and has not changed for fifty years.[7] The Swedish welfare state is not so very different from that of many other European countries, and yet the Russians and the Germans do not seem to have suffered the same uninformed criticism.

The British Welfare State: The Single Floor

After the Second World War the Labour government reorganized the system of social security, both social insurance and social assistance, making it quite comprehensive. Instead of the net to catch those who fell into certain categories, a floor was provided for all. But it was the introduction of a comprehensive scheme of medical care through the National Health Service that aroused most interest. Doctors and dentists, pharmacists and hospital administrators, all found themselves in a position to offer free attention to everyone, regardless of need. Part of the cost (13 percent in 1964–65) is defrayed by individual flat-rate contributions paid together with social insurance, but the main share (80 percent) is paid for out of taxes. In 1946 the National Health Service was estimated to cost about $1,200 million; by 1964–65 it was costing over $3,500 million a year.

The chief innovation of the British system has been the blurring of the traditional distinction between social insurance and social assistance. In Sweden and France, medical care costs are met through social insurance. In Britain the National Health Service is, in effect, a vast program of social assistance administered by

---

[7] The figures have been compiled from Ernst Michanek, *For and Against the Welfare State: Swedish Experiences* (Stockholm: Swedish Institute, 1964).

the state. (This is not readily apparent because a part of social insurance is earmarked for the Health Service.) Another interesting feature of the British system is the emphasis on the doctor as general practitioner. In Sweden medical care is for the most part provided by hospitals that have large staffs of full-time specialists. The Swedes until recently were spending six times as much as the British (proportionate to population) on hospital construction. In doing so they conserved manpower, encouraged specialization, and discouraged emigration.

The postwar British welfare state was successful in its attempt to substitute a floor for the net in the provision of social services. Twenty years later, however, the single floor appeared inflexible compared with the various floors for different categories in such Continental welfare states as Sweden and Germany. Once again Britain seemed backward.

How had this come about? The main weakness of the British system seems to have been its stress on redistribution of the national income (perhaps due to the influence of Keynesian economics) rather than on economic growth. The Labour party was determined in 1945 to abolish the hated means test of the 1930's that seemed to imply that the millions who were victims of the depression were paupers. The party dismantled the Poor Law, workhouses, and indeed the whole apparatus that had, like some temporal hell, awaited those members of the working class who suffered deprivation of income. It also tried to eradicate the image of two Britains: the one with its family doctor and "voluntary" (that is, private) hospitals, the other with its insurance panel and gloomy public institutions. In blurring the distinction between social insurance and social assistance, the Labour government hoped also to blur the distinctions between social classes. By establishing a free National Health Service for all and by placing all except teaching hospitals under regional hospital boards, the government intended to further the sense of equality and community (and of one England, or rather of one United Kingdom) that wartime privations and rationing had engendered. Temporarily this policy might upset the middle class—who could and sometimes did opt out of the National Health Service—but the long-term advantages of integrated health services for the community as a whole were thought to outweigh any short-term offense to the susceptibilities of the prosperous. (American governments were later to attempt a similar policy of social fusion in the integration of white and Negro children in schools, sometimes with similarly unsatisfactory results.)

Successive British governments failed to see the implications that economic growth, inflation, and balance-of-payments difficulties all had for the British welfare state. The principle of social equality became in fact subsistence benefits, and those who could do so enrolled in private schemes of social insurance and hospitalization. The two Britains did not disappear. Instead of a "leisure class" and a "working class" on the prewar model, there was now the Britain of the able-bodied, young, employed, and independent on the one hand and the Britain of the sick, aged, unemployed, and dependent on the other. Benefits were not related to an expansion of the gross national product or the cost-of-living index (as they were in Germany). Individual contributions remained small and with the rising cost of drugs and hospital care the burden on the exchequer became increasingly heavy. In addition, the benefits themselves were inadequate because they were spread thinly over the whole population instead of being directed to those in need. The most obvious example of this problem was the subsidies to tenants of council houses, who were once poor but now were often affluent.

By the 1960's there was a reappearance of categorization of benefits. Graduated pensions were introduced in 1961 by an act of 1959, a quarter of a century after they were established in the United States. The problem of the "new poor" remains unsolved, however, and it is complicated by the arrival of so many colored immigrants. There is no intention of returning to the principle of the net, but the single floor has proved inadequate. The new Labour government is trying to remedy its defects.

The French Welfare State: Emphasis on the Family

The most famous feature of the French welfare state is its system of family allowances. Many other countries, the United States being a notable exception, now pay such allowances, but the French allowances are distinctive by their generosity in comparison with those of the other countries and even more in comparison with other benefits in France, such as pensions. Moreover, they are financed out of the contributions of employers, not from general taxation.

Another notable feature of French social security is its financial basis. Instead of the flat-rate contributions so long favored by the British and instead of the willingness of the central government to pay much of the costs, French social security is defrayed by the graduated contributions partly of employees and to a much greater extent of employers. It has been estimated that social security contributions add 30 percent to the total wages bill in France.[8]

France has established social services in accordance with its own peculiar circumstances. It has long been a country that, like the United States, has large areas that are primarily agricultural. The coverage of the social services is thus less comprehensive than in Britain and Sweden; there is, for example, no French unemployment insurance. Another feature of French society is the widespread unwillingness to pay direct taxes. French governments have therefore traditionally relied on indirect taxes. French family allowances, like Swedish day-nurseries, have their origin in the fear of population decline, a matter of great importance to a country whose rival and neighbor, Germany, has for a century been so powerful and energetic. (There is even a Ministry of Health and Population in France.) Some of the defects in the French social security program (pensions, for example, often amount to only 20 percent of normal working income) have their origin in the lower standard of living in France compared with countries like Britain and Sweden. France has no national health service, though there is an attempt to reimburse medical costs through a system of public insurance. This system covers most hospital costs, but it meets only half the bills presented by doctors and druggists and only 10 percent of dentists' bills.

The French social security system has three other unusual characteristics. First, like the Americans, the French distinguish between categorical and residual (or general) assistance, the latter being awarded at local discretion. Second, like communist states, France enables those who are insured to participate in the management of social welfare funds, mainly because social welfare was at one time the responsibility of trade unions. Finally, despite their reputation for centralization, the French have permitted a considerable amount of decentralization in the administration of social security.

---

[8] Frederick F. Ridley and J. Blondel, *Public Administration in France* (London: Routledge and Kegan Paul, 1964), p. 287.

The Liberal Economy of the United States Versus
The Mixed Economies of Britain, France, and Sweden

There is a distinction between the United States and European countries in the attitude toward state control of the economy. Of course the United States is not a country of laissez faire, where private entrepreneurs regard government as something that they can freely manipulate in their own interests. "Big government" is here to stay and, as the steel industry was one of the first to discover, is a power in the land. But the acceptance of controlled capitalism by Americans, whereby the government may if it wishes regulate the economy, does not mean that the United States has approved of nationalization of industry (or socialization as it is aptly called in the United States). America is rather different from most European countries (and from Canada), where for one reason or another there has been some support for actual government operation of sectors of the economy. Hence the term "mixed economy" to describe the public and private sectors that exist in most European countries. For want of a better term we may call the controlled capitalism of the United States a "liberal economy."

The differences between the two forms of economy must not be overestimated. There has probably never been a government that did not intervene in some form in the economic life of the country it governed. Taxes have economic effects; so has devaluation. As a spender, a government influences the economy nearly as much as it does in its capacity of collector of revenue. Protective tariffs are a direct and deliberate interference with the normal course of business; so are subsidies. But there is enough truth for practical purposes in the description of the nineteenth and early twentieth centuries as a free-enterprise era. France and Germany interfered more in their economies than did Great Britain or the United States, the latter, with its high tariffs and its great assets of public lands, more than the former. But all four powers, especially the last two, assumed that the government had no right to interfere directly with the working of the economic machine and, consequently, no duty to see that it worked well.

The twentieth century has changed all that. All governments now interfere directly in the management of the economy; all governments profess to provide economic benefits such as full employment; all governments openly use tax and tariff policies to steer the economic development of the nation in the way the politicians think it should go. By the 1960's the American government had adopted the Keynesian notion of deficit financing when a recession seemed imminent.

What caused this shift? Some weight ought to be given to the influence of socialist teaching and preaching. It was widely argued and widely believed that private ownership of the means of production was unjust and produced intolerable economic anarchy and an unstable and incoherent management of the affairs of the community. Political democracy was of no importance if it was not accompanied by economic democracy, the means to which were described in a famous British Labour party program as "the nationalization of the means of production, distribution, and exchange."

But it would be unwise to attribute too much importance to the influence of socialism. Germany had never been converted at the level of its governing class to the full doctrine of *laissez faire, laissez aller* ("let people do what they want," "let them alone"). The German states owned a great deal of property which they administered, and in 1914 all the railways of Germany had long been nationalized, while only a fragment of those of republican France had been, and none were nationalized in the two most advanced democracies, the United States and Britain. Nationalization was not a matter of pure doctrine. The complexities of the modern economy, the arrival on the scene of the great corporations —the "trusts"—not allowed for in classical economic theory, the rise of powerful trade unions, the demand for what we now call social services, all diminished the appeal of a system of government that washed its hands of any share of decision-making in the economy. In Britain, the establishment between 1906 and 1914 of unemployment insurance, health insurance, old-age pensions, the intervention in strikes, and the special rights given trade unions made the picture of Britain as a laissez faire economy implausible. Even in the United States the establishment of the Federal Reserve System in 1913 gave the government important power in the banking system. The railroads were already regulated, and in 1916 they had to accept the settlement of a railroad strike by an act of Congress giving the railroad workers what they wanted.

The British and American Economies

The real force that accelerated government intervention in the economy was the First World War. Had the war lasted (as was expected) only a few months, the old order might have stood. But for Britain it lasted four years. And as each year passed, the government's share in the direction of business and labor grew. It took a larger and larger share of national resources; it imposed more and more controls over the use of raw materials; it imposed rationing. People became accustomed to the idea that the government could and should interfere and control. Even in the United States, where the war made comparatively little impact, the government interfered in unprecedented ways—fixing the price of farm products, taking over all the railroads, drastically raising taxation, and controlling foreign trade.

In both countries one legacy of the war ensured that the governments would have to take a more direct part in the running of the economy. What were by the standards of the age immense national debts had been contracted during the war; that meant the continuation of what was, again by the standards of the times, very high taxation—and taxation is a very important economic force indeed. It was no longer merely a matter of raising revenue by the most efficacious method but of doing so "justly," an ambiguous term usually meaning that the rich should pay proportionately more of their income in taxes than the poor; they could better afford it. According to the next stage of the argument (more openly advanced in Britain than in the United States), the rich should pay higher taxes to diminish the inequality of incomes. Tax policy became central to government policy, and the impact of tax policy on the economy became part of the raw material of politics.

If the United States could make an attempt at a formal return to "normalcy" following the First World War, Britain could not. From 1920 it was plagued by serious unemployment that unemployment *insurance* schemes could not handle, since many of the claimants had been unemployed for years and had exhausted all their claims on the insurance funds. What was to be called "the dole" came into existence: a small payment to any unemployed man or woman, not based on any past payments to the insurance funds but on mere need. Local tax systems were adjusted to encourage business, marketing schemes were sponsored, and the government was further involved in economic decision.

With the depression of 1929, the British government was faced with still greater problems, all of which seemed to demand more government intervention—or tinkering. In the United States the administration of President Hoover tried for a long time to resist pressure to force the federal government to intervene. But states and cities soon ran out of revenue and borrowing power. The pressure of mass unemployment mounted. By establishing the Reconstruction Finance Corporation the government put itself into the center of business decision by lending money to businesses that could get it no other way. The decisive step had been taken. The federal government had now a positive duty to support the economy.

With the New Deal, further steps were taken in the direction that Britain had already turned. The Public Works Administration and the Works Progress Administration were federal efforts to create work for the unemployed. The National Recovery Act undertook to manage the industrial economy in its general lines, and the Agricultural Adjustment Act did the same for agriculture. Some of these schemes worked well, some ill; some were declared unconstitutional. But the point to note is the degree of responsibility that the federal government was now assuming.

In both countries the Second World War greatly accelerated the process. In Britain, under siege for five years (1940–45), a highly controlled economy was created. There was conscription not only of men but of women. Rationing was rigorous. There were elaborate controls on the allocation of raw materials and of labor and complete control of industrial financing and the allocation of capital. Far more than Nazi Germany, Britain experienced complete economic as well as military mobilization. In the United States the revolution was not so complete. America was not besieged. It had immense natural resources and immense "slack" to take in as the war endured. Unemployment disappeared. Wartime controls over wages and farm prices were more or less accepted. Far more than in 1917–18, the federal government controlled the economy, often in petty detail.

In both countries one result of the Second World War was to accustom the masses to new governmental functions. Government intervention might be unpopular, but people saw its necessity. In Britain, if not in the United States, some government interventions, as in rationing, had made a good impression. With the coming of victory there was in the United States a fairly rapid dismantling of controls. The British government gave up conscripting women, but most controls were kept and some were even added; thus bread, never rationed in war, was rationed in peace. There were two reasons for the different tempo in the two countries. In 1945 the British electors chose a Labour government formally committed to socialism, so some of the delay in dismantling controls came from a desire to keep the hand of the government on the wheel. But far more came from necessity: Britain emerged from the war desperately impoverished, and even a Conservative government would have had to do many of the things that the Labour government did. Some of these actions necessitated very drastic interventions in the decision-making powers of private business. Thus many firms were forced to produce for export only; none of their products were to be sold on the home market.

One experiment in direct government control of the economy was judged by public opinion (including a great body of Labour voters) to have failed. After its victory in 1945, the Labour government nationalized the railroads, the coal mines, most road transportation, most air transportation, and finally steel. The results were not thought to be satisfactory either by the customers of the nationalized industries or by their employees. The railroads ran into increasing deficits, and there was no general belief that service had improved. Coal was scarce for a long time. It became and remained expensive. The airlines needed subsidies, and the nationalized truck service fought, after the Conservatives came back to power, a difficult battle with independent rivals. The workers found the government not very different as an employer from the old capitalist owners. It was not usually noted that the two most dramatic nationalizations—those of the coal mines and the railroads—were of industries declining all over the world. Perhaps nationalization made no difference either way, but it got a black eye all the same.

The nationalization of the natural monopolies, electricity and gas, was financially more successful, but that made little impact on the public mind. For the moment, British opinion was against direct government management of any new sectors of the economy.

The situation in the United States was both formally and practically different: formally, because there was no serious body of public opinion committed to "socialism"; practically, because the United States had fewer government controls to demolish, fewer businesses for the government to get out of. But the role of the government in the economy was very important—much more so than before the war. First of all, quite apart from collecting taxes to pay interest on the immense war debt (more than ten times the war debt of 1917–18), the government became by far the biggest purchaser of goods. From the Korean War on, the government spent half its tax revenue on defense, and the defense budget mounted to the prodigious figure of seventy-five billion dollars a year by 1967–68. The policy of the Pentagon, what weapons were bought—and where—affected the whole economy and the prosperity of even the great corporations like General Motors. It was vain to talk of "free enterprise" under these conditions.

The federal government was also committed to a whole series of important interventions in the economy. It supported farm prices. It indirectly subsidized air travel and highway transportation (thus making the competitive position of the nonnationalized but declining railroads worse). It was under constant political pressure to use its expenditures to benefit one area rather than another. What the British government did openly—forcing businesses to go to Liverpool or Glasgow instead of London or Birmingham—was done less directly in the United States by acceding to pressure to put defense plants where the need was greatest and by keeping plants in operation even when their production was in the wrong place—economically speaking—or not wanted at all. Rare was the congressman or senator who, having cried: "Get the government out of business!" obeyed his own principles when an arsenal or air field was to be shut down in his district or state or when a new source of employment was located in another state.

We can nevertheless see that Britain is visibly further down the road of government control of the economy than the United States is. Its economy is much more vulnerable; it is in a state of constant economic siege, and in a siege the free play of the market forces would be disastrous. It is not only that the Bank of England is nationalized and takes its orders from the Treasury but that the government has kept other weapons in its arsenal, weapons not available to the American government in what is still a liberal economy.[9] In 1964 the new Labour government established departments of economic affairs and technology to assist in the overhaul of the economy and to help the economy withstand the pressures on it. After reelection with a larger majority in 1966 the government prohibited wage and salary increases for six months: the ban was still in force in 1967. Temporary devices such as the Selective Employment Tax were introduced in the hope of diverting manpower into essential export industries.

The liberalism of the American economy is in part a result of the federal system. Much of the taxing power is in the hands of the states and, by permission of the states, in the hands of the cities. Thus sales taxes are entirely state or local. The federal government could, no doubt, impose a sales tax, but it would be extremely unpopular in the states that already have one—as well as in those that do not. The British equivalent of the sales tax, the purchase tax, is levied only by the central government, which can and does use its power to tax in order to control the direction of the economy, sometimes encouraging the purchase of durable goods (washing machines, cars, and so on) by tax reductions, sometimes damming up the demand by making the tax prohibitively high.

In addition to the purchase tax the British government, like the American, levies excise duties, mainly on luxuries such as drink, tobacco, and gasoline. It also raises a substantial revenue from legal gambling. It taxes bets on the race course pari-mutuels, bets made with licensed bookmakers, and bets made in the betting shops now authorized by law. And it taxes the "investments" in the most popular form of gambling in Britain—the "football pools" on professional soccer results.

On the continent, governments often own and control such revenue-raising operations as tobacco and alcohol manufacture and football pools. But in Britain outright nationalization is mainly confined to transport and utilities. Today, in Britain, as in many other liberal democracies, the emphasis is on state control of the commanding heights of the economy rather than ownership of the means of production.

---

[9] For example, the Industrial Reorganization Corporation Act was passed in December 1966 to enable the British government to buy blocks of shares in private corporations. In January 1967 the new corporation bought stock in Rootes Motors, which otherwise might have become a wholly owned American (Chrysler) subsidiary. This absorption happened to the British Ford Company in 1960–61.

The American economy today would seem to have four salient characteristics that affect planning. First, there is the diffusion of responsibility among various institutions. Congress ultimately controls the purse strings, but it depends very much on guidance from the president. The legislative branch is divided into two houses that must agree on policy. The executive comprises the treasury and the Bureau of the Budget as well as the president and his cabinet, to say nothing of the Council of Economic Advisers. The president and Congress can regulate the economy by raising or lowering taxes, but monetary policy in the form of changes in the rate of interest is the responsibility of yet another institution—the Federal Reserve System, which enjoys greater autonomy than most central banks do today. And even if the whole federal political system is agreed on policy there remain the fifty states and their local governments. The financing of education, for example, which is one of the most expensive modern social services, is predominantly the responsibility of the states.

A second feature of the American economy is the existence of a number of very large private corporations. These can be regarded as a potential threat to the public interest, but in the context of diffused political responsibility the corporations do provide national policies of their own that to some extent offset the fragmentation of decision-making encouraged by the political system. All these corporations, however large, are subject to regulation by the third feature of American fiscal policy-making—federal agencies, such as the Interstate Commerce Commission and the Federal Communications Commission. Their role demonstrates the American preference for government control of private enterprise rather than nationalization of the economy.

The fourth characteristic of the American economy is the part played by defense spending, to which may be added expenditure on space research and the development of nuclear weapons. It is true that private corporations are awarded large and lucrative contracts, but the big decisions are made by governments, not by the firms themselves. In the field of defense expenditure the federal government has the power to direct the American economy. There is at the same time a danger that the military leaders and the heads of large corporations may concert their efforts in such a way that the public interest is endangered, as President Eisenhower warned in his Farewell Address. On the other hand, the large defense budget and the regulatory agencies give the administration a planning power that it would not otherwise possess under the traditional American separation of powers.

The British economy, which is often assumed by Americans to be under the direction of a powerful cabinet, is difficult for government to control because of what may be called *ideological diffusion,* as distinct from the *institutional diffusion* characteristic of the American system. Since 1945 there have been numerous attempts to incorporate planning into the governmental structure, culminating in the establishment of a Department of Economic Affairs in 1964 and the allocation of regulatory authority to the Prices and Incomes Commission in 1967. But there has rarely been consensus on the proper steps to be taken to control the economy. Some observers regard sections of British industry to be responsible for the sluggishness of economic development; some blame the trade unions for an unwillingness to modernize their structure or adequately to control their members. Others blame the "dead hand" of the treasury, which still controls the civil service and the budget. Various official bodies have been set up to get around the opposition or apathy of business, labor, and the civil service, but the main result seems to have been the alienation of all three. There has been little of the concentrated drive that has enabled the French technocrats to marshal all three interest groups behind a determined policy of government-directed modernization.

Successive British governments have found themselves unable to balance the country's international payments, with the result that British policy is to some extent determined by its foreign creditors. In 1965 the new Labour government produced a national plan with emphasis on economic growth. A new payments crisis led to its hasty abandonment and its replacement by deflationary policies calculated to slow down growth but to get Britain out of debt.

The French Economy

The role of the government in the development of the French economy has been much more important than it has been in either Britain or the United States. Past French governments had established state monopolies of tobacco and matches, not as examples of planning but as a means of raising revenue. One important

French railroad was nationalized just before the First World War, and all were nationalized by 1936. After the Second World War not only was the Bank of France nationalized but also a number of big private banks and insurance companies, as well as gas and electricity. The coal mines were nationalized—as was the great Renault automobile plant, on the grounds that its owner, Louis Renault, had collaborated with the Germans. So the French government had its hands on a number of economic levers. The state-owned enterprises were given a good deal of autonomy; for example, they borrowed for their expansion on the open market, largely by special loans. The Renault firm is run, with great efficiency, like a private corporation whose sole stockholder happens to be the French Republic. The same is true of the nationalized airplane plants.

But the most important intervention in the French economy was the "Monnet Plan."[10] The sectors of the economy that most needed and deserved help, it was decided, were transportation and heavy industry—steel, machine tools, automobiles, and the like. Given preferential access to credit, these industries entered into a period of boom and modernization that transformed France from a stagnant agricultural and small-business economy to one of the most rapidly growing great industrial powers in the world. It should be noticed that the *Commissariat du Plan* did not impose "norms"; it merely set targets which the various business enterprises, public and private, could aim at, and it helped, financially, to aid them to hit those targets. Two criticisms can be made of the working of the plan: it was probably one of the factors in the series of inflationary crises that led to successive devaluations of the franc, and Monnet skillfully avoided any form of parliamentary control. He spent money without direct authorization; he reported after the event, not before it. This meant cutting out a lot of red tape. It avoided parliamentary meddling and possible jobbery. But it also meant that the Fourth Republic never got credit for the things that its servants did well—for the French railroad system, the fastest and best in the world; for the great hydroelectric plants like Donzère-Mondragon; for Renault cars and Caravelle jets. The discredit into which the Fourth Republic fell was in part due to the concentration of public attention on the

---

[10] Jean Monnet, originally a businessman, has shown one of the most inventive minds in international politics. He is the chief begetter of the European Common Market.

things it did badly, not on the things it did well or permitted to be done well.

Nevertheless, the Monnet Plan and its successor, the "Hirsch Plan," transformed France. They were helped by Marshall aid and by the general upswing in European productivity that began around 1952. France had even the good luck to bring in one or two minor oil fields and a great natural gas pool in the Pyrenees that transformed the fuel situation. Grave difficulties remain, however. Although French agricultural methods have been revolutionized (it is possible that France today has too many tractors), there are in France (as in the United States) too many farmers on uneconomic farms. France, unlike any other major European country west of the iron curtain, has big agricultural surpluses that are in need of markets. One of the main reasons for France's entering the Common Market was to get a chance to sell its surpluses to Germany, the argument being that if French industry was to be exposed to the bracing competition of German industry, it was only fair that German agriculture should have to stand the competition of French agriculture.

In 1966 the government inaugurated the fifth plan to be completed by 1970. Before the plan was started, the nation's reserves had been increased from $630 million in 1958 to $5,500 million in 1965. At the same time, foreign debts had been reduced from $3,300 million to $450 million. Individual purchasing power had risen by 40 percent. The Common Market had provided a challenge to French industry that the government met by a policy of vigorous modernization and an increase in productivity.

The French system has been given the title of "technocracy" because of the important role played by highly trained specialists in the top echelons of the civil service and business. It is true that unlike the Americans the French have an elite corps of civil servants and unlike the British administrative class the French senior civil service is not composed of generalists. It is also true that instead of having two middle-of-the-road parties, which try to reach a compromise in the Anglo-American tradition, the French have strong parties on the left and right that approve of firm central direction. But the plan itself is the product of careful and prolonged discussion over several years by numerous committees on which hundreds of prominent men of affairs sit. The planning commissariat plays a guiding role, but the French plan is far from being the brainchild of a small civil service elite that imposes its will on a passive public. In any case the plan is an *indication* of where the government hopes the economy will go. It is not a *directive* on the Soviet model.

How much the French owe their plans for the economic growth of the past twenty years is hard to say. At the very least, the plans have enabled the French to set realistic targets, to observe the economies of other countries, and to discover their own shortcomings. The plans have provided a sense of national purpose. To some extent French planning seems to have been accidental. The political parties of the Fourth Republic were unable to agree on a comprehensive welfare state but were willing to allow the planning commissariat to function. The European Economic Community gave further impetus to planning. The French were fortunate in that the reorganization of their economy was achieved just at the time the large postwar generation of young people came into the labor market.[11]

According to Andrew Shonfield, the difference between French and British planning stems from a different political and economic philosophy. Traditionally the French have been mercantilists, encouraging senior civil servants and leading businessmen to work together for the good of the state. The British have thought their success lay in free trade and laissez faire (and they defeated Napoleon and a much larger France). Thus the French government as minority shareholder in the Compagnie Française des Pétroles insisted on its management rights. In contrast the British government, despite a 51 percent holding in the Anglo-Iranian Oil Company (later British Petroleum), abdicated from its management responsibilities.[12] British governments have not given their planning staffs the responsibility and prestige allotted to their counterparts in France. British planning staffs have even been denied official information. (A trade union leader referred to planning as "lad's work".) In planning as in so many areas, the British have not believed that power and influence should go too readily to qualified specialists. The expert should be on tap, not on top, as the phrase goes. The democratic spirit and consensus have prevailed over technocracy and state direction of affairs.

---

[11] It may be no coincidence that the attributes associated with Gaullist France have been discipline and dedication. The gay, carefree atmosphere that used to be associated with Paris is now to be found in London, where the postwar generation appears to take a very different attitude to life.

[12] Andrew Shonfield, *Modern Capitalism* (London: Oxford University Press, 1965), p. 82.

The Swedish Economy

As far as Sweden is concerned, the term "social democracy" is associated not only with social welfare but with economic planning. But surely, it may be argued, if a country is as socialist as Sweden appears to be, then it should have a fully socialized economy where the state (or cooperatives) owns everything and where wages cease to be the result of hard bargainings between capital and labor. This may be pure socialist doctrine, but, except in communist countries, it bears little relation to socialist practice. And in Sweden, as in Germany, the Social Democrats have even abandoned socialist doctrine, contenting themselves with social reform.

Indeed, perhaps the most interesting feature of the Swedish economy is the *absence* of government interference in collective bargaining. One consequence of "Organization Sweden" is the ability of the great social groups to work together without consulting the government. In contrast to most other free countries, the Swedish Employers' Federation and Trades Union Congress carry out negotiations for the whole of the industry, not just one sector such as steel or mining as is the practice in Britain and the United States. Like the Americans (but unlike the British and the French) the Swedes sign contracts that remain in force for a definite period of years.

As for socialization of the economy, there has been nothing comparable to British nationalization, which transferred ownership and operation of a number of important utilities such as gas, electricity, coal, and the railways to the state. The Swedish Social Democrats set up a socialization commission in 1920 when they first took office but abandoned full-scale nationalization after they formed their first majority government in 1933.

This is partly because nationalization was not necessary. In Sweden, as in Russia under the tsar, some of the nation's basic resources, such as forests and water, belonged to the crown and were developed by the state instead of being handed over to private enterprise. Whereas in the United States private companies, aided by the federal government and supported by foreign as well as American investors, were able to throw a network of railroad lines across the continent, in Sweden, as in Russia, the prospects of profit were often dimmer, and many lines had to be built by the state.

Today five large state "trading agencies" partly organized on civil service lines are responsible for post offices, telegraphs, and railroads, generate 40 percent of the hydroelectric power, and own and exploit 25 percent of the forests. The state railways also operate 40 percent of the country's buses. The last of the large trading agencies, the Power Board, was set up in 1909—several years before the Social Democrats formed their first government.

Another reason for the decision not to nationalize the economy has been the pragmatic temper of the Swedes. Although in a number of other fields the state has part or complete control, each decision has been made on an *ad hoc* basis, not as part of a plan. There are over a score of "state companies," some of them large industrial undertakings in the iron and timber industries competing with private enterprise—and cooperating amicably when it is to both sides' advantage. Several companies, for instance the football pools and lottery companies, are fiscal monopolies, and it was for fiscal reasons that the Tobacco Monopoly was created by a Liberal government in 1914 and the Wine and Spirits Monopoly by a Conservative administration in 1917. The Tobacco Monopoly paid for the Liberal government's pension program; the Wine and Spirits Monopoly was part of a campaign to eliminate the motive of private profit from the sale of alcohol, alcoholism being so serious a problem in Sweden that citizens were strictly rationed in spirits consumption until 1955. Occasionally the state appears to act on principle, as in the decision in the 1920's to put broadcasting under public control. More recently there has been participation in the Scandinavian Airlines System together with the governments of Norway and Denmark.

Public enterprise raises the question of adequate public accountability. It has been pointed out how Sweden separates public administration from the government. This has numerous economic advantages for the trading agencies that, although part of the civil service, are autonomous in structure and, unlike the administrative agencies, control their own operating budgets. The state companies are given even more freedom, being outside the civil service altogether and organized like private companies with their own boards of directors and shareholders. This raises certain political difficulties. Presumably the real shareholders are the taxpayers, or at least Parliament on their behalf. In practice it is often the appropriate minister who acts as sole shareholder and whose nominee attends the annual general meeting. One can hardly imagine the United States Congress allowing the executive branch such power. In setting up the state companies the Swedes have abandoned the principle of the separation of the executive and the public administration and have given ministers what is in practice individual ministerial responsibility on the British pattern. But they have gone further. By retaining the company form of private capitalism they have argued that the state companies are not in fact part of the public administration at all and have restricted the right of the legislature to supervise this part of the public sector of the economy.

It is tempting to compare the Swedish system with the British public corporation (or nationalized industry), but it is not really possible. The British corporation (which by definition is a public body) is a peculiar product of British law, and there is no place for it on the European continent. It certainly is not part of the civil service, but neither is it a company governed by articles of association. Each nationalized industry has its act of Parliament and issues bonds (stock) but not equities. The intention behind both company and corporation, however, is much the same—the avoidance of civil service red tape on the one hand and private irresponsibility on the other. Whether either has achieved the best of both worlds is a matter for debate.

One thing is becoming increasingly clear. The size of the public sector of the economy is often denoted by counting the number of people it employs—10 percent of the labor force in Great Britain and 5 percent in Sweden. By this definition Swedish public enterprise, which employs about 120,000 people in the trading agencies and 40,000 in the state companies, is comparatively small. But a very different figure is obtained if reference is made to the money invested. Twenty-three percent of Sweden's gross national product was invested in 1963, nearly 10 percent in the public sector. This compares with a public sector investment of just over 7 percent in Britain and France.

Controversy over the advantages and disadvantages of a planned economy is likely to continue for a long time to come. The supporters of the planned economy argue that private capitalists, if left to themselves, look after their own interests instead of the general interest, and there is considerable evidence that in many parts of the world this has been the case. What better way of improving the situation, so the argument runs, than transferring decision-making from the boardrooms of private capital to the people themselves through their government? For is not government responsible to the public in a sense in which business is not?

The opponents of planning at one time used the old argument that far from private interest being opposed to the general interest it was part of it: the sum of the private interests of members of the community, which meant by definition the sum of the private decisions of people such as businessmen and others, could not conflict with the common good. This argument is rarely used today because decision-making is concentrated in comparatively few hands, as price determination of a number of important products clearly indicates. The private interests of a small and successful minority may conflict with the common good.

There is, however, another argument that has acquired importance since the defects of nationalization and government control have become apparent. This is that it is naïve to assume that the government represents the public interest: governments, and more especially their economic planners, develop their own private interests, which may be just as inimical to the public interest as those of private firms. It is true that in the long run government is amenable to popular pressure, but in the short run it is far more monopolistic. Opponents of planning have therefore suggested that there should be several foci of decision-making, not just the government itself.

It does not take much reflection to realize how sensible it is to distrust the government and its vested interests. In many ways the capitalist system was an escape from the shackles of the bureaucratic mind. To hand back economic decisions to the civil service would seem, on the face of things, to be an abandonment of the dynamic approach to economic development that the industrial revolution introduced.

The story does not end here. While western Europeans wonder whether nationalization is altogether quite such a panacea as they had hoped, they are not sure whether a return to private control is the solution either. The world rarely goes back to a system that has once been abandoned. Though there is obviously need for new ideas on the question of the role of government and the economy, the case for the abandonment of control has not been fully made. For one thing, the publicly owned Renault and (until recently) Volkswagen companies were fairly strong competitors of privately owned American and British companies, while the publicly owned

B.O.A.C. seems able to hold its own with American airlines. For another, one cannot ignore wartime experience. When emergency arises, it is to the government that everyone turns. And no one is horrified that atomic energy and the exploration of space even in the United States are the prerogative of the federal government. Lastly, if planning is as defective as some people seem to think it must be, then the Russian challenge is a very puzzling one indeed. Our conclusion must be that the old stereotype of the bureaucrat needs modification. Somehow wartime Washington and London produced public service tycoons capable of winning a war, and in the Soviet Union no one thinks of the managers of the great combines as anything but very tough operators indeed.

Conclusion

The welfare state and the mixed economy are still far removed from the communist notion of social welfare and economic planning. Other countries have not chosen the extensive welfare arrangements of the Soviet Union or its completely socialized economy because the people have been free to choose and have in fact preferred partial to full socialism—even in so-called socialist Sweden.

One may or may not like planning, but to oppose it merely because the Russians find it useful is like refusing to build freeways because Hitler constructed *Autobahnen*. The British did not refuse to adopt social insurance merely because Germany, their archenemy, had introduced it. Americans are not only willing to copy the German missile program: they engage the engineers and scientists formerly employed by Hitler. Americans emphasized quality in education, particularly in science, once the Soviet Union had sent up the first satellite in 1957. Yet by some quirk Americans are unwilling to believe that in the field of social relations, whether it be welfare, control of the economy, or the problem of ethnic tensions, there is something to learn—or even that there is much to be learned—from the Europeans. Somewhere there is a logical fallacy at work. It does not follow that because lemons and daffodils are yellow lemons are daffodils. Because Russians and Americans have social welfare and government intervention in the economy does not mean that Americans are becoming Russians, or even communists.[13] The world is changing all the time, and neither country can stop itself from constantly shifting its policies and learning from the other. The ideological debate over planning ought soon to work itself out and decisions be made according to what works best.[14] Social welfare is not a matter of ideology: it raises humanitarian issues.

---

[13] See Zbigniew K. Brzezinski and Samuel P. Huntington, *Political Power: USA/USSR* (New York: Viking, 1964).

[14] See Daniel Bell, *The End of Ideology: On the Exhaustion of Political Ideas in the Fifties* (New York: Free Press, 1959).

5

INTERNATIONAL ROLE

Imperialism, Old and New

The past fifty years have witnessed a dramatic shift in the external power of the leading liberal democracies. Where once the Mediterranean Fleet of the Royal Navy kept the route to the East open, the United States Sixth Fleet now patrols. Instead of the Royal Navy's China Station based in Singapore, there is the United States Seventh Fleet off Formosa. New imperialisms, so it would seem to many of the people of the world, have replaced the old, and American troops fight communist guerrillas in the jungles of distant Asia now abandoned by the European powers.

The American empire, if such it may be termed without offense, is the most precarious that has ever existed.[1] Its power is based not on colonial conquest but on the willingness of independent nations to tolerate American bases and American business corporations on their soil. Should they change their minds, as de Gaulle has done, then the bases must be closed. This power is precarious for another reason. Most modern empires—the Spanish, the French, and the British especially—have existed for at least a

[1] See Richard W. van Alstyne, *The Rising American Empire* (New York: Oxford University Press, 1960).

century and usually for a much longer period. But America emerged as a world power only in the 1940's. Barely half a generation later a powerfully armed Soviet Union sent its first Sputnik into space and served notice that American hegemony was not to go unchallenged. To make the situation even more complicated, power was now concentrated in weapons of mass destruction possessed not only by the United States but by her chief allies and opponents.

The British empire has dissolved in a most remarkable fashion. In the half-century after the American Civil War the former white colonies (Canada, Australia, New Zealand, and South Africa) became the Dominions, and in 1931 the Statute of Westminster formally defined their independent sovereign status. After 1945 it was the turn of the colored colonies and dependencies, led by India, to gain their freedom, and nearly all those that have wished to become free have done so. Most have abandoned the monarchy, but few have left the Commonwealth. Ireland, Burma, and South Africa are the most notable exceptions. The loose association of the Commonwealth will grow looser still as time passes and the British-educated elite loses influence; it may disappear if the Commonwealth is weakened rather than strengthened by its multiracial character.

No one knows to what extent the newfound freedom of the colonies will result in a worsening of Britain's trade position as German or Japanese firms gain a foothold in what were British preserves. It is against the background of a changing Commonwealth that Britain's proposed entry into the Common Market should be viewed. If the British people find themselves becoming steadily poorer by comparison with their North American and European neighbors they may react vigorously and even unexpectedly. Extremism is not a political virus against which the British have been miraculously inoculated by a benevolent deity.

The French have experienced much the same situation as the British, with their empire in the Far East and Africa attaining similar independent status within or without the French Community. The strains have in fact been far greater, for Britain has really had no counterpart to the Dien Bien Phu debacle in Indochina or the protracted large-scale rebellion in Algeria. France nevertheless prospered in the 1950's, and its international position has been ably sustained by de Gaulle. But both France and Britain, like Italy and Germany before them, are being forced by circumstances to regard themselves primarily as European powers. This is also true of the Belgians and the Dutch. After five hundred years, the age of European empires, which seemed so secure and almost eternal to Bryce in 1912, is almost over.

And what of Sweden? Here is a country that, like Switzerland, can claim to have been at peace for a long time, undisturbed by either world conflict of the twentieth century. It was, and still tries to be, a neutral country, anxiously believing that its neutral position is all that permits its neighbor, Finland, to remain free despite the Russian shadow.

In the old days, when wars were between rival great powers, Sweden's neutrality made sense. Sweden was off the main trade routes, and as its territory was not suitable as a battlefield it avoided the fate of little Belgium, caught between France and Germany, or Poland, partitioned by Prussia, Austria, and Russia. Today, however, the conflict is ideological as well as military. As far as the communists have been concerned Sweden cannot, by definition, be neutral. To the communists a country is either capitalist or communist, and no one can deny that after thirty years of social democracy Sweden remains 90 percent capitalist.

Nor does Sweden escape criticism on other counts. In a world almost overwhelmed by poverty and overpopulation Sweden is an underpopulated country with almost the highest living standard in the world and with less poverty than the United States. She is a "have" nation in a world in which the "have nots" are becoming increasingly vociferous. Moreover these nations are not only under-privileged but colored: Sweden is overprivileged and white. There are no neutrals of the traditional Swedish sort today, and so Sweden too must adjust to a new world very different from that of 1939.

The Conduct of Foreign Affairs

Britain and the United States

In the histories of the two countries, foreign affairs, until very recent times, have played parts of very different importance. For Britain, foreign affairs have been paramount. The condition of Europe, and more recently that of the entire world, has been a matter of extreme urgency. Again and again, Britain has been threatened with invasion from abroad. One defense against that invasion, second only to the Royal Navy, has been the prevention of the creation on the continent of Europe of one power or a group of powers strong enough to concentrate superior forces against the island. Philip II of Spain in the sixteenth century, Louis XIV of France in the seventeenth, the first French Republic and the empire of Napoleon I in the late eighteenth and early nineteenth, and the Germany of Wilhelm II and of Adolf Hitler in the twentieth threatened, by their own power and by that of their allies and satellites, the independence of Britain. These threats were averted by the stirring up or acceptance of allies who could divert the strength of the attacker—allies such as Holland, Austria, France, and the Soviet Union.

Previous to this century the United States had been in no such danger and had had no such need to put foreign affairs among the first of national preoccupations. Except during the Revolution, when it was necessary to get the aid of France, and during the Civil War, when it was necessary to prevent the intervention of Britain and France on the side of the Confederacy, the United States was never in danger from foreign aggression. It could afford highly incompetent secretaries of state and even more incompetent ambassadors and ministers. Of course, the American foreign service (or its equivalents) had some highly qualified people. The State Department had to have one or two permanent officials who could guide the newly appointed politicos. One of these served from Andrew Jackson's time to the time of William McKinley. There had to be one or two good linguists both in Washington and abroad.

In contrast, the British foreign service was overwhelmingly professional. All ranks were usually filled by professional civil service officials. A good knowledge of at least French and German was insisted on. It was, of course, a highly exclusive foreign service (apart from the consular service, which was long separate and socially inferior).

There was an even more important difference between the British and American systems than the caliber and training of the executants of policy. In Britain, control was highly centralized. The foreign secretary was always a politician of the first rank. He had an independent position of his own. He might not rival the prime minister in public fame or support, but he ran close to him. If he didn't, there was no point in giving him so great a post as that of foreign secretary. A prime minister of exceptional force might dominate his foreign secretary, but this was regarded as a bad thing, reflecting credit on neither person. In making appointments abroad, the foreign secretary had no patronage troubles, no politicians to placate. If he was fit to command, he could command.

In the United States, however, the president was always the boss of his cabinet. Many of its members might have been unknown to him and to the country at the time of consideration for appointment.[2] They might have had important political positions, but they were all agents of the president. In a showdown, they could not win. That meant that the last—and sometimes the first—word in foreign affairs went to a man who had a hundred other things to do—most of them, in what were called normal times, of more immediate importance to the United States—and to the president—than any foreign question could be. The authority was divided not only between secretary and president but between the administration and the Senate. The constitution provides that treaties can become effective, part of the "supreme law of the land," only if ratified by two-thirds of the senators voting.

The British institutions are very different from the American. There are no standing committees comparable to the Senate Foreign Relations Committee in the House of Commons. Such control of the conduct of foreign affairs as there is comes from occasional debates and frequent questions that force the government to explain and, if it can, defend its policy. Yet it is possible that the House of Commons and even the House of Lords do more to act as educational forums than do the two houses of Congress. For in both the Senate and the House, foreign affairs has become a specialist's job for members of the committees. A representative or even a senator who is not a member of either committee may hesitate to intrude. Of course, the committees freely and firmly examine the secretary and his assistants in open and in executive session. But if one of the functions of a representative body is to educate the voters on the burning and dangerous issues of the day, the House of Commons probably does it better than either the Senate or the House.

With brief intervals from 1914 on, both the United States and

---

[2] It is said that Dean Rusk had never met President Kennedy until he was "inspected" for the office of secretary of state.

Great Britain have been given little temptation to think that foreign affairs do not matter. The realization of this truth has led to reforms in both the United States and Britain. In the United States, a series of laws have created a unified foreign service, composed of qualified civil servants who, except at the highest level, do not get their jobs or promotions for political reasons.

In Britain, similar changes have been made. All the various servants of the Foreign Office—clerks in London and attachés and consuls abroad—have been united in one service. The private income qualification has long been abolished, and, since the end of the last war, a deliberate effort has been made to recruit outside the charmed circle of Oxford and Cambridge graduates. The foreign services of the United States and Britain are now more alike than they have ever been.

But it must be said in conclusion that behind the foreign service, behind the secretary of state or the foreign secretary, must in every case lie the head of the executive: the president or the prime minister. And if there is no firm and adequate policy lead from the very top, then no skill, no devotion, no cunning outside the White House or 10 Downing Street can supply the lack.

France

In the French Foreign Office the most treasured relic is the desk of Charles Vergennes. Vergennes was the great foreign minister who made the alliance that secured the independence of the United States and, more than Talleyrand, is thought of as the ideal director of French foreign policy: prudent, exact, limiting himself to attainable objects. These are the classic characteristics of French diplomacy, despite the aberrations of Louis XIV, Napoleon I, and Napoleon III.

But the memory of Vergennes has another significance. When he was minister of Louis XVI, France was the most powerful nation in Europe—and the richest (the government was bankrupt, but that is another story). Today the case is altered. Although France is rapidly becoming rich again and the government is not bankrupt, the power of France is a shadow of what it was. Whatever President de Gaulle may say in his moments of haughty public meditation, France cannot "go it alone." Not all the skill of the carefully selected, carefully trained diplomatic service, with the oldest tradition in Europe, can conceal the fact that, in many parts of the world, in Asia and Latin America, the word of France counts for very little where once it counted for a great deal.

With the dissolution of the old French empire the main attention of French diplomacy is concentrated on Europe, especially on relations with West Germany. This was true before General de Gaulle returned to power. It is truer than ever today. But there are aspects of de Gaulle's foreign policy that draw criticism, and that criticism finds its voice in the Senate. However, as long as the Gaullist regime lasts, the final decisions will be made by the president. In a deep sense, no one is sitting at the desk of Vergennes.

It is seldom remembered that France has, since the end of the war, spent more proportionately of its government income on underdeveloped countries than have either the United States or Britain (this does not include the billions poured out in Indochina or Algeria). This aid has gone overwhelmingly to French Africa. In short, the French empire has been a burden on the French economy, not a source of profit for the French state—whatever it may have been for individual Frenchmen. Has aid been intelligently given and intelligently used? The French empire was traditionally protectionist, and both French exports to the colonies and imports from them were priced above the world market. Even since granting Senegal membership in the French Community, France has bought Senegalese peanuts at above the world price— which is a form of aid. Another form of aid has been the French pressure on its partners in the Common Market to give preferential prices to exports from the former colonies. Germany, it is felt, should buy its bananas from the former French colonies, not from the former British colonies. The spectacle of West Germany with a vast surplus for investment abroad evokes envy. If France only hadn't an empire—or a former empire!

On the other hand, the fact that so much of Africa has been trained by France, that only one out of the numerous colonies offered their free choice by President de Gaulle chose to quit the French Community altogether, is a matter of pride.

To sum up France's strengths and weaknesses: France is an intrinsically rich country, with a great deal of fertile soil, a good climate, great natural resources such as the Lorraine iron field (one of the greatest in the world) and the natural gas field at Lacq, and, above all, an industrious and ingenious people who, for the first time in over a century, are rapidly increasing in numbers.

But a number of weaknesses are also evident. France has been living beyond these resources, playing the role of a great power when it might have been better to concentrate on home affairs, to "cultivate our garden," as Voltaire put it. Another weakness goes back to the French Revolution: the destruction of any "consensus" among Frenchmen, the survival of old feuds and the creation of new ones. This has accounted, as much as military disasters, for the instability of French political institutions. There is no evidence that this instability (even though offset by the excellence of the civil service and the stability of local institutions) has been cured. All central institutions are in the shadow of one great man. Whether they will survive his death or retirement no one can say. It used to be common form to prophesy that with the death or retirement of de Gaulle, French politics would fall back into the parliamentary form of the Third and Fourth Republics. But de Gaulle's reelection in 1965 made this much less certain. The prestige of Parliament as the voice of the people has diminished.

Sweden

When the British observer contemplates proposals for greater parliamentary control of foreign policy, he instinctively thinks of America's experience of interfering congressional committees. He is thankful that in Britain—as in Sweden—the conduct of foreign affairs is the prerogative of the crown.

There is, however, an important difference between the two European monarchies. Such parliamentary control of foreign policy as exists in Britain is exercised either informally or in general debates on foreign affairs. There is no House of Commons select committee on foreign affairs as there is on the nationalized industries or estimates. In Sweden, by contrast, there is a foreign relations committee of the legislature such as is found in the United States. In fact there are two committees, different in origin but identical in membership.

The Permanent Advisory Council on Foreign Affairs, set up in 1921, is the modern successor of the ancient "Secret Committee" of the estates that the crown consulted on confidential issues. As the Standing Committee on Foreign Affairs, which was formed in 1937 as a counterpart to the other joint standing committees of the Riksdag, the members are available for ordinary consultations. Neither committee is comparable to the Senate Foreign

Relations Committee because the Swedish Parliament has no specific constitutional responsibility for confirming diplomatic appointments or ratifying treaties. The government has full responsibility for foreign policy.

The committees are therefore consultative and deliberative rather than checks on the executive. The joint Standing Committee on Foreign Affairs has been less influential than expected because a large number of important decisions affecting Sweden's international position are in fact the responsibility of the other (and older) standing committees.

It is sometimes thought that one advantage of parliamentary government is that it provides a better forum for debate than the American Congress. This is not so in Sweden. Until recently there was no real counterpart to the British general debate on foreign policy in the House of Commons. Members may oppose a government bill, put forward their own motions, or ask questions, but the constitution allows no motion of censure. It is sometimes said in Sweden that the Riksdag is relatively ineffective in controlling foreign policy, but there can be no agreed criterion of effectiveness. Moreover Nils Andrén insists that "on the whole the part played by the Riksdag in the sphere of foreign policy is greater today than at any other time in modern Swedish parliamentary history."[3] Its role may lack the dramatic qualities of the House of Commons, but through its committees it possesses an element of that independent expertise and judgment so characteristic of the United States.

No countries have more consistently supported international cooperation for peace and United Nations action to relieve political tensions and economic distress than Sweden and her neighbors. At the present time comparatively little of the aid to underdeveloped areas is channeled through the United Nations and associated agencies. Individual great powers prefer to take credit for their generosity and sometimes to retain some measure of supervision over what is distributed. If ever the decision is made to establish an international program of development to replace national competition, countries like Sweden will have a considerable contribution to make. Already there is little doubt that the recipients of aid would rather receive help through an international agency and be associated with the smaller independent powers. The numerous

---

[3] Nils Andrén, *Modern Swedish Government* (Stockholm: Almquist & Wicksell, 1961), p. 148.

African and Asian visitors to Sweden testify to the great interest that these countries have in the achievement of Scandinavia in creating a modern economy without the ugliness and misery that accompanied industrial revolutions elsewhere, and in retaining a stable society where increasing wealth is distributed among the whole population.

Should visitors from developing countries ask for the secret of liberal democracy, the answer is not simply "freedom of the individual." For as some writers have pointed out, there are many today who resent the burden that individualism sometimes imposes. In France, which appears to foreigners to be a nation of individualists, liberal democracy does not flourish in a manner that would be recommended for export. The secret of the more successful liberal democracies such as the United States, Great Britain, and especially Sweden, lies in their ability to temper the effects of individualism with a sense of group solidarity. Not only are the people of these countries patriotic in the best sense, but they bring political influence to bear through the groups of which they are members—the trade unions, employers' organizations, farmers' associations, and even churches. Liberal democracy thus has two facets, the individual at the ballot box and the group bringing pressure to bear on political parties, the legislature, and even the executive itself. The African or Asian leader who opposes tribalism, religious sects, and any organization that presumes to differ from the views of the dominant party may justify his actions by an appeal to the individualism of liberal democracy. He could do worse than pay a visit to Organization Sweden.

PART TWO

THE
COMMUNIST
PATTERN

Three Variations:
The Soviet Union
Yugoslavia
China

PART TWO

THE
COMMUNIST
PATTERN

Three Variations:
The Soviet Union
Yugoslavia
China

6

PRINCIPLES:
A Revolutionary Doctrine

Evolution or Revolution?

Stable democracies such as the United States, Great Britain, and
Sweden have had two features in common: the development of
representative government over a long period of time and the
gradual extension of suffrage until everyone over twenty-one is
now eligible for the voters' lists. As far as representative government is concerned, all three countries had powerful legislatures
before the French Revolution transformed Europe. The thirteen
colonies were hardly political novices in 1775; the four estates
helped to govern Sweden during the so-called Era of Liberty from
1721 to 1772; the British Parliament challenged Charles I to battle
in the 1640's and won. But democracy in the form of universal
suffrage came much later, taking from 1832 to 1928 in Britain,
from 1866 to 1921 in Sweden, and being completed in the United
States at the present time as southern Negroes are having their
voting rights assured.

When a revolution replaces autocracy with representative government and universal suffrage, the result is often unstable government, for there may be no opportunity for the people or the main
institutions of society to become adjusted to the new order of

things. The balance of social forces is upset, and it is with considerable difficulty readjusted. France is the most obvious example of a country in the Western democratic tradition where even after nearly two centuries the social forces remain in antagonism. No political system there has obtained general and lasting support. The 1789 eruption was only the first of many, and although there has been nothing in the present century quite comparable to the revolution of 1848 or the uprising of the Paris Commune of 1871, France is by no means an extinct political volcano.

The Attractions of Revolution

For many people still oppressed by reactionary regimes in nineteenth-century Europe, France's turbulent upheavals appeared far more relevant than the gradual improvement characteristic of America, Britain, and Scandinavia. The revolts of 1848 and 1871 exercised a peculiar fascination over those who sought an escape from autocracy, not the least among them Karl Marx. To him the events of 1789 symbolized the end of feudalism and victory of the bourgeoisie. The risings in Paris in 1848 and 1871, by contrast, were interpreted as the unsuccessful attempt of the proletariat in its turn to seize the reins of power. *Liberté, Egalité,* and *Fraternité,* the rights of the individual, wars between the great powers—all these seemed to Marx to be of less significance than the class struggle.

Marx may have been right—at least as far as some countries were concerned. But in parts of western Europe the emergence of new social groups or classes (so clearly apparent by the end of the nineteenth century) did *not* cause an explosion because they had a flexible political structure that soon found room for the lower-middle class—and ultimately the workers—on electoral rolls and in the legislatures. Consequently, the doctrine of class struggle had only spasmodic success during the period of adjustment. Since 1945, in countries like Britain, where even the largest businesses have felt at the mercy of the Labour government, the slogan "the state is the executive committee of the bourgeoisie" has lost its appeal as the weakness of the owners of the means of production has become clearly apparent. In many other liberal democracies, including the United States, no class, not even the most economically powerful, can feel wholly secure in its long-term political position, as the events of the New Deal era showed.

Russia's political development, like that of much of central and eastern Europe, has had far more in common with the French revolutionary tradition than with the gradualism of the other leading democracies. It was in Russia that Marx's doctrines took root and were adopted to the Russian tradition of violent and conspiratorial opposition to the regime. The tensions between government and people were much greater than those in western Europe where responsible social democratic parties took part in parliamentary governments. The end of tsarism in 1917 was almost as dramatic as the fall of the Bourbons. There had been no real democracy and little experience of representative government, despite the setting up of a legislature (the Duma) in 1906. Serghey Yulyevich Witte, the tsarist prime minister and author of the October Manifesto of 1905, had been able to congratulate himself that the creation of the Duma as a representative assembly meant that there was a constitution "but a conservative constitution and without parliamentarism."[1]

All the problems associated with modern politics, where the people wish to have a say in their affairs, were to be found in Russia and by the third year of the First World War were clearly insoluble without an upheaval. Early in 1917 the tsar was compelled to abdicate, and a provisional government was formed. Whereas the Paris Commune had failed, the autumn rebellion of the soviets or workers' councils (led by the Bolsheviks) in Petrograd and Moscow, the two great cities of Russia, was an easy success. Blood did not flow down streets as it had in Paris less than fifty years before. According to the communists, 1917 witnessed both the bourgeois revolution (February/March) and the proletarian seizure of power (October/November).[2] The communist revolutionaries were sufficiently a part of the old Russia to appeal to the masses in terms that they could understand. Instead of the abstractions of the French Revolution there were the concrete proposals of peace, bread, and land. (Whether either revolution gave the people what they expected is still debated.)

Events in Russia were not without their impact on central and

---

[1] B. H. Sumner, *Survey of Russian History* (London: Duckworth, 1944), p. 68.

[2] The October Revolution is commemorated in November because until the Bolsheviks seized power the Russians used the old Julian calendar and were eleven days behind Western countries. The Gregorian calendar had been adopted in 1582 by the Roman Catholic countries and in 1752 by Britain and the American colonies.

eastern Europe. Finland experienced civil war between Whites and Reds; communist regimes were briefly established in Hungary, Bavaria, and Slovakia; and in Italy as well as Germany there was the threat of proletarian violence following the end of the war. Out of the fear of communism emerged nazism and fascism in central Europe, while the new countries of eastern Europe were to be torn increasingly between the two forms of totalitarianism and to become doubtful of the support that the liberal democracies would be prepared to give them.

The Results of Revolution: How Stable Is Communism?

In the United States, Great Britain, and Sweden gradual democratic development has been accompanied by an underlying governmental stability; in France the revolution left the nation unsettled. What of the Soviet Union? It is of course too soon to be dogmatic. It is possible that fundamentally the U.S.S.R. is no more stable than France. The Russians may have simply exchanged one autocracy for another, and the Communist regime may merely have bottled up the passions of men even more effectively than tsarism itself. (The Chinese communists are sometimes accused of introducing a new Confucian authoritarianism.) On the other hand, the U.S.S.R. has now lasted over half a century. Why have the Russians not revolted against their new masters? The following answers to this question have been offered: one change of system in a lifetime may be enough for most people; the Russians have had to spend much energy defending their homeland against invasion; the Communist party is far more efficient and ruthless than tsarism (which had exiled V. I. Lenin for only three years in 1897 and let him keep in touch with his friends); there has been a great increase in the strength of the country and, above all, a rise in the standard of living. The number of opportunities offered to the rising generation may more than compensate for the limitations on personal freedom. In any case, it has been suggested, few Russians have ever cherished Western political ideals.

Some people have taken a different view of communist autocracy and have argued that communism is infinitely superior to tsarism (and many Russians certainly seem to think it is). The main problem facing the Bolsheviks was the choice not of ends but of means, not liberalism or totalitarianism but disunity or discipline. In Russia, as in France, the constant threat of disintegration, within and without the party, was clear before and after the Revolution. There had been disagreements between the parties before 1917, and even the Social Democrats themselves were divided from 1903 into Bolsheviks and Mensheviks. The 1920's were to show that there was no unity even within the victorious Bolshevik faction. Lenin felt compelled to establish his unquestioned authority, and Joseph Stalin in his turn drove out his rivals. The phenomenon was repeated yet again in the 1950's when Nikita Khrushchev achieved power. Firm leadership alone, it has been argued, has prevented instability.

Let us suppose that any one of these three men had failed to impose his will. It is possible that some balance of forces, some give and take, might have replaced personal domination as seemed to happen in 1964 when Leonid Ilyich Brezhnev and Alexei Nikolaevich Kosygin replaced Khrushchev. But it is equally possible that instead the result would have been warring factions and chaos. At best there would probably have been a conflict over fundamental principles as in French politics. Today we are more aware than ever before that countries like those of northern Europe and North America have been fortunate in their heritage and that it seems to be the lot of a great many other nations to be unable to find agreement even on the general principles of government. However, even England itself was once engaged in a bitter civil war—to say nothing of its troubles in Ireland. The United States has also suffered civil war. What is loosely termed totalitarian government, the antithesis of liberal democracy, has in some countries provided an element of stability, at least for a time.

Unhappily, the lessons of 1640–60 in England and 1775–87 in America that were learned within the English-speaking world were not always grasped outside it. The former colonies of the Spanish empire and of other European powers have not enjoyed such peace and progress. The abandonment of nazism by the Germans and fascism by the Italians came about only through war and conquest.

Politically the Russians have not been part of the Western world and were largely untouched by the democratic ideals of the French Revolution. Instead they have suffered setbacks in wars with other powers, which have led to important social changes at home. The Crimean War was followed by the liberation of the peasants, the 1904 war with Japan by the creation of the Duma, and the First World War by the Revolution itself. It is idle to speculate whether defeat in the Second World War would have led to the end of the Communist regime.

The basis of the present Soviet political system, therefore, was not the gradual development of democratic government but the violent overthrow of autocracy—little more than fifty years ago. Moreover, instead of the assimilation of the various social classes and groups by participation in the political process, there was the domination of one group, the Communist party, which claimed to represent one class, the proletariat. And instead of an adjustment to a modern industrial society based on capitalism or what the communists called bourgeois society, there was the overthrow not only of tsarism but of the liberal (provisional) government that succeeded it. What is now called totalitarianism had arrived.

The Communist Ideology

It is possible to explain the victory of communism as the communists themselves do—as the result of the inevitable processes of history whereby feudalism gives way to capitalism, which, as this in turn develops internal contradictions, is superseded first by socialism (the dictatorship of the proletariat) and later by communism (the withering away of the state). Why should communists look at life so differently from the way we do? Why should they believe in inevitability—or believe that, to quote the constitution of the U.S.S.R., the most active and politically conscious citizens "voluntarily unite" in the Communist party? The answer, in a word, lies in their ideology.

For most of us communism is a matter of belief: either one believes the world is moving inexorably toward socialism or one does not. Communists themselves do not consider their doctrine to be a belief at all. They prefer to think of it as something akin to knowledge, though they recognize its different quality from mathematical and scientific knowledge by the use of the term "ideology." They consider those who disagree with them to be men who are unable to see the truth. Needless to say, this makes any attempt at reconciliation or compromise, except on secondary matters, extremely difficult.

The importance of the communist ideology is obvious. Instead of saying, as democratic socialists do, that they believe in socialism but that every man is entitled to his own opinion, which he may express in free elections, the communists assert that every right-thinking man, unless he is tainted by class prejudice, cannot help but see things their way. This assertion has been rejected in non-communist countries, but some observers have been troubled by the reports of brainwashing in Korea, which suggested that a significant number of Allied soldiers were demoralized by a clever process of indoctrination.[3]

The insistence on the scientific validity of its doctrine makes communism worthy of far more attention than the fascist mystique of race or national destiny, even if one disagrees with Engels' verdict that Marx did for the social sciences what Darwin achieved for biology. It is true that, in practice, those people living under communism who have rejected the ideology have been subject to the same terror as those who opposed nazism. But in theory any oppression has been the result not of love for violence or dislike of minorities (which caused the Nazis to destroy the Jews) but of concern for the preservation of truth. Noncommunists are considered not as false prophets but as political alchemists who want to be let loose in an expensive laboratory where scientists are at work. (Of course true scientists might be prepared to let the alchemists demonstrate their incapacity.)

The Establishment of Communism

It may be that practice is more important than any amount of abstract theory, but the attraction of communism for many people has been its theoretical explanation of world events. In the field of ideas there is very much a "communist world." On the other hand, the ability of communists to hold on to power once acquired appears ultimately to lie in their control of the means of oppression—whether these be the army, the Soviet secret police, or the Chinese Red Guards. Moreover, communism owes its success originally to the October Revolution, which was largely due to the organizing genius of Lenin. In view of the short time that elapsed between the bourgeois and proletarian revolutions in 1917 it would seem that someone persuaded the historical forces to

---

[3] For a discussion of the literature see Albert D. Biderman, "The Image of 'Brainwashing,'" *Public Opinion Quarterly*, XXVI, No. 4 (Winter 1962), 547–63.

operate with unusual haste; indeed, there were many Social Democrats, mostly Mensheviks, who believed that the time was not ripe. Yet if it had been Lenin alone who was responsible, it is doubtful whether the regime he instituted would have survived his early death and the death of his successor—or would have been copied elsewhere. The Bolshevik party that he organized and led was a disciplined instrument. It proved capable not only of conspiracy and revolution but of sustaining the regime through civil war, foreign intervention, economic and social chaos, fifty years of rapid industrial expansion, and a great war that strained the country to the utmost.

There is probably no single explanation of the rise of communism. Certainly the capacity of both Lenin and Mao Tse-tung for leadership played an important part. Moreover, their preeminence in the revolutionary movements was established not with the aid of any party bureaucracy, secret police, or regime of terror such as gave Stalin his opportunity to defeat his opponents but through strength of will and determination (and some chicanery). Lenin was able as an *émigré* to dominate the movement both inside and outside Russia, a truly remarkable achievement. Looking back, one also feels that in a quite extraordinary way he understood the implications of the social and economic forces at work in Europe. For one must not imagine that he and his friends were the only opponents of tsarism. There were other groups, some far more important than the Bolsheviks until the closing months of the old regime. The Social Democrats, of which the Bolsheviks were a part, spent a great deal of time and energy attacking the liberal Constitutional Democrats (Cadets). As interesting as the success of the Bolsheviks is the failure of the liberals or the peasants (represented by the Social Revolutionaries) to determine the destiny of Russia.

The Russian background is clearly very different from that of the Western powers. It would be difficult enough to understand a nation that so recently has revolted against centuries of autocracy, that has been so little affected by the ideals, such as freedom, current in western Europe since before the French Revolution, and that has been so ambivalent in its attitude to the West. When to this is added the ideology of Marxism-Leninism, the important and unique role allotted to the Communist party as the vanguard of the proletariat, and the very personal nature of political leadership since 1917, then it is clear that here is a political system totally outside our own experience.

It is evident that elsewhere in the world the success of communism owes much to Russian aid and even intervention. Until the Second World War the Soviet Union was the only communist country; after the war the communist form of government was established throughout eastern Europe. It is sometimes thought that all communist governments owe their creation to the might of Soviet arms, but in fact Yugoslavia and Albania liberated themselves from Germany and formed communist governments independently, and the Red Army withdrew from Czechoslovakia two years before the 1948 coup by the Czech communists. The Chinese communists owe much to Russian encouragement (at times), but Mao Tse-tung established his Communist regime independently when he conquered China in 1949. Yet it is true that for the most part the governments of eastern Europe depended heavily on Russian support and for some years were dubbed satellites by people in the West. They called themselves people's democracies to indicate that they had not attained the Soviet Union's status of a proletarian soviet system.

In recent years the countries of eastern Europe have gradually established their own identity. Czechoslovakia experimented with a new form of economy in 1965. In 1967 Rumania refused to sign a statement condemning Israel for its war with the Arab states. It is no longer possible to lump all the countries of eastern Europe together or even to assume that they will always adopt the policies prescribed by the Soviet Union.

The first country to establish its national independence was Yugoslavia, and that country has been the most interesting variation on the Soviet pattern to be found in Europe. For the first few years after the war Yugoslavia was vigorously anti-Western and pro-Soviet. It was only when the Russians proposed the integration of the economies of eastern Europe that the alliance between the Soviet Union and Yugoslavia fell apart. The Yugoslavs refused to sacrifice their national independence; from that time on they were accused of the heresy of "national communism." They were expelled from the Cominform and subjected to economic sanctions. An attempt was made to persuade the Yugoslav communists to overthrow Tito. The attempt failed, and the Yugoslav people, both communist and noncommunist, found themselves united against Stalin as previously they had been in support of Tito's partisans against the Germans.

In its doctrinal position, Yugoslavia has tended to be pragmatic, if that is possible for a communist society. Its first five-year plan, introduced in 1947, was bold to the point of brashness; it came to a halt after the eastern bloc ceased to provide aid for and to trade with its erring neighbor. Instead of struggling along alone, the Yugoslavs (who in the days of the Marshall Plan had been the only east European country apart from the Soviet Union to oppose the plan unreservedly) appealed for aid to the United States and Britain, and this was granted. They did not immediately begin a new five-year plan in 1952 but planned ahead one year at a time. In 1953 the Council of Producers was formed to guard against the excesses of bureaucracy and to restrict the influence of noncommunist specialists on government. Because this innovation did not succeed, it was dropped from the new constitution of 1963. In 1957 the Yugoslavs introduced a second five-year plan in which the usual emphasis on heavy industry was conspicuously absent. Whether Yugoslavia has abandoned Marxism or has merely adapted it sensibly to a changing world has been a subject for heated debate in the communist world.

Although Yugoslavia was the first communist state to reject Soviet leadership, easily the most important non-Soviet communist country is China, which became communist in 1949. Its importance lies partly in the fact that there are twice as many people in China as in all the other communist states combined.

In some ways China's experience has been analogous to that of Yugoslavia. Like Tito, Mao Tse-tung fought as a partisan for many years and came to depend on the peasants for support. Consequently, Chinese communism was not founded on hostility to the peasants or the villages as such. The regime since its inception has been led by a national hero most of whose colleagues have remained loyal to him since their days together as partisans. Both Tito and Mao are proud men who stood up to Stalin and who on his death refused to allow Khrushchev to inherit Stalin's preeminent position as leader of world communism. For Tito the death of Stalin meant little change until the new Russian leaders themselves made their peace with him in 1955. But for Mao the situation was very different. He felt that on Stalin's death he became the senior figure in the communist world, not only because he ruled China but because of his contribution to communism thought. The quarrel between China and the Soviet Union came out into the open in the early 1960's, twelve years or so after the breach between the U.S.S.R. and Yugoslavia, and there had been no sign of reconciliation by the time of the fiftieth anniversary of Russia's 1917 revolution.

If China resembles Yugoslavia in its peasant orientation, the partisan origins of its rulers, and its unwillingness to obey the Russians (though for several years after their revolutions both countries slavishly imitated the Soviet model), it is very different in other respects, particularly in doctrine. From the Russian point of view, China's aging leaders are still wrapped in the cocoon of Stalinism. To the Chinese, the Russians and still more the Yugoslavs are revisionists who have abandoned Marxism-Leninism.

The Chinese seem to have passed through two stages. During the first, which lasted until the Great Proletarian Cultural Revolution got underway in 1966, they distinguished "theory" from "thought." Theory, which they attributed to Marx, Engels, Lenin, and Stalin, was universal in its applicability and could be described as pure ideology. Thought applied universal theory to particular national situations and enabled pure ideology to be translated in practical ideology. Only thus could communist theory be translated into communist fact. The significance of this gloss on communist theory was that it placed the earlier Russians, Lenin and Stalin, in the communist pantheon but prevented Stalin's successors from claiming to be heirs to the Marxist heritage. After Stalin there was an ideological vacuum. Mao proceeded to fill this void with his thoughts on national communism.

The second stage became apparent when Lin Piao (said to be Mao's successor) made a speech in 1966 in which he referred to Mao's *theory*. If this speech was as important as some observers believe, then Mao is being placed by the Chinese in the communist pantheon. No living Russian is accorded this honor. In other words, having challenged the Soviet Union's claim to be the sole or even main repository of the Marxist canon, the Chinese are claiming for themselves, or at least for their leader, direct descent from Lenin and Stalin. This means that communists everywhere should look to China for inspiration and should ignore the post-Stalin Soviet Union. Not surprisingly this claim has annoyed the Russians intensely. In December 1966 the Central Committee of the Communist party of the Soviet Union denounced Mao's international policy as having nothing in common with Marxism-

Leninism. Two months later *Pravda* accused Mao of being not only nationalist but racialist in his attitude.

International Communism in 1967

By the time of the fiftieth anniversary of the Russian Revolution, three remarkable developments in the international status of communism were discernible. Firstly, the Russians had lost much of their revolutionary fervor and in some ways were beginning to behave as a "have" nation with a vested interest in peace and prosperity. It is true that they were actively assisting the North Vietnamese in the Far East and the Arabs in the Middle East, but they seemed to be doing so with unusual circumspection.

Secondly, despite the effective suppression of dissent in eastern Europe by Russian tanks in 1956, the east European countries were no longer satellites. Instead, there were various forms of national communism of which Yugoslavia's was but one. The Communist parties seemed to be the one unifying force in a traditionally unstable region where the main reason for solidarity among the various nationalities was fear of invasion from the West, a fear that seemed to be receding. The Communist party leaders throughout eastern Europe and the Soviet Union kept in close touch, but the European communist world was becoming more like a commonwealth and less like a Soviet empire.

Finally, there remained the enigma of China. Here revolutionary fervor was still actively encouraged, and Communist parties in other countries were being criticized for revisionism or for a toning down of the revolutionary spirit. There was no question of dismissing the Chinese as dissenters from the agreed party line. They were schismatics, and communists elsewhere had to decide whether to recognize the Chinese or the Russian interpretation of Marxism-Leninism as correct. For the most part, they continued officially to support the Soviet Union. But in many ways the Chinese experience seemed to have more relevance for the underdeveloped regions of the world. The Chinese disagreed with the Russians over the need to adapt to a changing society, over what constituted national interest, over who was supreme authority, and over foreign policy. Increasingly the Chinese were trying to identify the Soviet Union with the West—with the Caucasian race, the

European cultural heritage from Greece and Rome, and even the Judaeo-Christian tradition.

One thing seemed clear. The claim of the earlier communists to have overcome national rivalries had not been substantiated. The split between Moscow and Peking might yet prove as significant for the history of the world as the schism between Rome and Byzantium nine hundred years earlier.

7

POLITICAL PROCESS:
The Organization of Politics

The Role of Social Groups

By comparison with other illiberal systems, communism seems to have greater staying power. This is partly because it attaches itself to the largest social groups—the workers and (less successfully) the peasants—and partly because it actually eliminates the upper and middle classes who control the means of production. The groups that have been at the bottom of the old society form the basis of the new. But the Communist party also pays particular attention to the educated persons who govern the new society. It refuses to consider them as a separate class (on the grounds that they do not own the means of production) but has allotted them an old and honorable Russian title—the intelligentsia. The organization of politics is taken very seriously indeed.

Whereas Swedish society consists of a number of important organizations such as trade unions and farmers' cooperatives, each of which tends to be identified with a political party, the people of communist countries are all organized *politically* by the Communist party. There are, however, a number of organizations in the Soviet Union, such as trade unions, cooperatives, and cultural societies, that are said to participate in the nomination of candidates for the soviets. These organizations represent the three main occupational groups in the U.S.S.R.: the workers, the peasants, and the so-called intelligentsia. Although the Russian political process centers on the Communist party, it involves each of these groups to a greater or lesser degree. They are allowed participation in the electoral process within the limits of the "democratic centralism" that determines the role of the party, and they are "guided" and "protected" by the mass media that the party controls at all times.

It is interesting that the constitution of what is supposed to be ultimately a classless society does in fact—unlike liberal democratic constitutions—recognize the existence of certain social groups. Actually, Article 1 of the Soviet constitution ("The Union of Soviet Socialist Republics is a socialist state of workers and peasants"), like that of China, recognizes only two. The communists themselves maintain that as the means of production are nearly all state- or cooperatively owned there is no economic exploitation. Consequently classes, in the Marxist sense of exploiters and exploited, no longer exist: only social groups remain. The economic objective has been achieved. There are no landlords left in the U.S.S.R. and no nobility. There are no private stockholders in Soviet business and no capitalists. As Article 2 of the Soviet constitution succinctly puts it:

> The political foundation of the U.S.S.R. is the Soviets or Working People's Deputies, which grew and became strong as a result of the overthrow of the power of the landlords and capitalists and the conquest of the dictatorship of the proletariat.

The Chinese have been a little more specific and even optimistic about their landlords and capitalists. Article 19 of their constitution declares that the state provides them "with a way to earn a living in order to enable them to reform through work and become citizens who earn their livelihood by their own labor." In Yugoslavia, where capitalism has had little opportunity to develop, the conflict has been between landlords and peasants. The former were dispossessed of almost all their land in 1945. But collectivization of the peasants, as elsewhere in eastern Europe, has been far less successful than in the Soviet Union and China.

The abolition of classes in the Marxist or economic sense does not mean that there will be no distinct social or occupational groups, at least not until socialism (from each according to his ability, to each according to his work) gives way to communism (from each according to his ability, to each according to his need). Great stress is laid by the critics on the unequal incomes and styles of life in communist countries, not excluding the Soviet Union. To liberal democrats, these social distinctions are what really count and they are based on differences in income as much as on "the ownership of the means of production." Whether "class distinction" in the usual sense of social snobbery will be eradicated in the communist world is a moot point.

To a communist, differences of income and status are less important than the "elimination of exploitation." Social class does not mean to him what it means to the average American or western European. This is not only because of his Marxist heritage but because exploitation and class distinction were far greater in tsarist Russia and old China than in western Europe or North America. The vast mass of ordinary folk in Russia and China were peasants treated somewhat like the Negro slaves in the United States before emancipation, as chattels rather than as persons. Even after the Russian emancipation in 1861 the serfs were given a very inferior status. Nor was the proletariat, which grew in numbers as the century progressed, in a different position, for its ranks were filled with peasants who had drifted to the towns. Neither peasantry nor proletariat had been integrated in Russian society by the time of the Revolution. The result was that the old, educated classes (some members of which were so divorced from the life of the mass of their countrymen that they insisted on conversing in French) were replaced by the two groups that considered themselves outcasts. By comparison with the deep sense of grievance that so many poorer Russians and Chinese have felt toward their masters, the nuances of a modern American or European suburb appear trivial indeed. But the modern Russian equivalents of suburbanites *do* have a guilty conscience over the great differences in income and status. To many Russians, socialism does mean egalitarianism.

The creation of the Duma in Russia a decade before the Revolution did little to overcome the class divisions so long recognized even in law. The system of an electoral college (Curia) used for the elections meant that electors voted according to their class for class representatives. Manipulation of the electoral college reduced the representation of the peasants from 42 percent to 22 percent and of the workers from 4 percent to 2 percent. (The comparatively small number of industrial workers effectively prevented the Social Democrats from becoming the powerful political force they were in Germany and Scandinavia before the First World War.) The absence of a parliamentary system, or even the quasiparliamentary system of the Kaiser's Germany, made any peaceful adjustment between the new and the old social groups impossible. There was no strong group of moderates or liberals; therefore, instead of the pull toward the center that is so marked a feature of liberal democratic government there was a tendency for left and right to become poles apart. Neither side behaved in a way that would have been tolerated in a liberal democratic legislature.

The polarization of politics between reactionaries and potential revolutionaries that occurred in Russia between 1905 and 1917 has become a commonplace in many countries since that time. It paved the way for fascism and nazism in Europe, it has prevented France from enjoying stable government, and it is a marked feature of many developing countries from Central America to the Middle and Far East. In China it seemed for a time as though the Kuomintang might provide the necessary element of moderation missing in Russia, but despite its auspicious beginnings under Sun Yat-sen and the efforts of Chiang Kai-shek, it gradually became the instrument of reactionary forces. A later generation lost interest in an increasingly corrupt regime similar to those that China had experienced for centuries: the way was open for the communist victory. Mao Tse-tung expressed the feelings of many Chinese in his famous words of 1949:

> To lean to one side is the lesson taught us by the forty years of experience of Sun Yat-sen and the twenty-eight years of experience of the Communist Party. We firmly believe that, in order to win victory and consolidate victory, we must lean to one side. . . . Not only in China, but in the whole world, one leans either to the side of imperialism or to the side of socialism. Neutrality is a hoax, and a third road does not exist.

One of the main aims of the "nonaligned" countries is to escape this stark choice. But it remains to be seen whether the nationalist leaders in other countries such as India and Indonesia will be any more successful than the Russian provisional government of 1917 or the Chinese Kuomintang in transforming their ancient societies into powerful modern states and able to show that other roads (not only a third) do exist.

The discovery that stable government depends on the absence of extremes of rich and poor and on a strong middle class is nothing new. Aristotle made it. There is a modern fallacy that to defeat communism it is only necessary to raise the standard of living. But a nation, like a family, requires more than prosperity. Neither Finland nor France is particularly poor, and yet communism has long flourished in each. Where a group of people feel apart from the mainstream of society, whether they are intelligentsia in St. Petersburg, engineering workers in Helsinki, or dock workers in Marseilles, and where class divisions are marked, communism has its appeal. The polarization of politics is as much a question of social psychology as it is of economics.

It has been said that fascism has been strong in more advanced countries while communism thrives in backward societies where an appeal can be made to an emerging "proletariat." This last word, rarely used except in abuse, like the word "vulgar," has a strange sound in Anglo-Saxon ears. It seems to be popular enough elsewhere, however, and has become part of communist folklore. The "dictatorship of the proletariat," whether it means anything or not, is the communist equivalent of the liberal "equality of man." Just as the notion of equality still has its mystique in status-conscious America, so the notion of the proletariat has its appeal in communist countries.

Workers

THE SOVIET UNION

According to the *National Economy of the U.S.S.R. in 1963* (Moscow, 1965), 74.3 percent of the people of the Soviet Union were "manual and office workers." Three-quarters of those engaged in industrial production seem to have been manual workers (though the statistics are not very clear on this or on many other points), the class that, until Stalin declared it no longer existed, was called the proletariat. He argued that the toilers of the Soviet Union do not sell their labor: they apply it to the socialist economy that they collectively own.

This class has always been ideologically the most important in postrevolutionary Russia. According to communist doctrine the overthrow of capitalism means not only the elimination of the bourgeoisie—the owners of the means of production—but the transfer of economic power to the proletariat. Yet in a backward country the proletariat may be comparatively insignificant. This has caused difficulties in the U.S.S.R. and even more in China. In the Soviet Union the speed of industrialization was so great in the early years of the twentieth century (over two million workers were enrolled in sick benefit funds in 1914) that Lenin and his followers were convinced that it was only a matter of time before the proletariat became the most important class in the economy. Stalin's massive program of industrial expansion did indeed create a large class of industrial workers. But it may be a long time before the peasants in China become a minority.

Since the Twenty-first Party Congress of 1959 the Soviet Union has officially been a "state of all the people" rather than a "dictatorship of the proletariat." The Russian communists have been well aware of the difficulties involved in ensuring the dictatorship of the proletariat under their leadership even though the number of workers has increased. For one thing, as soon as a man or woman becomes a party organizer or a government administrator, he ceases to be a worker and becomes in fact a "former worker." One defense of the infrequency of the meetings of the Supreme Soviet is that it enables people from the factory floor to attend—unlike liberal democratic legislatures that often require a man to give up his job.

More serious, however, has been the emergence of a new group of what are called specialists, people with higher or at least specialized secondary education. These are hardly proletarians except perhaps in ancestry, yet they play a vital part as leaders in the economic and political life of the country. According to the 1965 statistical yearbook, their number rose from 521,000 in 1928 to 12,066,000 in 1965. American social investigators, with their theories of the managerial revolution, the organization man, and the power elite, have taken account of this phenomenon in the United States. Indeed, it is common to all advanced countries. The industrialization of eastern Europe also is transforming its social structure; Polish sociologists have argued about its implications. Unfortunately for the Russians, their Marxist ideology has no real place in society for their most important group, who now number over a quarter of the working population. They are considered to be in the same category as workers and are now sometimes defined as "workers by hand and brain." Yet the very notion of an intellectual proletariat would seem to be a contradiction in terms.

Today there is emerging a third generation of postrevolutionary Russians—the sons and daughters of specialists who have held superior positions. The children feel themselves entitled to a better education and better jobs than their proletarian fellows. It is difficult to forecast the role of the dictatorship of the proletariat except as part of the revolutionary myth. According to official figures, 404 (26.6 percent) of the deputies to the Supreme Soviet are workers and 294 (19.4 percent) are peasants. The average age of deputies has changed over the years. In 1937 only 27 percent of the deputies were over forty; in 1958, 70.5 percent; and in 1966, 60 percent.

YUGOSLAVIA AND CHINA

The workers have been given prominence in both Yugoslavia and China. Workers play an important part in the economy of Yugoslavia by service on Workers' Councils. In China, where traditionally the worker has had little prestige, the Communist party has indoctrinated the people with the proletarian ideal in accordance with the tenets of Marxism. Neither country has been communist-dominated long enough for a third generation of well-educated young people to emerge, but there are indications that the dictatorship of the proletariat has run into difficulties in both societies. The Yugoslav writer Milovan Djilas complained of the "new class" as early as the mid-1950's, while in China the Communist party has been struggling to complete the transformation of the people by means of the Great *Proletarian* Cultural Revolution.

Peasants

THE SOVIET UNION

Outside the Europeanized and Americanized part of the world the overwhelming mass of mankind earn their living from the land, often precariously. In 1917, 80 percent of Russians were peasants. In 1955 only 40 percent were estimated to belong to peasant families and in 1962, 25 percent. Whatever the constitution may say, the Russian peasants have never been given the political power to which their numbers would seem to entitle them. Partly this is because the practice of serfdom held back their development: like the southern Negro sharecroppers, they have had a long tradition of oppression and passivity. And like the sharecroppers, the peasants have been rapidly declining in numbers. Some Russian reformers in the later nineteenth century did try to arouse the consciousness of the peasant masses but gave up in despair. Most of them were very different from the American farmers of the Midwest or the Swedish peasants whose representatives sat in Parliament.

Nevertheless, it is easy to underestimate their capacity, as the Russian communists seem to have done. It was these rural folk who emigrated in millions to Siberia, who formed cooperatives whose number and national organization worried the tsarist regime, and who secured a number of land reforms, notably when the government in the years after 1906 encouraged individual ownership of farms. They were more individualistic than the Chinese peasants. In the only truly free election in Russian history, that of the Constituent Assembly in November 1917, the peasants' own party, the Social Revolutionaries, won twenty-one million votes compared with the Bolsheviks' nine million.

It is possible now to be aware of the dilemma facing the Bolsheviks in 1918. Had democracy won the day the peasants would have demanded the allocation of scarce resources to agriculture, just when the Bolsheviks were anxious to transform the country into a mighty industrial power by the development of heavy industry. The Bolsheviks therefore disbanded the Constituent Assembly and passed a new land law. Ten years later Stalin ordered the replacement of individual holdings by state and collective farms.

Industrialization increased the number of urban mouths to be fed, and by 1928 there was a shortage of food. Unable to satisfy the peasants by producing consumer goods in exchange for farm products, the communists used force. The peasants were compelled to deliver up their grain and cattle without adequate recompense. The first five-year plan of 1928–33 emulated American large-scale farming by the introduction of collective farms instead of peasant small holdings. If there was need for increased agricultural production, the methods adopted were hardly successful. The more prosperous among the peasants who owned their own farms were labeled *kulaks* and were liquidated; the peasants as a class showed their resentment by killing off their cattle and refusing to collaborate with the government's schemes. In the Ukraine a bad harvest led to the deaths of countless country folk. And the burden of Russian industrialization continued to be borne by the peasantry.

It was to be a long time before Soviet agriculture recovered from this severe conflict of interests, and to this day it remains the weakest spot in the economy. *The U.S.S.R. Economy: A Statistical Abstract* (1956), which in some ways magnifies Russian achievements, tells the unvarnished story about the results of the 1928–33 five-year plan:[1]

(in millions)

	CATTLE	PIGS	SHEEP AND GOATS
1916	51.7	17.3	88.7
1928	66.8	27.7	114.6
1933	33.5	9.9	37.3
1941	54.5	27.5	91.6
1955	67.1	52.2	142.6
1966	97.1	58.0	141.0

Economically it might have proved wisest to have left the peasants alone, but there are observers who regard collectivization as primarily political in intention. In a society devoted to social production the individual initiative represented by the old peasant economy posed a threat to the regime. Another table in the *Abstract* (page 19), which is shown here on the next page, tries to fit the complex Soviet social structure into simple Marxist categories and seems to be presented with something like pride.

Unlike the Chinese communists, who were peasant-based at the time of their revolutionary seizure of power, the Russian Communist party after 1917 was to some extent hostile to and suspicious of the peasantry. After collectivization (and liquidation) some of these suspicions were removed and in the new constitution of 1936 the peasants were given equal status with the proletariat. The east European satellites seem to have blindly followed the Russian example during their "Stalinist" period (1948–53) when they copied the Soviet Union's policies of heavy industrialization and state ownership of the economy. When Imre Nagy came to power in Hungary in 1953, over half the members of the collective farms left the collectives within a year. In Poland,

---

[1] From the English translation published in London in 1957 by Lawrence & Wishart, p. 118. Also published in the United States as *Statistical Handbook of the U.S.S.R.* (New York: National Industrial Conference Board, 1957). The 1966 figures, calculated as of January 1, 1967, are taken from *Pravda*, Jan. 29, 1967.

	1913	1928	1937	1955	1963[2]
Total population (including families)	100	100	100	100	100
Of which:					
Manual and office workers	17.0	17.6	36.2	58.3	73.6
Collective farmers and cooperative craftsmen (*kustari*)	...	2.9	57.9	41.2	26.3
Individual peasants (excluding *kulaks*), working craftsmen and artisans (*remeslenniki*) not in cooperatives	66.7	74.9	5.9	0.5	0.1
Landlords, large-scale and small-scale urban bourgeoisie, traders and *kulaks*	16.3	4.6	...	...	...

Wladyslaw Gomulka had argued against collectivization ever since 1946, and when he returned to power in 1956 a halt was called to collectivization in Poland also. The result, according to Brzezinski, was that "the only class in the socialist society to enjoy appreciably better living conditions are private landowners."[3] He added that the present muddling through cannot be a long-range response to the problem—an indication of the dilemma facing states that try to take off into industrialization without the backing of the peasantry.

The industrial-agricultural conflict is not without its parallels in other countries. It is a commonplace that the industrialization of Britain caused the import of food products in return for manufactured goods on such a scale and at such low cost that English agriculture was only rescued from its depression by the First World War and by the realization that an island cannot afford to import the bulk of its food supplies. In the United States, where the farmers were more powerful, resentment against the

[2] The 1963 figures are taken from A. I. Aitov, "Some Peculiarities of the Changes in the Class Structure of the U.S.S.R.," the *Soviet Review*, VI (Winter 1965–66), 3. (Translated from an article in *Voprosy filosofii*, No. 3 [1965].)

[3] Zbigniew K. Brzezinski, *The Soviet Bloc: Unity and Conflict*, rev. ed. (Cambridge, Mass.: Harvard University Press, 1967), p. 361.

commercial and industrial interests of the East stimulated Populism and later radical movements.

Two things distinguished the Russian conflict. Instead of being a struggle between manufacturers or bourgeoisie against the farmers it was between the proletariat (led by the communists) and the peasantry. Some critics have even suggested that the Communist party and its nominees are the bourgeoisie under another name—a "state bourgeoisie" instead of a "private bourgeoisie." The other unusual characteristic is that neither the Americans nor the British were ever faced with the prospect of farmer-dominated political systems as the Russians were by the victory of the Social Revolutionaries in the 1917 election. In Sweden the Agrarians were able after a long struggle to liberate the farmers from the main burden of taxation and military service in 1891, but the farmers did not enter the government until their great coalition with the Social Democrats in 1933—by which time they were a minority group. Nevertheless it is of interest that in 1933 when the industrial workers and farmers in Sweden were joining forces the Russian peasants were facing their worst ordeal at the hands of the workers—or at least the Communist party, which claimed to act on their behalf.

It is possible that if the Russian peasants had been as progressive as the farmers of Sweden, Britain, and the United States, they might have received better treatment. It has often been suggested that the peasants of eastern Europe have been of a different kind from western farmers, being reactionary in politics and separated from the urban population by obscurantism and traditionalism. In the Soviet Union many still belonged to the *mir*, the village community that controlled the local economy much as tribes do in Africa today. Just as the rising proletariat could find no means of accommodation with the old upper and middle classes, so it could find little in common with the peasantry. Once again, instead of a gradual social adjustment, revolution—this time revolution in agriculture—was thought to be necessary.

Some of the peasants' bitterness has declined in recent years as Khrushchev and his successors, showing an understanding of the peasantry that Stalin lacked, have replaced the stick with the carrot. The Machine Tractor Stations, the symbol of the new industrial society, were for a long time manned by technicians trained in communism and able to control the activities of the ostensibly autonomous collective farms. Now they have been dissolved and their equipment placed under the jurisdiction of the farms themselves. Even more important from the peasants' point of view, farmers are still allowed to care for their own plots and to sell their produce. Individual enterprise, the aim of the peasant throughout the ages, has not been eliminated. At one time Khrushchev hoped to transform the peasantry into a proletariat by the creation of "rural towns," or *agrogorod*, in which farmers could enjoy urban amenities and develop the same cast of mind. In Britain and America the farmers already share the outlook of townsfolk, and the term "peasant" is never used. But in many other countries, including the Soviet Union, the gulf remains wide. One of the most interesting experiments in the communist world, in China as well as in the Soviet Union, is the attempt to provide urban amenities in rural areas. In so doing the communists hope to eliminate forever the peasant mentality—and to create a genuinely classless society.

YUGOSLAVIA AND CHINA

The Yugoslav communists gave up the idea of transforming the peasantry into a proletariat in the 1950's. The peasants opposed it, and in view of their contribution to the partisans' guerrilla war the party had been reluctant to enforce collectivization. When the large estates were broken up, the land was distributed to the peasants, the maximum holding being little more than one hundred acres. Later, collectivization was imposed, but it did not work and land was handed back to the peasants. Since the early 1960's a balance seems to have been struck between individualism and collectivism by the use of General Cooperatives through which alone the peasants can purchase new machinery and obtain credit.

In China there had been little peasant opposition to collectivization, partly because the proportion and power of the *kulaks* were less than in the Soviet Union and partly because the Chinese learned from the Russians' mistakes and introduced reform gradually. The Chinese had a further advantage in that the communists in China were peasant-based to begin with. However, this advantage was thrown away. Expectations of a large crop in 1958 encouraged the Chinese Communists to consolidate the 800,000 collective farms into 26,000 communes in preparation for the transition from socialism to communism. Whether the bumper crop failed to materialize because of natural causes or because the peasants resented being communized is hard to say. At all events the commune experiment failed, the Great Leap Forward ground to a halt, Mao lost prestige, and the Chinese were com-pelled to import grain from Australia and Canada. Since 1960 no official statistics of Chinese production have been published.

Intelligentsia

By getting rid of the feudal landlords, the bourgeoisie, and the "lackeys of the bourgeoisie," the communists at first imagined that only workers would be left. They soon learned that it takes more than workers and peasants to run a modern state and that administration demands more than the ability to transfer memo-randa from the "In" to the "Out" tray. In the Soviet Union, the communists set about the education of the "new Soviet man," as he is sometimes called.

THE SOVIET UNION

Originally a dictatorship of the proletariat and from 1936 to 1959 a society of workers and peasants, the Soviet Union, as we have seen, is now a "state of all the people" and recognizes a third social category or stratum that it calls the "working intelligentsia." Indeed, the revised constitution of the Communist party, unlike the Soviet constitution, refers explicitly to this group in its open-ing sentence. In the nineteenth century the Russian intelligentsia comprised the professional people and intellectuals—for example, writers, doctors, and teachers—who opposed the autocracy of the tsar and found the social and political orthodoxy of the bureau-crats and businessmen uncongenial. Like both these groups, how-ever, it was separated in way of life and outlook from the mass of the people. Indeed its inspiration, unlike that of other educated Russians, was largely foreign, for it was strongly influenced by Western culture and political ideas. There seems to be something similar to this intelligentsia in many underdeveloped countries.

It is today often suggested that the term "intelligentsia" is a misnomer in the modern Soviet Union because, in addition to the intelligentsia proper (that is, the intellectuals), it tends to com-prise the managers of industry and the civil servants in the state administrative machine, in fact all those sometimes euphe-mistically called specialists. Hugh Seton-Watson's term "state bourgeoisie" distinguishes these three sections of the so-called intelligentsia from the "private bourgeoisie" of intellectuals, businessmen, and civil servants in liberal democracies. The term "intelligentsia" has, of course, been adopted in the Soviet Union because of its association with a group that, like the proletariat, was hostile to the old regime. In contrast, the term "bureaucrat," like kulak or "landlord," has unpleasant associations in the Russian mind.

The refusal of the communists to accept the term "bureaucracy" in its neutral sense is connected with their refusal to accept Western sociology generally, Marx alone being to them the father of the social sciences. It may make things clearer to refer to the communists' new "intelligentsia" in quotation marks, to show that the term is not used in its strict sense. It is probable, to judge by recent writings, that many intellectuals, members of the intelligentsia proper, oppose the communist regime, but it may be a mistake to assume that there is the same general hostility as in tsarist days. The communists seem to have been successful in creating a fairly homogeneous elite in which intellectuals have a place of honor. There is considerable intercourse of a horizontal sort between its various social groups—the civil servants, industrial leaders, and professional people. Leading artists and scientists receive as great rewards and prestige as do engineers and senior bureaucrats. In 1966 there were six scientists on the Central Committee of the Communist party and 123 doctors or candidates of science elected to the Supreme Soviet. Over 70 percent of the Supreme Soviet's 1,517 members had received a higher or secondary education.[4]

Nor is the elite, or "intelligentsia," separated from the people as a whole as it was formerly; the amount of vertical movement in Soviet society remains considerable. One consequence of the great purge of 1936–38 was to accelerate the promotion of the newly trained Soviet "intelligentsia" to posts formerly held by the traditional elite that Lenin had been compelled to keep in being after 1917. The transformation of Russian society is all the more remarkable when it is remembered that in 1926 the illiteracy rate in the Soviet Union was still about 50 percent—the level of southern Negroes at the turn of the century.

It is a matter of conjecture whether, together with the communist leaders (who are forming what Djilas called the new class

---

[4] See "Data from the Credential Committees' Reports," *Current Digest of the Soviet Press*, XVIII, 31, p. 5, for details.

with a sense of class solidarity), members of the "intelligentsia" are anxious to perpetuate their status through their children by means of educational privileges. So far, Russian society, like that of America, has been remarkable for its social mobility based on the belief that a man gets ahead on his own merits and not on those of his ancestors. It may be that a more stratified social structure will emerge as the economy stabilizes and the need for mobility lessens. In America there are some observers who detect not only the expansion of the college-educated population but a trend away from egalitarianism and the emergence of a new conservative middle class. But by integrating the intelligentsia proper as well as the "intelligentsia" into Russian society and the Soviet economy, and at the same time making the basis of the state the workers and peasants, the communists have tried to remove the barriers that traditionally separated these classes from those in power above them and the masses below. It is presumably partly to avoid the emergence of a new and dominant class that makes the Russians hesitate to recognize the existence of a separate "intelligentsia." However, even if it could be proved that there was a new privileged social class, the communists would argue that this was not a class in the Marxist (economic) sense of an exploiting group.

Whether there remains any sizable intelligentsia proper that desires liberty and feels itself outside Soviet society is hard to say, though the reaction of Stalin's daughter to a reading of Boris Pasternak's *Doctor Zhivago* would seem to indicate that the old spirit of independence survives.[5] It may well be that the urge to derive ideas from the West remains; certainly the efforts to prevent the free dissemination of Western ideas in the U.S.S.R. would seem to indicate that there is such an urge. And presumably it is the intelligentsia proper rather than workers, peasants, or Soviet managers that is most anxious to know about the outside world. On the other hand, it is always the function of any intelligentsia to be critical of the society in which it lives; it is only when it finds life intolerable that it endangers the regime. There is not much evidence that the Soviet intelligentsia as a whole has reached this point.

The intelligentsia of eastern Europe has been less restrained

---

[5] Svetlana Alliluyeva, "To Boris Leonidovich Pasternak," trans. M. Hayward, *Atlantic Monthly*, CCXIX (June 1967), 133–40.

than the Russian intelligentsia so easily cowed by Khrushchev and his successors. A Pasternak or Dudintsev, a Daniel or Sinyavsky, can be accused of being unpatriotic. In proud Poland it is the Communist party that has to avoid the stigma of being unpatriotic. Here the intelligentsia delightedly embarrasses the regime by taking the mantle of nationalism upon itself. And the 250,000 people who lined the streets of Warsaw in 1959 to greet the American vice-president perhaps indicated where the sympathies of the Polish public lay.

Some observers think the Russians have on the whole managed so far to escape stratification of the capitalist variety because, although managers have more money than workers, they have had few opportunities for conspicuous consumption. Not only have houses and automobiles been scarce, but there has been considerable social pressure on those better off than their fellows. It would seem that just as in America there is no place for a European-style upper class so in the U.S.S.R. there has been no room for an American-style middle class; so far, at least, there is evidence that in its ethos or political culture it still is very much a proletarian country.

YUGOSLAVIA AND CHINA

Although Yugoslavia and China have experienced communist revolution much more recently than the Soviet Union, the two countries have already been faced with the problem of the intelligentsia in both senses of the term. It is a Yugoslav, Djilas, who has been one of the most vociferous intellectual critics of communism, having abandoned the new intelligentsia, his "new class," for the old intelligentsia proper. Like the rest of eastern Europe, Yugoslavia is finding itself increasingly influenced by the social norms of western Europe rather than of the U.S.S.R. But it is improbable that eastern Europe will become fully Westernized, if only because (like the Americans) the east Europeans have abolished the upper class of the type that still has a significant social role in western Europe. The east Europeans can hardly copy the United States either, because (like the Russians) they have abolished the traditional middle class of the type that governs America. They therefore have to create a new society; if it cannot be classless as Marx hoped or proletarian in culture as the Soviet Union still hopes, it may well have to be a society with a new class. This could combine features of both the new and the old intelligentsia.

The assimilation of both intelligentsias presents as great a problem to the Chinese. Pride in their ancient civilization has been essential for the self-respect of the Chinese during the last century in which they have been made increasingly aware of their technological backwardness. It has been necessary for the communists to encourage pride in past Chinese achievements without giving too much respect to the custodians of China's heritage—and to develop science and technology without separating the new class of experts from the workers and peasants. This in part explains the Great Proletarian Cultural Revolution. To some observers, that revolution has appeared as a nostalgic attempt to turn the clock backward to simpler days, but from a different viewpoint it seems to have been one of Mao's periodic attempts to jolt his people and to prevent them from sinking back into the old ways, living on the past.

Unlike the Russian intelligentsia proper, Chinese intellectuals traditionally do not seem to have experienced the same long period of futility. They have had a status and respect and tradition of public service unrivaled elsewhere in the world. No doubt the Chinese Communist party assumed that the intellectuals could be persuaded to serve the new regime as they had served successive dynasties. The party carefully left the term "intellectual" undefined. But the Chinese have had to create a new intelligentsia of scientists and technologists, very different from the old literary bureaucrats steeped in the Chinese tradition. Whereas the college-educated party elite understands the mentality of the old intelligentsia, it finds the new breed of scientists with their cosmopolitan scientific culture difficult to understand. Thus the scientists are not as close to the political leaders as they are in the Soviet Union.[6]

Today throughout the communist and noncommunist world there seems to be emerging yet another intelligentsia. This consists neither of creative writers and scientists nor of creative entrepreneurs in industry and the civil service. It comprises countless young educated people who are potentially vital members of society but who feel alienated from it. They find that their awareness of the world differs from that of their government and of what they

---

[6] See John M. H. Lindbeck, "The Organization and Development of Science" in Roderick MacFarquhar, ed., *China Under Mao: Politics Takes Command* (Cambridge, Mass.: M.I.T. Press, 1966), pp. 333–67.

call "the Establishment." Many of these young people are critical of both capitalism and communism, and some have symbolized their rejection of the values of their society by simply "dropping out" of society.

The Communist Party

The Soviet Union

Unlike liberal democracies, communist systems usually tolerate only one party. If there are other parties, they play a very secondary role. In the U.S.S.R. the Communist party alone exists as the vanguard of the proletariat. Provided one accepts the exclusively class basis of political parties (as the Swedes almost seem to do with their division of bourgeois and workers' parties) it is possible to believe that conservative and liberal parties, as representatives of the bourgeoisie, have no place in a workers' society. Agrarian parties too can be called bourgeois on the grounds that they represent only the richer farmers—the *kulaks* or their equivalent. This leaves only the workers' parties.

But it is difficult to see how a peasantry can be said to be represented by communists, the party of the urban proletariat; not unnaturally the peasants, especially in eastern Europe, have been somewhat uncooperative. Even more difficult to grasp is the claim of the communists that they and not the social democrats should represent the working class. In the Soviet Union and China there was no strong non-Marxist social democratic movement before the communist seizure of power. In eastern Europe, however, political life was more mature, and it was necessary at first to form broad alliances under communist leadership: hence the invention of the term "people's democracies" to distinguish these countries from the one-party Soviet state. The communists argue that the social democratic parties in Scandinavia, Germany, and western Europe generally, have betrayed the interests of the workers by becoming lackeys of the bourgeoisie: the communists alone have kept to the right path. (How the communists know that they are right and their rivals wrong is an interesting question.)

Since 1962 there has been a commission to revise the Soviet constitution, now that proletarian democracy has been transformed into a democracy of all the people. Certainly the Communist party of the Soviet Union has been transformed—from a small band of conspirators into a party of twelve million, among whom are nearly all the elite. Some people criticize this transformation, but it is hard to see how the party would have survived if it had remained a group of old bolsheviks and had not moved with the times. It must be much more difficult to manage a large Communist party, and on the whole the Communists appear to have been successful in keeping the party alive and vigorous. It is still comparatively weak in rural areas, but since the 1930's its rule has been largely unquestioned even there.

Members of the party belong to small primary organizations, as they are called. In a government department the minister and the janitor, if he is a member of the party, may belong to the same cell. The leaders of the party form its Central Committee, which is formally elected by the party congress and in 1966 numbered 195 full members. The Central Committee in turn elects a small Politburo[7] in which most of the main policy decisions of the party (and thus of the state) are taken. The precise role and relation of the Politburo and Central Committee at any given point in time in a particular country is a matter of conjecture. What is clear is that at each level of the party hierarchy the permanent secretaries play a vital part. Their appointment must be confirmed by the party Secretariat, which is under the general secretary; thus the general secretary usually controls the party. Stalin demonstrated the power inherent in this post in the period of flux after Lenin's death. There are some who think that this experience caused the triumvirate that succeeded Stalin to look for a buffoon who could never dominate the party as Stalin had done; they selected Khrushchev, and he lasted nine years.

It is sometimes suggested that there are two separate hierarchies in Russian communist society, one of permanent party officials and another of Soviet bureaucrats and captains of industry —clergy and laymen as it were. This is not so. According to David Granick, three-quarters of the Central Committee elected at the 1956 party congress in the U.S.S.R. had held major career positions outside the party.[8] Clearly the party does not form a separate caste. There was some evidence, however, that the best road to the top of the party hierarchy was not via industrial management.

---

[7] Called Presidium in Khrushchev's time.
[8] David Granick, *The Red Executive* (New York: Doubleday, 1960), p. 313.

Only 20 percent of the Central Committee had ever been in industry. When the Central Committee was enlarged from 175 to 195 full members in 1966 the number of party functionaries remained stationary at eighty. The number of government officials rose from fifty-eight to seventy-three. The remaining forty-two members included fourteen representatives of the armed forces, one member of the secret police, and twenty-seven "others." The Central Committee now represents the Soviet elite.

Yugoslavia

A new form of communism has been devised in Yugoslavia, and the state is called a socialist democracy. The Communist party is as strong and influential as elsewhere, and in times of crisis it is clear that the main decisions are taken by the party. But Yugoslav communism has several distinctive features that may have worked to strengthen rather than weaken its hold on society. The party has not been primarily a vehicle through which the proletariat has established its domination over other classes of society. If anything, it has been a unifying factor, the one organization that cuts through the traditional ethnic and religious rivalries that throughout history have plagued the peoples who form the modern Yugoslavia and that prevented the interwar Yugoslavia from becoming a stable state. The party has also been relatively unobtrusive. By refusing to take the credit for all the country's positive achievements it has escaped taking the whole blame when things go wrong. Finally, like the communist parties of other east European countries, the Yugoslav party has shown a greater flexibility than the Soviet party through its willingness to work with other parties in the Socialist Alliance. It is true that other parties must accept the leadership of the League of Communists, but the very existence of other parties provides a safety valve for both communists and noncommunists that may one day prove useful.

An important feature of Yugoslav society is the deep religious faith of many of the people, whether Catholic, Orthodox, or Moslem. The refusal of the Serbs to abandon Orthodoxy during centuries of Turkish rule (though this meant remaining serfs instead of becoming citizens) was a warning to the Communist party not to tamper with religious freedom as such. The communists have deprived the various churches of their property, but religious bodies can obtain state financial support, particularly for historic buildings. In 1965 the Vatican resumed relations with the Yugoslav government after a break of fourteen years.[9]

China

Owing to its period in the wilderness, the Chinese Communist party was far less conspiratorial than the Russian and was largely peasant-based. From less than a million members before 1949 it expanded to twenty million full and candidate members by 1966. In China the difficulty has been to recruit enough *urban* members; the ratio of peasants to proletarians remains four to one. As in the U.S.S.R., the Communist party in China is the only politically alert and active group amid a vast sea of humanity.

As far as its political process is concerned, China remains a mystery. It is known that the Communist party plays a much greater role than in the Soviet Union (whereas in Yugoslavia it is relatively inconspicuous, working through the massive Socialist Alliance) and that the vast peasantry is not treated as it was in the U.S.S.R. at a similar stage of development. China's chief social problem appears to be that of urbanization resulting from industrialization. As a higher proportion of people join the ranks of the "experts" who alone can operate a complex modern economy, enthusiasm for the simple life to which the older communists became accustomed during the Long March tends to diminish. People are not as "red" as they were. Hence the attempt to combine education and ideology through the slogan "red and expert."

The Organization of the Communist Party

The formal organization of any communist party, like that of parties elsewhere, is hierarchical, extending from small local groups to the party congress, which meets every three or four years. In many ways, however, it is very different from liberal democratic parties—in its method of election, its claims on its members, its role in government, its dependence on a hard core of permanent officials, and above all its principle of democratic centralism.

---

[9] For further discussion of Yugoslavia, see G. W. Hoffman and F. W. Neal, *Yugoslavia and the New Communism* (New York: Twentieth Century Fund, 1962).

In fact, it is best not to think of the Communist party as a party in the liberal democratic sense at all. In some ways it has been compared with a medieval church or order. Its high priests (the party theoreticians) maintain the orthodoxy of the monarch (the general[10] secretary who, like the queen of England, is defender of the faith); their congregations of the faithful (party members) set the tone of the society in which they live. Men and women do not simply join as members of the party as in liberal democracies: they must pass rigorous tests of character and loyalty to party doctrine before admission. There are indications that admission has become less rigorous, but in the past it has been more difficult to join the party than it is to become a member of most churches. Perhaps the church analogy can be taken further. Deviant members are excommunicated; revered leaders are canonized after death. Already, as between Rome and Byzantium, there are schisms—first between the U.S.S.R. and Yugoslavia and later between the U.S.S.R. and China over whether the U.S.S.R. is the leader of the communist bloc. There have been heretics since the days of Leon Trotsky and the numerous deviationists of left and right. Those of us outside the communist camp are miserable heathens whose grandchildren, according to Khrushchev, will one day accept the Marxist-Leninist testament. Meanwhile, should any noncommunist, in Hungary or elsewhere, dispute the "march of socialism," he is branded as a counterrevolutionary.

Democratic Centralism

The most interesting and distinctive feature of communist organization is the principle of democratic centralism. In addition to the Soviet Union, communist parties elsewhere, including those in China and Yugoslavia, have adopted the principle. Article 19 of the Communist Party of the Soviet Union (C.P.S.U.) rules states that the principle signifies:

   a. the election of all leading party bodies, from the highest to the lowest;
   b. periodic reports of the party bodies to their party organizations;
   c. strict party discipline and subordination of the minority to the majority;
   d. the absolutely binding character of the decisions of higher bodies upon lower bodies.

[10] Only Khrushchev was *first* secretary.

The first two clauses are the democratic elements, and the last two indicate centralized control. As the Chinese party constitution (Article 19) puts it, "Democratic centralism means centralism on the basis of democracy, and democracy under centralized guidance." Together centralism and democracy distinguish the party from purely authoritarian organizations such as the Nazi party and from liberal democratic parties. The Nazi rank and file accepted orders from above; the liberal democrats believe in the sovereignty of the people or their parliamentary representatives. But the communists try to have both participation by party members *and* central direction of policy. Thus the role of the secretaries at various levels, which is abhorrent to liberal democrats, fits into the doctrine of party discipline and direction from above. Democratic centralism also permits certain restrictions in party elections, for although each body formally elects the one above it, each level in the party has a dual responsibility—a responsibility to the one above as well as to the one below. This means that the nomination of candidates for office is not left entirely to the discretion of the lower bodies but is controlled by the bodies above them.

Many observers regard democratic centralism as a travesty—or even the negation—of democracy. The U.S.S.R. is to them a totalitarian machine disguised by democratic phraseology. John Hazard[11] has suggested that it makes more sense to describe the communist political system as one that incorporates democratic forms but counterweights these with totalitarian controls. The advantage of his interpretation is that it makes room both for many communists (for example, the millions of agitators at election time in the U.S.S.R.) who believe that there has never been such popular participation in government before and for the party functionaries who clearly manipulate the system in the interests of the party leaders. Only they understand the realities of political power. Given this dichotomy in communist politics it is difficult to persuade communist leaders that similar machinations do not take place in liberal democracies to make sure that the "capitalist imperialists" retain effective control of the political machinery, whatever party is in power.

---

[11] John N. Hazard, *The Soviet System of Government*, 3rd ed. (Chicago: University of Chicago Press, 1964).

At times it has, nevertheless, been hard to see how any thinking Russian or Chinese can regard the political structure as more than a façade. Hazard's framework is not wholly satisfactory. When censorship was temporarily lifted in Poland in 1956 even the Communist party press ridiculed the Sejm (Parliament) for always voting unanimously. Stalin more than "counterweighted" inner-party democracy when in the great purge he liquidated over half the Central Committee—the committee that had formally appointed him and to which he was responsible for his actions. It is more useful to follow Alfred Meyer's example and to compare the Soviet Union with a capitalist business corporation.[12] The leaders are comparable to a board of directors; the state apparatus is equivalent to the managers; and the rank and file represent the stockholders. A large corporation shuns publicity, demands corporate loyalty, and has a democratic façade symbolized by the annual general meeting.

But in one important matter the business firm and the Communist party are different. The business exists to make a profit; the party exists to promote communism. Despite all the talk of "convergence" and of comparable problems of economic growth, profitability remains a secondary aim so long as the party remains in control.

Whether the permanent purge is a general communist phenomenon or a peculiarly Russian one (with other communist states merely copying the Soviet example) it is too early to say. Most twentieth-century totalitarian systems seem to have adopted a policy of violence at an early stage, but not all have used the purge as a means of revitalizing the party. Hitler's bloodbath of June 30, 1934, in which he decimated his Brownshirts, was succeeded by a long period, which lasted until the führer's death, during which there were fewer changes in the top leadership of Nazi Germany than in that of any other great power. Recent stress on "legality" in the U.S.S.R. indicates that many Russians are anxious for a more constitutional form of government. Nevertheless, it is in the very nature of totalitarianism that it can at any time revert to extreme policies as the experience of China and the rampaging Red Guards in 1966 and 1967 would seem to confirm.

---

[2] Alfred G. Meyer, *The Soviet Political System* (New York: Random House, 1965), pp. 112–15.

Elections

The principle of democratic centralism is apparent in the organization of elections. Those of the Supreme Soviet, the Soviet Union's legislature, take place every four years. Since 1936, when the peasants were admitted on equal terms with the workers and when reactionaries were assumed to have been eliminated, the formal electoral arrangements have been much like those of liberal democracies. In contrast to party elections, which are indirect (and of course confined to party members), election of members of the Supreme Soviet is direct, by all citizens aged eighteen and over. For those who want privacy, curtained voting booths are provided. China has not yet reached this stage; elections to the National People's Congress are still indirect—through provincial, regional and city congresses. Incidentally, China is a unitary state, and the lower congresses replace the quasifederal structure of the Soviet Union's fifteen union republics.

Yugoslav elections are direct, as in the Soviet Union, and Yugoslavia is a federal state. It has gone one step further than the Soviet Union by permitting electoral contests among Communists. There are signs that this innovation may be adopted by other communist countries if it succeeds in providing a means of replacing older Communists by younger members of the party.

To liberal democrats one of the mysteries of communist politics is the way in which the communists manage to secure such a large turnout at the polls (such as 99.98 percent), especially in the absence of competition. It would seem that there must be some exaggeration of the actual figures. Yet it is probable that a very high proportion of electors do vote. Part of the explanation lies in efficient organization by the party. Ballot boxes are available everywhere (including trains), and numerous agitators encourage the slothful. Election day is a holiday, and voting is regarded as a demonstration of national solidarity to impress the outside world.

Another explanation of the turnout is that, in the Soviet Union at least, the electorate has in fact had more participation in the electoral process than a glance at the single name on the ballot paper would suggest. Not all candidates are Communists; some are independents classified as members of the "nonparty bloc." None is formally nominated by the Communist party

A number of organizations may nominate candidates and in fact do so. The result is that the ballot paper indicates a candidate's name, sponsoring organization, and party membership (if any). It is during the nominating process that discussion of the merits of various candidates takes place, and it is here, presumably, that the pressures at work in Russian politics come into play. The campaign is for nomination rather than election. But it is doubtful whether the various organizations have any real say if the party knows its own mind. Paragraph 67 of the party's rules is quite explicit about the role of party members in elective bodies: ". . . and in all elective bodies of Soviet, trade union, co-operative, and other mass organizations having not less than three party members, party groups are formed whose task is to strengthen the influence of the party in every way and to carry out the party policy among the non-party people." In fact, therefore, the party indirectly controls the nomination of all candidates.

However, to imagine that the Communist party alone determines which candidates will be nominated and that a docile public is merely called upon to vote for these is not quite correct. Electors vote against a candidate by scratching out his name. In the 1966 Soviet of the Union elections 143,570,976 votes were cast for the candidates and 345,643 against them. In local elections, where the party sometimes fails to do its homework properly, a majority of the electors occasionally scratches out the name of a particular candidate and in these instances, and when there is not the legally prescribed poll, he fails to be elected. Recently in the Soviet Union there have been proposals for contested elections with more than one name on the ballot. If the candidates were both Communists, the innovation would merely extend the competition already possible at the time of nomination. But if one were a nonparty candidate the procedure could be used to reduce the power of the party.

Suppose a candidate wishes to do more than run as an independent member of the nonparty bloc. Suppose he is against the party. At that point the party (officially, the Election Commission) draws the line and refuses to allow the nomination to go forward. In this respect, and it is a very important respect, elections are not free. No one is allowed to oppose the official ideology; such persons are branded as counterrevolutionaries, reactionaries, or at least deviationists. In the U.S.S.R. there neither are nor can be opposing parties as there neither are nor can be opposing classes. Here again is that bland, extraordinary assertion that politically conscious citizens voluntarily unite in the Communist party.

This is very different from the restrictions on the Communist party enforced in some liberal democracies. In these countries there is no restriction on competing parties as such and no assertion that one party stands for the truth. Only those who, if given the opportunity, would put an end to party freedom are in fact proscribed.

The Press

Just as in Sweden, there is in the communist bloc a party press, but since there is in effect only one party this means that control of the whole press (and mass media generally) is in the hands of the Communist party. Social democrats elsewhere have long complained of the role played by a hostile capitalist press, and some of them believe that no individual, however well-intentioned, should be allowed control of an important newspaper. Nonetheless, very few countries outside North America and northwest Europe have a free press even of the capitalist variety. The communist solution to the problem of the control of mass media is, however, more of a warning than an example; it entails not only a government monopoly as a replacement of a certain amount of competition but also the suppression of news for reasons of state. The Russians go so far as to deny the right of any individual as such to publish anything at all, even a book or a handbill. Although a newspaper in a liberal democratic society can be indicted for libel, it does not have to pass a censor. Such freedom to publish is not allowed by communist governments.

Unlike many other totalitarian regimes, however, the communists seem anxious to keep in touch with public feeling. "Letters to the editor" are an important feature of their newspapers. Presumably the comparatively minor criticisms of the administration that are published appear to many readers to be a sign of freedom. Communists no doubt look on public criticism of their regime, as distinct from comments on administrative shortcomings, with something of the distaste that patriotic British people reserve for those who criticize the queen.

The Soviet Union

The leading Russian newspaper is *Pravda* ("Truth"), the official organ of the Communist party, with a circulation of over six million. It is national rather than local in coverage, and its news and views are reproduced in many other papers. The government newspaper *Izvestia* ("News") had a circulation of only two million until Khrushchev's son-in-law Alexei Adzhubei adopted interesting journalistic techniques. By 1965 its circulation had reached eight million. Other newspapers take their cue from the two leaders. On one occasion in 1954 *Pravda* and *Izvestia* startled the world, and possibly themselves, by actually disagreeing over Soviet policy. So dull is much of the press that unkind critics say that this explains the Russians' passion for books.

Yugoslavia and China

In Yugoslavia the newspaper *Borba* ("To Fight") is the organ not only of the League of Communists but also of the Socialist Alliance, and it has tended to reflect the comparative tolerance of the regime. Yet in regard to freedom of expression Yugoslavia is still a communist country. Djilas, once a close friend and collaborator of Tito, has been imprisoned on several occasions for his writings. In 1967 a young professor named Mihajlo Mihajlov was sentenced to four and a half years in prison and forbidden to publish anything for a further four years because he asserted that Yugoslavia was a totalitarian country where a small group of people had an absolute monopoly over ideas. Even so, Yugoslavia is not quite as closed a society as these cases may suggest. Djilas has been freed from time to time, and whenever he comes out of prison he publishes yet another criticism of the regime. And when Mihajlov appeared in court he said that although Yugoslavia was totalitarian it was ten years ahead of other communist countries and its totalitarianism was of a different kind. The Communist party in Yugoslavia does seem to be more tolerant than in most other communist countries. There have been no bloodbaths and there has been much interchange with the West.

The most quoted paper in China has been the *People's Daily*. The official party newspaper is the *Red Flag*. There are many other newspapers published throughout the country, all of course following the party line. The Cultural Revolution disrupted the press. In June 1966 the *Peking Daily*, the organ of the Peking Communist party, was reorganized and its staff purged. On September 3, 1966 publication was suspended and was not resumed until January 20, 1967, on which date an editorial denounced the "abominable crimes" of its former editors. A poster campaign occurred partly because the newspapers ceased to provide adequate news of what was going on.

Generally speaking, the world communist press is less monolithic than it was. Newspapers in Moscow and Peking denounce one another; there is confusion in China concerning what should and what should not be published; and in Yugoslavia and eastern Europe there are signs of greater toleration, though not yet of freedom of speech.

Groups and Individuals

One paradoxical feature of communism usually receives less notice than it deserves. This feature is the insistence on the one hand that socialist man is a social being and that therefore only as a member of a group has he any right to nominate candidates or to operate a newspaper, and, on the other hand, the notion that people may discuss shortcomings in the system (not the system itself) only as individuals and may not join forces with others in order to make this criticism effective. This peculiar reversal of the roles of the individual and the group has been very cleverly arranged. Even deputies prefer to intervene on behalf of their constituents rather than to air grievances of a general nature in the Supreme Soviet, or so it would seem. Socialist man must avoid partial associations: "democracy within the party" must not be abused by "antiparty elements."

The success of the communist system depends on the continued vitality of the party and the active sense of duty in each party member. For it is the party that has united workers, peasants, and intelligentsia, that has linked the nation's leaders to the masses, and that has given opportunities for ambitious young people to enter the elite. Quite simply, the political process of the U.S.S.R. and of all other communist states has been the

Communist party in action. Once the party ceases to be dominant, as is the case in Yugoslavia, there are demands for contested elections and a free press. The individual challenges the notion of group solidarity.

8

GOVERNMENT

The Unimportance of Government

In a liberal democracy policy is formed by the executive. The president of the United States and the cabinet of a parliamentary system are the governmental authorities responsible for decision-making at the highest level. Of course they derive many of their ideas from members of their political parties, especially those who represent the people in the legislature and who often sense the electorate's mood better than the leaders. They will be influenced too, for better or for worse, by the permanent officials in the civil service.

In communist systems any emphasis on the role of the executive and legislature is misleading. Policy is formed outside the governmental system: it is the responsibility of the Communist party at all times. The party does not express in a concrete platform the vague sentiments of a section of the electorate as in a liberal democracy; the party considers itself the appointed leader of the whole people and *the* dynamic political force in the nation. In practice the party's responsibility is borne in large measure by its top echelons—the Central Committee and, more especially, the Politburo and Secretariat. Only when there is a very big national issue, such as the need to diminish the role that Stalin played, is the party congress itself involved.

To the liberal democrat, accustomed to the governmental structure being paramount, the notion of a Stalin or a Brezhnev dominating Soviet policy even when not a member of the council of ministers appears anomalous. Yet there is nothing strange in this arrangement to a communist, for to him it is the party's Politburo, of which the general secretary is a member, that is the chief policy-making organ in the country.

The Legislature

The Soviet Union

Granted the superior role of the Communist party it is difficult to be sure of the role of the legislature, or Supreme Soviet as it is called in the U.S.S.R. The term *soviet* is Russian for "council" and there are local, city, county, and provincial soviets and Union-Republic supreme soviets as well as the Supreme Soviet of the U.S.S.R. itself. Formally, as the U.S.S.R. constitution indicates, the role of the Supreme Soviet is clear enough: it is the "highest organ of state power in the U.S.S.R." Its two houses, the Soviet of the Union and the Soviet of Nationalities, comprised 767 and 750 delegates respectively in 1966. They meet in Moscow about twice a year for a week at a time to pass laws, vote on the budget, appoint the council of ministers, and elect a Presidium of about 36. The Supreme Soviet seems to function like a delegates' meeting of an American trade union, where the leaders make speeches and the rank and file applaud, than Congress or Parliament, where the actions of the government come under constant scrutiny. But of course the Russians have had virtually no experience of a Western-style legislature.

Between meetings of the Supreme Soviet the Presidium acts on its behalf, and to judge from Article 49 of the constitution its duties are far more explicit than those of the Supreme Soviet itself. Yet even the Presidium appears to lack authority and to be regarded more as a substitute head of state or privy council than as a standing committee of the legislature. The whole soviet structure seems to play a subordinate role to the party, though it is less of a rubber stamp than formerly.

Yugoslavia and China

The Federal Assembly of Yugoslavia is unusual for eastern Europe in that, like the Russian, it has never been unicameral. Initially this was in order to represent the various national groups in the Council of Nationalities, but in recent years there have been experiments with other forms of representation of which nationality is only one. As has been noted, the Council of Producers was one such innovation. When it was abolished under the 1963 constitution it was replaced by no less than four new chambers each having 120 deputies elected by the communes. These chambers represent Economics, Education and Culture, Social Welfare and Health, and Organization. A fifth chamber, the Federal Chamber, includes the Chamber of Nationalities and has a total of 190 deputies.

In its form of government China modeled itself on the Soviet Union, though with a different terminology. The National People's Congress, for example, corresponds to the Supreme Soviet. The Standing Committee of the Congress corresponds to the Presidium of the Supreme Soviet. Each body is now larger than its Soviet counterpart. In 1964, 3,040 members were elected for a four-year term to the third National People's Congress. Its Standing Committee then numbered 112. Because of the Cultural Revolution the Congress did not hold its annual meeting in 1966. The announcement in August of that year that the Great Proletarian Cultural Revolution would be pursued in all sections of the community was made by the eleventh plenary meeting of the Central Committee of the Communist party—whose chairman was Mao Tse-tung.

The Role of the Communist Legislature

Two contrary explanations are often given for the peculiar place of legislatures in communist political systems, but neither is altogether convincing. Communists argue that the absence of class divisions means that there are none of the ideological conflicts that take up so much of the time of "bourgeois" legislatures. It is not required, therefore, to resolve social conflicts. But this is to assume that *all* or most arguments can be reduced to conflict between classes—which is clearly not the case.

Opponents of communism describe the communist type of legislature as a useless façade comparable to Hitler's Reichstag. Certainly no liberal democrat can approve of a system where a party is assigned the role that in liberal democracies is given to the legislature, because this means putting a particular party above the electorate as a whole. To communists, on the other hand, and perhaps to many Russians who now take the system for granted, it apparently makes sense to leave ideological matters in the hands of the Communist party, as the vanguard of the proletariat and the leader of society.

The system of national and local government fills the gap between the party and the people and has been called, together with the trade unions and other social organs, the transmission belt of the communist state. Presumably the party is the engine (the party Secretariat no doubt having its hand on the gear lever) and the toiling workers and peasants the wheels—the traditional "ship of state" in this mixed metaphor becoming the chassis. Communism is concerned with the implementation of communist policy through mass participation. It is not based on the liberal democratic notion of the party as a partial expression of public opinion. The liberal view is more one in which, to use a different metaphor, the flow of public opinion turns water wheels (parties) and through them the engine of state. In some countries, alas, there is not always enough water to make the wheels turn, but in the advanced liberal democracies the system is as powerful (and as complicated) as a hydroelectric power station. In China, by contrast, a number of mass organizations subsidiary to the party and political structure were created not because of a liberal notion of the sovereignty of the people but to enable the "radiating influence" of the Communist party to penetrate into as broad an area as possible.

It is very difficult to give a true assessment of the communist legislature's role, so different is communist society. It is probably fair to say that whereas the legislature in Britain and America mirrors public opinion and acts as a check on the executive, in communist systems, where the organization of politics takes the place of the doctrine of checks and balances, it is regarded as a device to keep the party in touch with "the masses," as the communists are pleased to describe the members of the public outside the party hierarchy.

The Ministry

An even more puzzling feature of communist government is the administration—the Council of Ministers in the Soviet Union, State Council in China, and Federal Executive Council in Yugoslavia. It is one thing to explain away the legislature as a transmission belt, but, the reader may protest, it is surely going too far to suggest that in the communist states the government does not govern. Yet the truth is that these states do not have a government in the liberal democratic sense. The communist system may perhaps be compared with one of those European business corporations that has a two-tier management, the top tier being policy-forming and the lower one responsible for the day-to-day operation of the business. In the U.S.S.R. policy is determined by the party Politburo: the Council of Ministers is administrative. In China it is argued that since the Communist party must at all costs retain its commanding position as the ruling group it would be both unwise and unworkable for the party to attempt to perform all the tasks of administration itself.

The Soviet Union

In practice there is not usually any great gulf between the Politburo and the Council of Ministers, the one at the apex of the party hierarchy and the other at the top of the state structure. The leading members of the Council of Ministers are often leaders of the party Politburo, and other ministers are members of the Central Committee. The two hierarchies are like two pyramids that partly overlap, especially at the top. Below the top, at the level of the U.S.S.R. Supreme Soviet, for example, perhaps 25 percent of the members will not be communists. At the bottom, in local soviets, the proportion of noncommunists may be as high as 70 percent.

There is thus an interlocking management of Soviet affairs that prevents the sort of conflict that might occur if there were two completely separate institutions, a party policy-making directorate and a management-oriented operating hierarchy. In the Ukraine there has been a tendency to appoint plant managers to the party's Central Committee. In Sweden, to be sure, one or two ministers are appointed from outside Parliament purely for their administrative ability. In the U.S.S.R. *all* ministers are appointed for their administrative competence, and a number are not members of the Supreme Soviet.

The U.S.S.R. Council of Ministers is a large body of over eighty members. It is large because of the number of state industries from timber and nonferrous metals to oil and railways that require a minister at the head.[1] (For a time under Khrushchev a program of decentralization replaced many of the ministries at the U.S.S.R. and Union-Republic levels with councils of the economy representing locally situated ministries responsible for all industry in their area.)

THE SOVIET–COMMUNIST PARTY PYRAMID

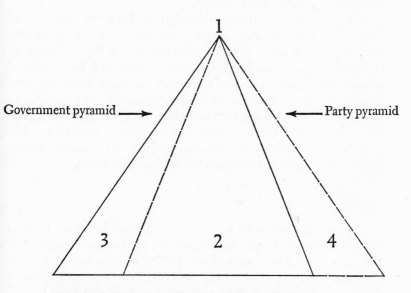

1. At the top, government and party interlock.
2. Many party members hold positions in soviets.
3. Some soviet members are not party members.
4. Some party members do not serve on soviets.

The Council of Ministers includes a smaller group of ministers who compose the highest policy-making body in the governmental structure and form a Presidium under the chairman of the Coun-

---

[1] In Britain nationalization led to the creation of new ministries such as aviation and fuel.

cil. In the early 1960's this chairman was Khrushchev in his other role as head of the governmental hierarchy, but since 1964 the chairman has been Kosygin. The Presidium includes the two first vice-chairmen and nine vice-chairmen.

Yugoslavia

The governmental structure in Yugoslavia differs from its Soviet counterpart in form and in fact. In form the system is "presidential"; that is to say, Tito is elected president of the Republic. (He was reelected in 1963 and 1967.) The administration is different in fact because Tito assumes leadership of both government and party. In the government he presides over the Federal Executive Council (the cabinet).

A controversy over Tito's succession has been indicated by the experience of his two long-time supporters and vice-presidents, Rankovic and Kardelj, both of whom had long been thought to be possible successors. In 1966 Rankovic, who had been chief of security for many years, was compelled to resign from the vice-presidency over a scandal involving the discovery of microphones in the rooms of high officials, including Tito. In 1967 the legislature resolved that the remaining vice-presidency, that of Kardelj, would be discontinued once the incumbent's term expired. In any case Kardelj could not be reelected to the same office.

China

Government seems to be more complicated in China than in either the Soviet Union or Yugoslavia. By now, noncommunist observers have grown accustomed to the relationship of government and party in communist countries, and they note whether the general secretary of the Communist party is also head of government (as Tito is and as Stalin and Khrushchev were for part of their tenure of office) or whether the offices of party secretary and the head of the government are separate as they are in the present-day Soviet Union. In China, however, there seem to be two governmental and two party structures, and the relationship between them is obscure. In the governmental sector the chairman of the Council of Ministers (the prime minister) is Chou En-lai. But there is also a chairman (or president) of the People's Republic of China who is head of state, Liu Shao-chi.[2] He succeeded Mao Tse-tung in 1959 and was reelected chairman in 1965. In the party the general secretary is Teng Hsiao-ping. These three men, Chou, Liu, and Teng, are thought to have taken over the government of China in 1959 after the failure of Mao's Hundred Flowers movement and the Great Leap Forward. Indeed in 1965 Mao is said to have moved from Peking to Shanghai. But Mao did not resign all his positions; he remained chairman of the Central Committee of the Chinese Communist party. Of the three other leaders only Chou En-lai is thought to be a member of the seven-man standing committee of the Politburo.

In addition, there are at least three important differences in governmental style between the Soviet Union and China that are worth noting. In China, as in Yugoslavia, regional government plays a prominent role. This was apparent after 1957 when decentralization of the economy occurred in both China and the Soviet Union. It failed in the latter but succeeded in China because the regions were strong enough to take command. A second difference is the division of the state into three branches: government, army, and judiciary. These are represented by the State Council, the National Defense Council, and the Supreme Court together with the Supreme People's Procuracy. In actual fact, the army has been far more important than the judiciary, and formal law is less important than in the Soviet Union. Thirdly, Chinese government is structurally more conservative than its Soviet counterpart but functionally seems to have been more flexible. Some very novel policies have been introduced, for example, in the decentralization of economic administration and management, without apparently changing the form of administration.[3]

Where Power Really Lies

The composition of the two Presidia and of the Politburo indicates where power really lies in the U.S.S.R. The Politburo of

---

[2] Until the 1965 appointment of Nikolai Podgorny to this position, the office of head of state had mainly honorific significance in the Soviet Union.

[3] Franz Schurmann, *Ideology and Organization in Communist China* (Berkeley: University of California Press, 1966), p. 174.

the Central Committee of the Communist party is the most important policy-making body; Stalin, Khrushchev, and Brezhnev have in turn played a leading part as secretary of the Central Committee in this small group of a dozen or so members. The Presidium of the Council of Ministers includes leading members of the party in their administrative capacity. Both Stalin and Khrushchev found it useful to be chairman of the Council of Ministers and to take an active part in its affairs. Stalin himself was never a member of the other Presidium—that of the Supreme Soviet, which in theory at least represents the Supreme Soviet as formal head of state. Until the appointment of Podgorny in 1965 the chairman of this Presidium was usually not one of the most powerful figures in the party leadership. Constitutionally the government of the U.S.S.R. (that is, the Council of Ministers) is responsible to this Presidium, but it would seem as formal an arrangement as the responsibility of the Swedish or British government to the monarch.

Just where power lies in contemporary China no one knows. Until the Cultural Revolution very little was known about the Chinese governmental system.[4] The exposures, accusations and counteraccusations publicized by the posters in Peking have been at the same time revealing and confusing. By and large they suggest that while Mao, like Tito, retains enormous respect, his colleagues of many years are becoming increasingly obsessed by the problem of succession. It has been noted that a man much younger than Mao, Chou, and Liu—Lin Piao—has emerged as a candidate for the succession. He is one of Chou's deputy premiers and a member of the standing committee of Mao's Politburo of the Central Committee.

There have been some interesting parallel developments in China and Yugoslavia. In China, as in Yugoslavia, the security services have been accused of placing microphones in leaders' rooms, including those of Mao himself. And in China, as in Yugoslavia, the minority groups (in such areas as Mongolia, Sinkiang, and Tibet) have expressed dissatisfaction with their position. Yet the solutions applied to the problem of succession in the Soviet Union, China, and Yugoslavia have been very different. Stalin applied the old Russian technique of terror; he died many years after his purges, leaving the succession unresolved.

---

[4] Schurmann, p. 9.

Mao seems to think the current conflict in China symbolizes the "peaceful contradictions" that characterize socialist society. The Cultural Revolution has been remarkable for the public restraint among the senior leaders. Very few have been removed from office, and none have been executed. Tito has been able to go one step further. Conscious of his secure position as leader, he has permitted the party and the Socialist Alliance to begin the process of preparing the succession without letting himself be personally involved. No doubt the problem will not be solved in his lifetime, but at least he seems to recognize the limitations of his position and has been wise enough not to place his mantle on any particular colleague. Some Yugoslavs even hope that the severe test of a transfer of power will not take place. The decentralization of power in the 1963 constitution, they assert, means that ultimately the federal government's power will wither away after the classic Marxist formulation.[5]

The structure of government in the communist bloc exhibits very clearly the vast difference between a liberal democracy and a totalitarian regime. The American and British party systems are ancillary to government, having developed (together with the extension of the franchise) as the intermediary between the executive and legislature on one hand and the electorate on the other. They help to lubricate the machine of state and to make sure that the parts fit smoothly together. In communist countries the state structure is ancillary and is the intermediary or transmission belt between the party and the people. The state is, according to Marx, in liberal democracies merely the executive committee of the bourgeoisie. What the communists have done is not only to eliminate the bourgeoisie but to transform the nature of the state, putting the emphasis on the party. Given the assumption that the party must be the driving force, the subordinate role of the state structure can be understood. The communist political system must be considered as a unity. It is useless to make piecemeal comparisons between, say, the United States Congress and the Supreme Soviet and to show how much the latter falls short of the former: the soviets are not intended to have the function of American legislatures.

The question to which one must always return, therefore, is

---

[5] Phyllis Auty, *Yugoslavia* (New York: Walker, 1965), p. 124. The number of federal employees was actually reduced from 47,310 in 1948 to 10,328 in 1956.

whether the underlying assumption of Communist party leader-ship is justified—the arrogant claim of a particular group to rep-resent the true interests of the people, whether the people think they do or not, and to have the right to prevent opposition from forming on the ground that their opponents must be "enemies of the people." In the short run, and in certain exceptional circumstances, as perhaps in the U.S.S.R. in the 1920's, the claim may be defensible on grounds of expediency. But to make the claim universal, a principle that is applicable at all times in all situations, is to stretch credibility itself.

Part of the fascination of politics in the United States lies in the public struggle for political power. Once every four years a number of men seek the presidential nomination and two of them ultimately fight it out in an election. Others run for Congress. At the same time, up and down the country men jostle for power in governors' mansions, state legislatures, county courthouses, and city halls. Not everyone may be wildly excited by some of the contests, but in many of them there is something like a free-for-all. Once the elections are over there are tussles between president and Congress, between president and Supreme Court, and of course within Congress itself. Less conspicuous is the bureaucratic infighting that sees the enlargement of certain agencies and the disappearance, like icebergs reaching warmer waters, of others. Of all the democratic political systems, none is so open to public view as the American, and none appears to foreigners so unruly, so disorganized—and so vigorous.

The communist world presents a startling contrast. To judge by communist publications there is no such struggle: everyone behaves in gentlemanly fashion and reason prevails. The elimina-tion of the class struggle, one is given to understand, involves the elimination of all struggle. This may indicate considerable naïveté or (more likely) reflect the notion current in many countries that have not experienced democracy that there are certain subjects that are not to be openly discussed: among these is the struggle between politicians or groups to influence those who make deci-sions. (Even in Britain there are many controversies that are carried on behind the scenes.)

So much secrecy surrounds the decision-making organization of the communist world that in order to find out what is going on in the Soviet Union observers analyze the positions occupied by the leading functionaries on the dais at May Day parades.[6] Those on the way up stand close to the leader: those on the way down may be inconspicuous or absent. When a leader dies the contest becomes really exciting. After Stalin's death a troika was set up with Georgi Malenkov as prime minister, Khrushchev as party secretary, and Nikolai Bulganin as minister of defense. Western observers with a sense of history compared the arrangement to the triumvirate of Stalin-Kamenev-Zinoviev that followed the death of Lenin. Within a few years Stalin, who controlled the party apparatus, ousted his colleagues; it was prophesied, with some accuracy, that Khrushchev as party secretary would do likewise. It is a matter of conjecture whether Khrushchev was expected to be more pliant and less competent than Stalin and therefore unable to establish yet another dictatorship. Certainly the nature of Khrushchev's rule was very different from Stalin's, being more open, more flexible, and more dependent on party support. Some commentators think that the Russian political tradition, going back to the tsars, favors autocracy; others suggest that it is in the nature of communism that whoever controls the party administration dominates the state. How long the partnership of Brezhnev and Kosygin will last is anybody's guess.

The Stability of Communist Government

Stability of governmental structure depends on unity within the party and on the subordination of other pressure groups to it. In the Soviet Union there is already evidence of stresses and strains within the party, and there seems to be some competition for power between the two main traditional party strongholds—Leningrad and Moscow—while the party organizations in the non-Russian Union-Republics are not always in agreement with Russian policies. There have been indications of some ideological disagreements between the Stalinists and new men who are less dogmatic in their use of Marxist theory, but no one knows how serious these are and whether they are more serious than the arguments that go on within any organization. It would be foolish at this stage to count on a split within the party.

---

[6] See, for example, Carl A. Linden, *Khrushchev and the Soviet Leadership 1957–1964* (Baltimore: Johns Hopkins Press, 1966), p. 94.

More serious is the threat to party harmony posed by other organizations. The liquidation of Lavrenty Beria shortly after the death of Stalin was a public indication that the secret police were not going to be allowed the power that enabled them to assist Stalin in the great purge of the 1930's, when thousands of leading party members were executed. The retirement of Malenkov from the premiership was a setback to the hopes of the industrial bureaucracy that it, rather than the party, would control the destinies of the Soviet Union. For a time it seemed that power might pass to Georgi Zhukov, whose armed forces had helped Khrushchev to overcome so much opposition, but the general's vanity proved his undoing, and when the time came Khrushchev was able to enlist the support of jealous generals who were happy to see the old warrior put out to pasture. Like Douglas MacArthur, he was a popular and able military man but no match for the politicians. Khrushchev in his turn was ousted after his administration had failed both domestically and internationally.[7]

So far the secret of the party's success has been its infiltration into all walks of life and its capacity to attract the ablest talent in the country to its service. Should the day come when the Soviet elite—scientific, industrial, administrative, and military—ceased to respect the Communist party, the structure of Soviet society would be threatened with disintegration.

In eastern Europe the Communist party seems less secure than in the U.S.S.R., but power on the whole lies with party secretaries who are amenable to Moscow. Occasionally, as in Poland, the Russians have to give way to nationalist demands, and then whoever gains power has the difficult task of trying to represent the wishes of his people without alienating the Russians. Increasingly, however, the various countries are pursuing their own national interests. The struggle for power has been between those political leaders totally subservient to Moscow and those who resort to Russian dominance. In Poland the Russians have had to tolerate Gomulka as party secretary and Cardinal Wyszynski as Roman Catholic primate; in Hungary for a time they permitted Nagy to govern. When there has been threat of a deep split Russian party pressure is brought to bear (by visits from high Soviet officials), and if this proves inadequate, as in Budapest in 1956, the ultimate

---

[7] Linden, Ch. 10.

sanction is the Red Army. Since Budapest it has been widely assumed in the West that the Communist parties in eastern Europe, unlike that in the U.S.S.R., are alienated from the people and are ultimately dependent on force—and alien force at that.

It is too early to pronounce on Yugoslavia's national communism. One day Tito and his colleagues who fought together as partisans will have to transfer power to a new generation whose experience will have been very different. It is by no means certain that the experiment will outlive Tito, and it may well be that the decentralization can operate successfully only so long as there is a single charismatic leader at the center. Early in 1967 there was further evidence that the traditional ethnic rivalries had not subsided when the Croat writers' organization complained that Croatian was being reduced to the status of a local dialect. The Communist party had to intervene and so later did Tito himself. In April 1967 six amendments to the constitution were passed giving greater powers to the Council of Nationalities.

On the other hand, unlike Stalin and Mao, Tito has not bottled up the passions of his people during his lifetime. In the elections of 1967, when he was reelected president by the Federal Assembly by a vote of 642 to 0 with two abstentions, several of his oldest and closest collaborators were defeated. Most of the new ministers were under fifty years of age. The shift of power seems already to have begun. But so long as Tito lives Yugoslavia has yet to prove that its communism can outlast the revolutionary generation.

Like Yugoslavia, China has yet to make the generational shift in its leadership from the revolutionary generation to its successors. Neither Tito nor Mao can copy Stalin, who was only fifty-six in the mid-1930's when he purged the Soviet Union of old bolsheviks and bourgeois remnants to bring on the new Soviet men of the technological generation. Tito and Mao were both in their fifties when they came to power, and today their lifespan is too short for them to be able to rely on the firm allegiance of a new generation. The shift in Yugoslavia may be taking place through the new system of limited electoral contests. In China something similar may be working itself out in the Cultural Revolution— though some observers think that Mao is taking the opposite method from Stalin, preserving the revolution in all its redness instead of giving responsibility to the technological experts. At all events—as has been mentioned earlier—the patterns of politics in both China and Yugoslavia cannot definitely be discerned until the present leaders have passed from the scene. And this applies to an even greater extent in the various small countries such as Cuba that have only recently experienced revolution.

9
ECONOMIC AND
SOCIAL PLANNING

The Communist Brand of Socialism

If there are two things that many Americans instinctively dislike about the socialism of western Europe, they are the emphasis on public ownership, which Americans call socialization, and the extension of welfare benefits to care for the whole population from birth to death.

As far as public ownership is concerned there is a great deal of difference between the practice of "socialism" in western Europe and the full-blooded socialism, say, of the U.S.S.R. Eighty percent of the people in British industry and over 90 percent in Swedish industry are privately employed: by contrast only 0.5 percent of the Russian economy is still in private hands. There are some Americans who still believe that there is not much to choose between the two forms of socialism, and in the sense that they both mean the replacement of private capitalism by public ownership, this is true. But there are two other important differences between social democracies and communist countries. In the former the extent of socialization depends on the willingness of the electorate to support it: the limited amount of public enterprise in Sweden, Great Britain, and France reflects the unwillingness of public opinion to go further in that direction. A second difference is that social democracies accept the principle of compensation when private companies are taken over. Nationalization involves the purchase of business undertakings at a fair price, not their expropriation.

It is difficult for most of us to imagine life without any private enterprise. There would be neither Macy's nor Woolworth's, no General Motors and no Standard Oil, no Prudential and no Cunard—and no commercial television. In a communist society there is no stock exchange, not a single private shareholder, no market price for goods in the sense that consumer demand determines supply and that together supply and demand determine the price structure, no fluctuations in currency values, and no balance of payments problem. The state decides what shall be produced and at what price it shall be offered (any surplus over cost of production providing the turnover tax that is the mainstay of the economy). It controls all imports and exports, expanding and restricting both in accordance with its economic policy. The price at which it imports commodities such as rubber is governed by the noncommunist world's ruling market price: in its exporting it can, if it chooses, select a price below that which is ruling elsewhere.

These differences are surely enough to indicate the gulf that separates American capitalism and European social democracy from communism. Some naïve people are surprised to find that, notwithstanding these basic differences, communist and capitalist economic life have much in common. As one would expect in two gigantic continental economies like the Soviet and the American, free of internal tariff barriers, possessing great natural resources and populations of considerable ability, there is the same zest for life, distaste for decadence, ambivalence toward the clever sophisticates of western Europe, and interest in the material things that men have devised. In business this produces an easy acceptance of innovation and an eagerness to overcome production bottlenecks, if necessary by flouting the law. The U.S.S.R. models its mass production economy after the American—like everyone else. The Russian consumer is uneasily aware that many decades ago Henry Ford offered Americans any color of car that they wanted so long as it was black and wonders how long it will be before he can buy even a black car. The American salesman wonders at the easy life of salesmen in the Soviet Union, where goods have always been in short supply. But times are changing, and in 1959 the Central Committee of the Communist party and the Council of Ministers issued a joint resolution: "Trading organizations do not sufficiently study consumer demand . . . and make serious miscalculations in drawing up orders for the production of these goods, which leads to unjustified cuts in the output of goods of various kinds which are in demand, or to the accumulation of excessive stocks."

Of course communist governments control their economies absolutely, and so far shortages are met by raising prices, surpluses by lowering them. (In the spring of 1962 the price of some foods in the Soviet Union was raised by nearly a third.) Not that capitalist economies altogether foreswear similar methods of government interference, if on a more limited scale. It is arguable that the difference between the modern government-regulated capitalist economy and the government-controlled socialist economy is one of degree rather than kind. Those who believe the United States to be the last home of free enterprise and Great Britain to be a managed economy that has slipped once down the slope to socialization and may be doing so again would do well to ponder the city columns of the newspapers more carefully. For example, the London *Times* financial editor noted in June 1960:

> Since most dollar commodities are either "administered" by their leading producers (especially for minerals) or stabilized by the United States government within its agricultural support policy, and since the prices of most sterling materials are determined in open markets, sterling prices now tend to be more volatile.

Perhaps more significant than this comparison between sterling and dollar is the fact that it is the products of advanced countries such as the United States and the U.S.S.R. that are administered, while it is those of underdeveloped and weak nations in South America, Africa, and Southeast Asia that are undetermined and therefore volatile. It is in these areas that free enterprise holds sway and the prestige of the capitalist system is damaged.

Where communist countries differ from the leading capitalist economies of the West is in their willingness to plan their economies ahead for several years. They consider that the production of targets at which to aim encourages economic growth—though it is also true that unplanned economies like those of Germany and Japan are capable of even more spectacular increases in production. A government that wishes to develop basic industry, if necessary at the expense of present consumption, can only do so by planning ahead. If the government can persuade the people to support the planned increase in heavy industry, the denial of immediate consumption may not be considered an intolerable imposition.

The Soviet Economy

Planning

In the Soviet Union the State Planning Committee (Gosplan) is responsible for drawing up the five-year plans that have been customary in the U.S.S.R. since 1928 and have since been copied in many other countries. Both the party and the soviet hierarchies are very much involved in the plan's formation and implementation. Khrushchev's attempt to decentralize the administration of the economy created as many problems as it solved. It did at least show a willingness to experiment and innovate that in itself suggests that the Communist machine had not lost its drive after thirty years of intense effort. There is some evidence, however, that the decentralization policy was carried out for another reason. Power was transferred from the industrial ministries in Moscow, where Khrushchev was weak, to the Union-Republics, where industry was under the control of the territorial party structure—and where most of Khrushchev's supporters were. Khrushchev's failure indicated that he lacked Stalin's power over the Russian people.

The Brezhnev-Kosygin regime that has succeeded Khrushchev's has proved remarkable for its cautious pragmatism, at least in comparison with earlier Soviet policy. The economy appears to be operating on much more rational lines. Long-term planning and Communist party control remain, but there is a greater willingness to adopt new techniques and to extend the market economy as advocated by Yevsei Liberman of Kharkov State University.

Collectivization

It is often alleged that in communist countries "everything is owned by the state." Actually the various countries differ considerably in their policies, and even in the Soviet Union by no means is everything state-owned and operated. There are a few craftsmen who work for themselves, and there is a large number of collective farmworkers with personal plots. Provided they do not employ (that is, exploit) other labor, citizens may make an independent livelihood, subject to a higher rate of tax than the remaining 99.5 percent of the population.[1] Peasants are allowed to sell their produce privately in the market, city dwellers may own their houses (a third of urban housing is privately owned), and personal possessions may be inherited. Presumably, as the people of the U.S.S.R. become more affluent there will be an accumulation of personal property. Private ownership is causing a number of problems in parts of eastern Europe where collectivization has proved unworkable owing to the hostility of the peasants.

In most communist countries the land itself, the factories, offices, and mines—in fact, nearly all the means of production— are publicly owned. But they are not always state-operated. This is particularly true of Soviet agriculture with its 11,600 state farms (*sovkhoz*) and 36,900 collective farms (*kolkhoz*) in 1965. There is a difference between the two methods of farming. In the *sovkhoz* the peasants own neither land nor resources but work for wages as in industry, under a manager appointed from above. Naturally this form of enterprise conforms more to communist theory and was until recently favored by the party, which would like to obliterate the distinction between state, cooperative, and collective farm property. In 1950, 76 percent of state farms were equipped with electricity compared with only 15 percent of the collectives. By 1959 the figures were 96 percent and 49 percent. But in the *kolkhoz* there is an element of individual ownership, and, as in other cooperatives, compensation for the produce sold replaces wages. Moreover, the management, at least in theory, is elected by the members of the collective.

There is little if anything in common between the collective farm and the old Russian village (*mir*) in which heads of families administered village affairs cooperatively, in some instances even redistributing the land to meet the varying needs of the families. The bulk of *kolkhoz* land is not individually owned at all, and the policy of the unit is determined by the national plan. The term

---

[1] Mysteriously enough, there are still personal servants in the U.S.S.R.

"artel" is sometimes used to distinguish the usual Russian type of collective farm from others—for example, the Chinese commune, which is much larger and attempts to be far more than a farmers' cooperative. Even though the average number of families in a collective increased from 81 to 411 between 1940 and 1963, the *kolkhoz* has remained a small affair in comparison with the Chinese communes. Just before his death Stalin was thinking in terms of a form of commune. There have been intercollective farm unions for the purchase of machinery and building materials, but the concept of the commune is still officially regarded with skepticism.

The state farm, the *sovkhoz*, is particularly useful where it is decided to develop a new technique or to exploit new territory. About half of the virgin land opened up in Kazakhstan during 1954–55 was plowed up by state farms. In places where young communists volunteer their labor for a few seasons such a system may be more suitable than the collective. It was reported in 1959 that the production of grain by state farms had trebled in six years. However, in 1962 it was officially reported that during the first three years of the seven-year plan agricultural production generally had fallen far short of the target. The year 1963 was a disastrous one for Soviet agriculture, and wheat had to be imported from Canada and the United States. Khrushchev's fall in 1964 was in part due to the failure of his agricultural policy. In 1965 it was announced that investment in agriculture would be substantially increased. To encourage the peasantry the system of state pensions was extended to cover collective farmers.

The U.S.S.R. paid a heavy price for agricultural collectivization. And it is not true that today the typical Soviet farm is a prosperous, fully mechanized collective showpiece in the midst of endless steppes, any more than Kansas is typical of the whole United States. Much of agriculture in the communist bloc remains backward. In 1963 three times as many tractors and trucks were used by American farmers as by the peasants of the U.S.S.R. By 1965 the output of cars, trucks, and tractors had not reached the million mark, and arrangements were made in 1966 and 1967 for automobile production lines built by the French and the Italians to be established in the Soviet Union.

The pattern of control in industry is more uniform than in agriculture. After the Revolution many Soviet workers believed that the new regime would give them control over their plants, but the workers' syndicates, the equivalent of the agricultural collectives, were replaced by what is called one-man management. There is an element of worker participation in industrial affairs, and no manager can afford to ignore the views of the workers; but the decisions and appointments come from above and not from below. In this way the party can ensure that its orders are carried out and the national plan fulfilled. Maximum production and efficient management have been given priority over industrial democracy.

A Reappraisal

Recent Soviet scientific and technical achievements have brought about a reappraisal abroad of the communist economy, which has long been underestimated. It seems strange that at one time many foreign observers believed that the communists would not be able to make a planned economy work at all. The Soviet Union's New Economic Policy of 1921–27, when the party went into reverse and allowed private initiative to help it out of its difficulties, was the first indication that all was not well. This was followed by the controversial first five-year plan of 1928–33, which aroused so much peasant hostility. Yet it is clear in retrospect that the main aim, industrialization, was achieved. Soviet statistics admit that industrial production in 1921 fell to one-third of the 1913 figures but indicate that it rose to eight times that figure by 1940. Production fell during the war but regained the 1940 level in 1948, and it has increased dramatically since. It is claimed that production actually quadrupled in the decade 1948–58 and that in the seven years 1959–65 industrial output increased by 84 percent and the national income by 53 percent. The current five-year plan, 1966–70, calls for a 50 percent rise in volume of industrial output and a 30 percent rise in real per capita income. It is no longer expected that industrial production generally will exceed that of the United States. Great weight used to be attached to basic industry in reaching estimates of the gross national product, but increased production of coal, oil, and electric power is not automatically translated into the sort of goods and services that go to make up the American standard of living. The rate of economic growth has slowed down in the 1960's as investment has shifted to "progressive" growth-inducing branches of industry such as chemicals, petrochemicals, and electronics.[2] There is greater emphasis on qualitative, rather than quantitative, growth.[3]

Since Stalin's death Soviet agricultural policy has been overhauled and a greater balance between industry and agriculture has been achieved. In return for the greater consideration shown them, the peasants have produced some of the meat, butter, eggs, and even grain that Khrushchev asked them for.

Yet agricultural production remains an unsolved problem in the U.S.S.R., as it is in most communist countries. It is one thing to create a new industrial base and to transform the peasantry into an industrial proletariat; it is quite another to change the way of life of a rural population rooted for centuries in the land. When the Europeans migrated to America, Argentina, South Africa, Australia, and New Zealand they did not adopt traditional peasant-subsistence economies. Instead they produced cash crops that were sold on the world market; many farmers made fabulous fortunes out of an agricultural revolution comparable in its implications to the industrial revolution about which much more is written. The east Europeans, the Russians, and the Chinese have not had the advantage of new lands to cultivate (except in marginal areas such as the virgin lands of the U.S.S.R.), and they have resorted to forced collectivization as a means of quickly increasing agricultural production. They do not seem to have succeeded, and the socialist stick has proved less effective than the capitalist carrot. But in comparing the communist countries with the liberal democracies we should not forget the many advantages, not least the possession of colonies, that enabled the liberal democracies to revolutionize their own economies less painfully.

It is often said that the quality of many Soviet products is inferior, and to judge by reports, this is true, especially of consumer goods and housing. But it may be because many of the workers are as yet comparatively inexperienced and have been encouraged to put quantity before quality. (It has taken a long time for Europeans to discover that American mass-produced goods are not necessarily inferior to the European handcrafted equivalent.) As conditions improve the standards already attained

---

[2] See *Current Economic Indicators for the U.S.S.R.*, prepared for the Joint Economic Committee of the Congress of the United States, June 1965, p. 2.

[3] United Nations, *Economic Survey of Europe 1965, Part 1* (New York: International Publications Service, 1966), p. 1.

in planes and rockets will no doubt be reached in other industries; it would seem that there has been less official interest in the consumer goods industries than in those that give the U.S.S.R. international prestige. The Russians, to say nothing of the Chinese, have a traditional reputation for inventive genius, and so the argument of poor quality probably has a limited life.

For a long time a most devastating argument against communist production methods was that labor and machinery were misused and that the need to reach targets led to wasteful methods and erratic production, often with overconcern for the present and not enough thought for the future. This has been confirmed by recent research and by the interest now shown in the "new economies" by the Russians themselves.[4]

It is clear that the communist system of priorities is different from that of advanced capitalist economies. Stalin publicly admitted in 1952 that profitable light industries were not being developed to the utmost because preference was given to heavy industries, some of which were altogether unprofitable.[5] (He defended his policy on the grounds that taking the national economy as a whole, and over a period of ten or fifteen years, this policy *was* profitable.) Public or state needs are put before private and capital investment before consumption. It is a social system where people have been taught that the state or society naturally comes before individual wants and where, as a result, interest in heavy industry and economic growth is as apparently genuine as the American businessman's interest in business. The Communist party of the Soviet Union claimed that the 1959 seven-year plan was discussed at 968,000 meetings by over seventy million people who made 4,672,000 observations. Even allowing for the grossest exaggeration there would seem to be far greater popular interest in and knowledge of the economy in the U.S.S.R. than in any noncommunist country.[6] Above all, like an earlier generation of

---

[4] "We see no credible alternative to the hypothesis that by 1953 efficiency was still at a very low level and that the rapid gains which followed represent in part the taking up of slack, as it were, left in the system at the time of Stalin's death." Richard Moorsteen and Raymond B. Powell, *The Soviet Capital Stock, 1928–1962* (Homewood, Ill.: Irwin, 1966), p. 289.

[5] Joseph Stalin, *Economic Problems of Socialism in the U.S.S.R.* (New York: International Publishers, 1952), p. 21.

[6] A young woman in Ilya Ehrenburg's *The Thaw* tells a visitor about her bedtime reading—all about the exciting new generators at the Kuibishev power station.

Western pioneers, the communists seem to have had an urge to sacrifice themselves for the creation of a better material life for their children. Soviet statistics make no attempt to hide the fact that the production of capital goods rose four times as fast as that of consumer goods in the years 1928–55.

It is true that there is greater pressure today for consumer goods, which is not surprising after all the years of deprivation. The members of the younger generation look forward to the surplus of commodities that they have been promised and to the day when the socialist principle of "from each according to his ability, to each according to his work" will be replaced by "from each according to his ability, to each according to his need." If and when this age of plenty comes, the final stage, communism, will be said to have arrived.

Things are changing rapidly. In 1959 time payments were introduced for the purchase of consumer goods, and it was announced that the value of consumer goods on the market was to rise by nearly 50 percent in the next three years. In 1960 it was decided to expand store construction and the import of quality foreign products. In 1966 there were plans to increase the production of cars, TV sets, and refrigerators. But the age of affluence has yet to arrive—still more the era of superabundance. The main decision is still made by the party leadership, which surveys the whole economy and determines the order of priorities. Some modification has taken place, but the principle that basic industry should come first has not been abandoned.

The Yugoslav Economy

Since 1945 Yugoslavia has experienced an industrial revolution. At the same time it has decentralized administration by giving power to its six republics (Serbia, Croatia, Slovenia, Bosnia-Herzegovina, Montenegro, and Macedonia), to the districts into which they are divided, and to the communes that are responsible for local government. The Federal Planning Commission has had its name changed to Federal Planning Institute and has been deprived of its executive and administrative powers. The most significant reform was the devolution in 1950 of economic power to the workers' councils of individual enterprises. It is this distinguishing feature of Yugoslavia that is the most famous: the modification of communist economic policy to make possible the operation of workers' councils. These councils, which are elected by the workers of each plant, factory, and office and which supervise the operation of each institution, may prove to be the country's most important modification of Soviet communism.

A workers' council consists of 15 to 120 members elected for a period of two years. The council selects a chairman who calls monthly meetings and who is not a member of the council's executive committee. The executive committee, elected by the council, has from three to seventeen members, three-quarters of whom are supposed to be production workers. The committee chooses its president, who draws up the agenda in collaboration with the director of the enterprise. Unlike a capitalist board of directors, the executive committee involves itself in the details of operation and in the appointment and dismissal of workers, as well as in planning and wage rates. To do this it must meet several times a week. Service on the workers' councils is unpaid, but members of executive committees are compensated for time lost from work. They serve at most two consecutive terms.

Plant directors are now appointed by the workers' councils and may be dismissed by them. Vacancies are advertised. In the early 1950's the workers' councils tended to be more concerned with distributing profits in the form of higher wages, but this has been checked by the government. Now wage increases and social welfare extensions must be linked with increases in productivity. The individual enterprises have also been made responsible for social insurance and depreciation allowances. Regular accounts have to be submitted to the communal bank. There is a complicated tax system that has frequently been changed in order to stimulate production.

Surprisingly, the tightening of control over individual enterprises and their workers' councils does not seem to have been accompanied by centralization of authority. Whereas in 1960 the councils controlled 20 percent of the total income of their enterprises, after tax changes in 1961 they controlled 55 percent. In 1965 enterprises were allowed to retain 71 percent, giving 29 percent to the various levels of government. Large enterprises have been subdivided into "economic units" to make direct control and self-government possible by workers at unit level. Wage policy has been changed. At first there was emphasis on equality; then differentials were introduced. More recently there has been emphasis on group performance. Now a group of skilled and energetic workers may earn as much as professional people or senior civil servants.

Such at least is the ideal of workers' control in Yugoslavia. It is still of course impossible to give an objective assessment of how it works in practice, particularly in the many institutions not engaged in measurable production as are factories. But in the productive sector it has certainly enabled one in every three or four workers to participate in management and to understand something of the difficulties that are encountered. It may also be partly responsible for the great increase in both productivity and wages in the 1950's. The Yugoslav workers, it has been suggested, would not wish to be deprived of the councils.[7] The 1966–70 five-year plan calls for an annual increase of 8 percent in national income, 9 to 10 percent in industrial production, and 5 percent in agricultural production.

As has been mentioned earlier, imposition of agricultural collectivization failed in Yugoslavia, and land was handed back to the peasants. Today nearly 90 percent of the farmland is in private hands, although the numerous small plots are not necessarily very efficient. Many of the peasants do belong to the General Cooperatives, through which they can buy equipment and obtain credit.

The Chinese Economy

The most dramatic episode in Communist China's history was Mao's new economic policy of 1958, which was given the title of the Great Leap Forward. At the time the Chinese were hoping to leap forward into communism, outdistancing the U.S.S.R. Economically the Leap was disastrous, and China's rate of growth declined instead of advanced. As a result there was some evidence of an attempted purge in 1966 and 1967. It is apparent that in China, as in the U.S.S.R., concentration on industrial production at the expense of agriculture has nearly brought about a catastrophe. It is curious that the Chinese should not have learned

---

[7] Phyllis Auty, *Yugoslavia* (New York: Walker, 1965), p. 160.

from Russian experience that an increase in the industrial population must be accompanied by a considerable increase in food production. Belatedly, the Chinese have realized that rapid European industrial development has only been possible because of the import of farm products from North America. And so, like Britain before them, they are now purchasing Canadian wheat.

Apart from the Leap there have been three other aspects of Chinese economic policy that distinguish it from the Soviet policy. According to Schurmann, there is the combination of vertical and dual rule, that is to say the responsibility of enterprises both to the ministry in Peking and to the provincial government. Vertical rule provides the bureaucratic chain of command that exists in the Soviet Union. Dual rule enables the provincial party organization to keep a general watch on developments in all sectors. It also enables the directors of enterprises as party members to meet other directors as party members at the provincial level and to look at the economy and their role in it through party eyes.

The second feature of the economy is the abandonment of the Soviet principle of one-man management in favor of collective responsibility. Schurmann comments that the U.S.S.R. was very much influenced in its formative years by the Ford Motor Company. Although the Chinese are not known to have studied General Motors, their system can in some ways be compared to that of GM in their preference for group decisions rather than one-man rule.[8] (One can also note the changes in Europe. Britain moved from the Board of Trade to a single minister and most recently has returned to the board system in its nationalized industries. The Swedes used group management in their colleges until the nineteenth century and have used the board in some of their state companies in this century.)

The third characteristic of China is its attempt to avoid the Soviet, and still more the Yugoslav, system of material incentives to persuade workers and peasants to increase output. Instead there has been a process of social mobilization as it is termed, one feature of which is the coining of slogans to arouse people to further activity.

---

[8] Franz Schurmann, *Ideology and Organization in Communist China* (Berkeley: University of California Press, 1966), pp. 298–307 raises this point.

The Communist Welfare State

The "socialism" of Great Britain and Sweden may not have led to full nationalization of the economy, but it has usually been associated with the welfare state. If communist states are to be truly socialist they too must pay great attention to social welfare— presumably with a reduction in personal incentive if the criticisms of the welfare state have any substance. How is the notion of the welfare of the people to be reconciled with the evidence of exploitation of labor over the years, an exploitation necessary in order that an immense increase in production could take place?

The skeptical explanation is that the U.S.S.R., to give the main example, has merely pretended to provide general welfare, for instance by operating a few sanatoria on the Black Sea coast. In practice, it is alleged, holidays and rest cures have been available only for a privileged minority, members of the party or leading workers. Where the facilities provided are adequate—for example, those for medical care—it is argued that this has been done to raise production and not out of concern for the individual. Were there genuine concern for employees, then safety arrangements in factories would be better and the accident rate reduced.

There is some truth in these criticisms. Only 707,000 beds were available in sanatoria and holiday homes in 1965, a small number in comparison with the population. Much, however, depends on the interpretation one puts on the figures. The scheme could be regarded as symbolic in its purpose—to show that the poor *can* enjoy what were once the privileges of the rich—or as a massive swindle, like the People's Car that Hitler promised the Germans.

In any case holiday homes are but a minor feature of the communist welfare state. There can be little doubt that a vast amount of money is spent on health, education, and cultural development. It may take second place to heavy industry and armaments, but it looms far larger in the communists' scheme of things than consumer goods. In stressing welfare the Russians enjoy certain luxuries denied to many Americans. Like the Swedes they send their children out of town to camp for the summer; during the rest of the year the children of working mothers are amply cared for by day nurseries. In view of the war devastation, the need to rebuild the economy, and the concentration on basic industry and the armed forces, the country's welfare achievements are impressive. The Russians claim to have halved the death rate between 1940 and 1955 and to have doubled the number of doctors and dentists (346,000 compared with 297,000 in the United States). By 1965 there were, according to the 1966 yearbook of the *Great Soviet Encyclopedia,* 485,000 doctors and 43,700 dentists. The number of hospital beds in 1955 was 1,290,000 (compared with 1,604,000 in the United States). The 1959 plan proposed that this figure be doubled within seven years; six years later (1965) there were 2,225,500 beds. China also has made health a fetish. Since the quaintly titled Battle of the Four Pests (flies, mosquitoes, rats, and sparrows) and the instillation of a new puritanism Chinese cities are clean and fresh instead of filthy and squalid.

Both communist countries have also, of course, paid particular attention to education at all levels. University professors and research workers are as highly paid as people in industry. Within a generation the U.S.S.R., once largely illiterate, has shown a determination to become the most highly trained (though perhaps not the best educated in the broad sense) nation in the world. The Chinese have put eighty million children in primary school and sent twelve million to secondary school; 600,000 are in colleges and universities. Communist tourists are notorious for pointing out the deficiencies in the cultural arrangements (for example, theaters and concert halls) of the West outside the capital cities.

The communist countries are not without their social security programs that provide for old age, accident, and sickness. In the Chinese cooperatives 2 percent of the income has been put aside in welfare funds for dependents. One great burden in the U.S.S.R. has been the disablement of so many men through war wounds and the need for greatly increased pensions from 1946 onward. As the number of old people increases (there are now eleven million over seventy years of age) so the bill for retirement pensions rises. Benefits are generous, ranging from 50 percent to 90 percent of earnings for trade unionists who fall sick. In one respect there is a gap in the provisions: there is no unemployment compensation. It is argued that the policy of full employment makes an elaborate scheme of unemployment compensation (the "product of a wasteful capitalist economy") unnecessary. There would seem to remain, however, the problem of frictional unemployment that accompanies the change of jobs and, more intractable, the seasonal employment of a number of people in agriculture. In the U.S.S.R., as in the United States, the agricultural laborer has been the forgotten man in society.

Social welfare in its widest sense includes not only medical care, education, and social insurance but also housing. Here the Russian record is less impressive; Russian cities are noted for their overcrowded conditions, two families often sharing a one-room apartment. Overcrowding was bad in tsarist times in the great cities, and the destruction of the war has made things worse. The problem of accommodation has been further aggravated by the influx into the cities of millions of country folk drawn into expanding industry. The urban population rose from 26 million in 1926 to 56 million in 1939, 88 million in 1956, and 122 million in 1965. This fivefold expansion in forty years gives some idea of the size and speed of industrialization in the U.S.S.R.

The efforts made to cope with the housing problem can be judged in two completely different ways. It is possible to compliment the Soviet authorities on increasing the amount of urban housing floor space from 216 to 1,128 million square meters from 1926 to 1963 and on almost keeping pace, despite the war and the many other demands on the economy, with the rapid increase in population. The 1959 plan was to more than double housing construction, and it was claimed that in the 1970's the housing shortage would be over. Alternatively, the communists can be criticized for not devoting until recently a much greater proportion of the nation's resources to the immensely important matter of housing.

It is not easy to form a fair judgment. It is odd that in Sweden, where the population has not changed so radically and where there have been no losses through war or revolution, there should have also been for a long time a chronic housing shortage. As late as 1939, when architects all over the world were praising the design of Swedish apartment blocks, 42 percent of new housing construction was of apartments with only one room and a kitchen. Different nations may give housing different priorities.

Less is generally known of the details of social welfare in Yugoslavia and particularly in China. In Yugoslavia, where the employer pays all the premiums (20 to 30 percent of the payroll), social security covers employees and members of cooperatives. However, since the peasantry still constitutes a large portion of Yugoslav society, full social security coverage is not yet universal in that country. China is a stage behind Yugoslavia. There is no unemployment coverage and there are no family allowances. Old age, sickness, disability, and survivor insurance is extended to workers "in larger enterprises." However, the extent of coverage is not known.[9] All this suggests that the welfare state may be less a function of ideology than a consequence of a nation's standard of living and stage of industrialization.

There has been, moreover, a lack of balance in communist planning. This imbalance has become particularly evident in the Soviet Union. The U.S.S.R. has achieved its objectives in the creation of a heavy industry able to sustain a powerful military machine, and its attainments in ancillary fields such as aircraft production and space research are also impressive. Like many other dictatorships since ancient times it has spent lavishly on public buildings, but instead of the pyramids or the palace of Versailles its monuments are ornate subway stations and government offices—and a large number of hospitals and schools. The fact remains that it has still some way to go before it feeds, clothes, and houses its people satisfactorily and provides them with the appliances and automobiles so many of them want.

The balance might have been different had the people been able to apply pressure through their trade unions. According to communist theory there is no need to bargain over wages because there are no capitalists anxious to employ labor as cheaply as possible. Collective agreements are signed by management and unions each year. Mikhail Tomsky, the trade union leader in the 1920's, was not convinced that the workers needed no protection against the new managers, and Stalin replaced him for refusing to be cooperative. There has been no place in the Soviet Union for the checks and balances, of which unions are one, to be found in liberal democracies. Yet it must be admitted that once private capitalism ceases to exist it is difficult to see how trade unions can be allowed to function in the traditional manner without engrossing for themselves the powers of the state. The unions of the U.S.S.R. appear, however, to have gone to the other extreme. Instead of looking after the interests of the workers as a group they now administer social insurance, supervise safety regulations,

---

U. S. Department of Health, Education, and Welfare, Social Security Administration, Office of Research and Statistics, *Social Security Programs Throughout the World, 1967* (Washington, D.C.: U.S. Government Printing Office, 1967), pp. 44–45.

and provide a channel for individual grievances—much as the oft-criticized "company unions" of the United States. After the unrest in eastern Europe in 1956 the Communist party of the U.S.S.R. did institute "permanent production meetings" in the factories in December 1957. These do not seem to have given trade unionists much say in affairs.

It may have been no coincidence that about this time, in the spring of 1958 (following a mining strike), a dynamic trade unionist named Svetozar Vukmanovic-Tempo was appointed president of the Yugoslav trade union organization, the Sindikat. It had been argued in Yugoslavia that the workers' councils eliminated the need for trade unions to protect workers against management. However, a report of the executive committee of the Communist party in February 1958 criticized the Communists for not paying enough attention to the importance of trade unions in worker-management relations. By 1967 trade union leaders and journalists were openly discussing whether unions should become more independent of the Communist party and even whether workers should have the right to strike.

In China the unions seem to have played a minor role. In 1956 industrial managers were given full responsibility for their enterprises provided they consulted with their workers' representative general conference. The trade unions merely arranged the meetings. Two years later individual management came under attack during the Great Leap Forward, and both the workers' conferences and the trade unions were revitalized. In the ensuing chaos as the Leap collapsed, one-man management was restored, and the professionals took over administration in China. It is too early to say whether the recent Great Proletarian Revolution has enhanced the status of the trade unions.

It is tempting to conclude a survey of the communist economy and social welfare program by repeating the platitude that whereas a liberal democracy puts the individual before the state the totalitarian countries put the state before the individual. This was more true of fascism and nazism than it is of communism—which in any case is more interested in social class than in the state as such. The communists have done a great deal for their people, and it cannot be said that what is good for the group, whether it be school or a hospital or a steelworks, is not in a sense good for it individual members. It is arguable that by putting these forms of capital investment, with their long-range benefits, before current consumption the communists have tried to interpret the "real will" of the public—a will that is distorted in liberal democracies by high-pressure advertising on behalf of consumer goods. However, it was necessary to create an industrial base before attempting to raise the general standard of living. This was equally true of nineteenth-century Europe, where the wage earners, if not the middle classes, had to go without many luxuries until the advent of the modern age of high mass consumption. Economically, at least, the antithesis of the state (or group) and the individual is not altogether convincing.

But the *political* implications of the communist system are profoundly disturbing. Liberal democrats realize that the individual alone is often powerless against a powerful group or the state. He needs freedom to organize—in his trade union, a farmers' cooperative, a chamber of commerce, or the National Association for the Advancement of Colored People. There is recognition of the importance of the group as a protection of the individual, provided he is free to select his own group. The communists, who otherwise are so group-minded, insist that no such organization is necessary: if a man has a complaint he must voice it as an individual but must not organize others whether in a breakaway union or a party faction. When it suits them, the communists are far more individualist in their philosophy than the liberal democrats.

10

INTERNATIONAL ROLE

Changes Since 1917

The international role of the communist world has changed remarkably since 1917. At first there was emphasis on the Marxist
principles of world revolution ("Workers of the world, unite"),
but when Stalin ousted Trotsky in the 1920's this missionary fervor
was replaced by a realistic determination to make a success of the
revolution initially in the U.S.S.R. Hence the slogan "Socialism in
One Country." Events seem to have proved the wisdom of this.
The rise of Nazi Germany in the 1930's posed a military threat to
communism in general and the U.S.S.R. in particular; no great
power felt more isolated and exposed than the Soviet Union. The
attack on the Russians in 1941 nearly succeeded. Russian morale
in the early stages was low owing to the purges and the inability
to defeat even Finland in the 1939–40 winter war except by much
effort. Throughout the Second World War the Russians depended
to a considerable extent on American material aid. Nevertheless,
had Stalin not laid the basis of modern industrial power in the
1930's it is unlikely that the Soviet Union could have withstood
the German onslaught—the like of which the Americans (and
even the British during the blitz) have never experienced.

The success of the Allies in the Second World War vastly improved the long-term prospects of the communist world. The U.S.S.R. was weakened but victorious—without the atomic bomb, it is true, but the proud possessor of a Red Army that could have overrun western Europe once the Americans withdrew. As it was, nearly half of Europe fell into communist hands and the "Iron Curtain" that descended to separate eastern from western Europe is only now being lifted. Under Stalin there was a determination to hold on to Russia's military gains and to impose communism on the satellite countries. By 1956 unrest in East Germany, Poland, and Hungary indicated how difficult it was to persuade more advanced nations to accept the creed that had been so successful in the more backward Soviet Union.

The success of communism in China, though it secured the flank of the U.S.S.R. and enabled the communists to claim that they now controlled a third of the globe, added strength to the argument that communism was a theory of government more suited to backward economies than to industrial nations. The threat of communism in France, Italy, and Japan receded as these countries became more prosperous.

The communist world thus moved from being an isolated backwater between the wars to a military threat after the Second World War and to a position of stalemate with the West in the late 1950's. The change was symbolized by the slogan of Khrushchev: "peaceful coexistence." Today it is difficult to assess the strength of that world. In the short term it would seem to be economically weaker than has been thought. The problem of meeting consumer demands has not by any means been solved, while even the supply of food, so plentiful in the West, is a constant worry. Partly this reflects a failure to appreciate the need to conciliate the peasants and the workers if overall production is to expand, but partly it stems from the misconception that the most important indexes in assessing a standard of living are such items as steel, oil, and electricity production. Men do not live by basic industries alone.

Yet the challenge presented by the communist world is as great as ever, and its international position shows every sign of being gradually strengthened, particularly in backward countries. Basic industry can supply the basic needs of more backward economies—and at the same time lay the foundation for a higher standard of living in the future. The exploitation of the Soviet Union's spectacular scientific achievements, the insistence that only the communists really understand the problems of developing countries, and the provision of financial and economic aid to other nations have all encouraged the new nations to consider the communist world to be a useful model worth examining, if not copying. Politically the communists may be conservative and even dogmatic in their ideology, but economically their massive mobilization of resources, their sense of purpose, and their passion for economic growth tend to strike a responsive chord. The communists have kept their countries armed and present the spectacle of Plato's "lean and hungry dogs," eager to ally with others against the fat and lazy capitalist powers of the West. Whether, in the event of world conflict, the communists' morale would be as high as propaganda paints it we cannot of course know, but the stoicism of the North Vietnamese under continual bombing suggests that it could be.

The Conduct of Foreign Affairs

The conduct of foreign affairs under communism is not a matter of public debate. In the liberal democracies there is a constant tussle between the executive, which is responsible for foreign policy, and the legislature, which does not feel that this aspect of the executive's work should be entirely free from legislative supervision. Resistance to legislative control has in most countries been greater and more successful in the foreign offices than elsewhere in the civil service, even in the United States—for obvious reasons. But no foreign minister outside the United States has to cope with anything like the Senate's Foreign Relations Committee.

In the communist bloc, as one would expect, it does not make sense to discuss decision-making under the rubric of executive-legislative relations. The Communist party determines external as well as internal policy, and even such a gifted foreign minister as Vyacheslav Molotov becomes little more than a mouthpiece of the party Politburo and the general secretary.

The party does not appear to allow the legislative branch of government more than a cursory examination of foreign policy. Among the Supreme Soviet's preparatory commissions are the Commissions for Foreign Affairs appointed by each chamber. Their duties, according to Andrei Vyshinsky, are to make "a preliminary examination of all matters connected with foreign affairs to be considered by the Supreme Soviet (and its Presidium)."[1] Instead of elaborating on this statement Vyshinsky proceeds to criticize the parliamentary committees of Britain, France, and the United States! Where mass propagandizing of a particular step, as for the Nazi-Soviet Pact of 1939, is required, it is brought before the Supreme Soviet. In other matters, as in the denunciation of the alliances with France and Britain in 1955, only the Presidium and Commissions for Foreign Affairs may be involved.

Foreign policy presents two aspects of the Soviet political system in startling contrast. On the one side there is the massive publicity given to certain aspects of official policy (for example, disarmament proposals and spy trials) and on the other a secrecy over policy formation and an unexpectedness in tactical execution that has earned the description "Byzantine." What is the explanation for this contrast? It would seem that a certain amount of participation by the people is necessary at the level of general strategy: they have to be informed of the need for Cold War or coexistence and if possible, through propaganda, persuaded of its rightness. But there is no tradition in communist society of a public general debate of actual decisions, for example, of the Hungarian intervention in 1956. There can be no greater contrast than the continuous noisy demonstrations in the House of Commons over the Suez invasion and the silence of the Supreme Soviet on Hungary in December of that year. Such secrecy is in the communist tradition and is assisted by the isolation of public opinion from foreign sources of information.

It may help in an understanding of the conduct of communist foreign policy to distinguish three levels of discussion. The *basic principles*—in particular, the principle that the world is moving toward socialism and that capitalism is merely a phase in its development—are taken for granted; every step the government takes is assumed to be "furthering socialism," and this underlying assumption is thought to require no debate. Members of the party and the public do, however, require enlightenment about current *strategy*, whether it is of temporary friendship (peaceful coexistence) toward capitalist states or hostility (Cold War). According to whichever strategy is adopted, the victory of socialism abroad

---

[1] Andrei Y. Vyshinsky, ed., *The Law of the Soviet State*, trans. Hugh W. Babb, prepared by members of the Institute of Law of the Academy of Sciences (New York: Macmillan, 1948), p. 349.

may be placidly awaited as inevitable, or it may be encouraged through speeches, trade agreements, the creation of international communist organizations such as the Cominform (the resurrected Comintern, buried for four years in 1943 and now reinterred) and Comecon (eastern Europe's response to the Common Market) or the infiltration of communists into positions of influence. Whether the socialist millennium needs to be hastened by more violent means is a matter of constant debate within and without the communist world. Trotsky's notion of world revolution made violence almost a principle, but he was successfully opposed by Stalin—who nevertheless, like Lenin, thought war inevitable between capitalist states.

The third level is that of *tactics*. The communists would be less than human if they did not take advantage of every opportunity that presents itself at the United Nations and elsewhere (for example, in Cuba) to achieve their ends. The general strategy of peaceful coexistence does not mean that the fundamental aim of the communists (the victory of communism) is abandoned, nor that local communists shall take a vow of pacifism as far as their tactics are concerned. In October 1960, Khrushchev said, "We recognize and support the just wars of peoples for their liberation." No communist can really abandon absolutely the cause of the workers and peasants in other countries where he thinks landlords and capitalists are exploiting them.

It is impossible to be sure at what point tactics merge into strategy or a change in strategy involves principle, but the notion of different levels prevents the easy assumption that Soviet policy as such has altered when it may be merely the adoption of different means to achieve the same end. Peaceful coexistence may have been adopted as good tactics to allay the suspicions of newly emerging nations. It may have been a strategic shift, transferring the main contest with the United States from the military arena where there was a nuclear stalemate to economic competition where the capitalist system was thought to be less efficient. Finally, it may have meant an abandonment of the principle that capitalism is doomed and an acceptance of its continued existence in the United States and western Europe. There is some evidence of this, and some of the differences between Peking and Moscow are over the assumed intentions of the capitalist powers themselves (that is, whether they will attack the communist states).

Yet it is not enough to note that foreign policy in the communist states is made by *the* Communist party. For each country has its own party, and since the death of Stalin the monolithic character of communist foreign policy has altered. Yugoslavia, as always, has gone its separate neutral way; China has sought the traditional Stalinist policies, in the formation of which, paradoxically, the Chinese communists claim an important role; and the eastern European countries have leaned toward Titoism at least to the extent of disputing the primacy of the U.S.S.R. In all the arguments a number of separate issues have been involved and occasionally confused—the acceptance of socialist unity based on Marxism-Leninism, the primacy of the U.S.S.R., and the division of the world into two hostile camps.

As far as the unity of all socialists is concerned, even Yugoslavia has felt compelled to toe the line. On the crucial question of the Soviet action in Hungary in 1956 Tito later signified his approval of the Red Army's second intervention and condemned Nagy for seeking help from the West. His embassy in unclear circumstances allowed Nagy to fall into the hands of the Soviet secret police. In other words Tito put the "defense of socialism" before individual rights, freedom, or national independence. Much to the dismay of Marxists who were disgusted by the events in Hungary, Tito was outmaneuvered by Khrushchev and proved unable to substantiate his claim to offer an ideological alternative to the U.S.S.R.'s version of Marxism-Leninism. Even Gomulka himself demonstrated the truth of Mao Tse-tung's dictum that there is no third road for communists: he too was ultimately persuaded to declare the Hungarian revolution counterrevolutionary.

It has been more difficult since Stalin's death to preserve the notion of the primacy of the U.S.S.R. Tito had already rejected Stalin's leadership in 1948, though a similar show of independence led to the fall of Gomulka in Poland in the same year. Yugoslavia established friendly relations with such uncommitted (and noncommunist) states as India, Ghana, Indonesia, and Egypt. Even more remarkable, it managed to obtain aid from the West and at the same time gradually to restore cordial relations with the Soviet Union. In 1955, with Stalin dead, the new Russian leaders came to Belgrade to apologize for the harsh treatment in 1948.

By 1956 the communist world had apparently so changed that the U.S.S.R. and Yugoslavia could sign a joint declaration stating that the roads and conditions of socialist development were different in different countries—and that "any tendency to impose one's own views in determining the roads and forms of socialist development [is] alien to both sides." The events in Hungary and Poland, however, estranged the two countries once more, the U.S.S.R. having made quite clear that neither country would be allowed to pursue a road similar to that of Yugoslavia. The open intervention in Hungarian and Polish affairs by the Soviet leaders mocked the idea of the equality of socialist states. Nagy's sin was to promote the deviation of "national communism." In Poland Gomulka walked a tightrope, declaring the U.S.S.R. to be the "first and mightiest socialist power" but obviously unwilling to admit the primacy of the Soviet Union. For a time it appeared that the Chinese might support the Poles, but conscious of the serious implications of rejecting Soviet leadership, Communist China publicly adhered to the principle that the U.S.S.R. was leader of the communist bloc. (It made little difference to Chinese policy, which went its own imperious way.) Had eastern Europe been allowed to put its own gloss on communist principles there might have been trouble over the postwar territorial settlement in which Hungary had agreed to forego Transylvania, Poland had accepted the loss of east Poland to the U.S.S.R., and East Germany had renounced the lands east of the Oder-Neisse rivers. It may not have been coincidence that revolt against Soviet imperialism occurred precisely in these three states.

Within a few years 1956 seemed but a memory. The various countries of eastern Europe enjoyed greater autonomy than ever before, and Yugoslavia was back in the communist fold. By 1965 Tito was cooperating with the Comecon. And in 1967 President Podgorny of the Soviet Union stopped to see Tito on his way to and from the United Arab Republic where he conferred with President Nasser after his defeat by the Israelis.

Internationally China has been underrated in recent years much as the U.S.S.R. was between the wars. Due recognition was given to the Communist party's ability to weld the people into a nation, and the size of the Chinese armed forces has always won respect. But in a nuclear world mere numbers do not count for very much, and Mao's refusal to recognize that thermonuclear war means mutual destruction has been regarded as an unwillingness to face the realities of the contemporary world. In 1967 China's position had suddenly to be reassessed when the Chinese detonated a thermonuclear device only two and a half years after exploding an atomic bomb. (The French had detonated an atomic bomb in 1960 but had not yet succeeded in exploding an H-bomb.) The belief that the Chinese might now be able to launch a nuclear attack on the United States in the early 1970's led to a decision to create an anti-ballistic missile screen against this possibility—but not against a threat from the Soviet Union. China's own interpretation of the significance of the detonation was given by the New China News Agency: "The success of China's hydrogen-bomb test has further broken the nuclear monopoly of U.S. imperialism and Soviet revisionism and dealt a telling blow at their policy of nuclear blackmail."

China has been cautious in its foreign policy in Korea and more recently in Vietnam. It has proved ruthless in regaining what it considers its own territory in Tibet and on the Indian border. It remains to be seen whether China will try to regain former Chinese territory now part of the Soviet Union. Both the United States and the Soviet Union are beginning to behave as though they had a new Nazi Germany on their hands, this time in Asia.

The problems of the communist countries have grown in size and complexity. Gone are the days of two blocs represented by Molotov and Dulles. Instead, while the United States faces increasingly restive allies in western Europe the Soviet Union has to tread softly in eastern Europe so that it may devote its energies to containing China's ambitions in the Soviet Far East and in Southeast Asia. The Russians find themselves competing with the Chinese in their attempt to support North Vietnam against the United States. They are aligned with the Muslim states of the Middle East and oppose Israel (which they regard as a satellite of the Western powers). Only in central Europe does some form of détente seem to have been reached. It is the common interest of all the powers to keep Germany divided and unarmed with nuclear weapons (though the declining strength of the American and British forces in Europe means that greater reliance has to be placed on Germany as a bulwark against communism).

The Russians are in a dilemma. Their Marxist dogma of class solidarity does not help them to resolve racial, ethnic, and national tension. The greatest failure of communism—and one that has passed almost unnoticed—has been the failure to incorporate all communist countries from East Germany to China in one vast Union of Soviet Socialist Republics. The consequence has been the creation of separate communist states and the emergence of traditional power politics between them.

CONCLUSION:
Implications for New States

The Variety of Patterns

The traditional view of liberal democrats has been that democracy as found in western Europe, the United States, and the British Commonwealth is the "natural" form of government to which all countries may be expected to aspire. Dictatorship has been assumed to be the hallmark of a predemocratic society. Communism, fascism, and nazism had all at first been dismissed as aberrations. Throughout the postwar period, states that have emerged from the old colonial empires have been equipped with Western-style constitutions and given at least the trappings of liberal democracy.[1]

More recently, however, there has been a gradual recognition that liberal democracy is not natural in the sense that newly independent countries will automatically find democracy the obvious choice of government. Liberal democracy has to be nurtured, and each state has to work out its own form of democratic political

---

[1] When the government of India was "technically" defeated (for the first time since independence) in the Lok Sabha in 1967, it referred to Thomas Erskine May's *Parliamentary Practice* for advice on what to do next.

system. Democracy may not succeed in all environments.[2] Even in those countries that have enjoyed liberal democracy for a long time, tensions arise that the traditional machinery is not always able to resolve.

Democracy, then, is not simply the "natural" form of government for all nations. Nor is dictatorship always predemocratic. Many an established liberal society has witnessed the emergence of a charismatic leader. Apparently, dictatorship is not in decline. A number of countries in recent years, including Ghana, Nigeria, the United Arab Republic, Indonesia, Pakistan, Brazil, Argentina, and Greece, have rallied behind a dictator or military junta. This traditional form of government has been given a new lease on life. (Military dress has of course long been popular on occasion not only with constitutional monarchs and viceroys but with such leaders as Churchill, de Gaulle, and Tito.)

Communism is no longer viewed as an aberration. (Nor is it regarded, as the communists would have us believe, as the final stage of development after feudalism, capitalism, and socialism.) Increasingly, the Communist party is being compared with laissez-faire capitalism as an instrument of social mobilization. The party has proved itself a very useful instrument for rapid economic growth and particularly for accomplishing an industrial revolution in countries that are largely agricultural and where the principle of "one man, one vote" would give victory to the peasants and the forces of tradition. Moreover, communism in the Soviet Union, at least, has demonstrated a capacity to survive the revolutionary generation. Even more important, Communist parties have evinced a certain adaptability to changing situations—even to the extent that in the 1930's Stalin copied some of the more unpleasant features of nazism, notably the purge. The result has been that new states interested in learning about communism have several variations to study.

Fascism and nazism, on the other hand, appear to be dead, perhaps only because of the defeat of Nazi Germany and Fascist Italy in war. None of the postwar dictators have modeled themselves on Hitler. This may be in part because the new countries are economically more backward than Nazi Germany and require different forms of social and political mobilization. Yet many of the characteristics of fascism and nazism linger on—for example,

---

[2] See, for example, Seymour M. Lipset, *Political Man: The Social Bases of Politics* (New York: Doubleday, 1959), especially Chs. 2 and 3.

economic self-sufficiency, management of the currency, propaganda, mobilization of the young, the one-party state, and terrorism.

In this book we have been concerned with the two main established political patterns of the mid-twentieth century and with the variations that occur within each pattern. From the point of view of American or Soviet foreign policy, or even from the standpoint of the branch of political science called international relations, the conflict between liberal democracy and communism may seem to overshadow everything else. But from the vantage point of the new states, and of the field of political science known as comparative politics, what is interesting is not the challenge that each pattern presents to the other but the convergence of the two that seems to be taking place and the nuances within each general framework. It is one thing to assert that the United States and the Soviet Union are still poles apart; it is another to draw clear distinctions between, say, France and Yugoslavia. New states will carefully examine the variations within both patterns and will no doubt evolve a type of liberal democracy or communism—or even a new pattern as yet not discernible—that meets their needs.

By way of conclusion, listed below are several main questions that we will attempt to answer in the discussion that follows.

1. Why, in the twentieth century, despite the attractions and successes of both liberal democracy and communism, their superior theoretical framework and their capacity for political or economic growth, have so many nations, old and new, relapsed into some form of dictatorship?

2. What are the lessons of communism as a political system? What are the implications of polycentrism?

3. How significant are the variations of liberal democracy? What is there in the liberal democratic model that deserves attention?

Dictatorship

A Response to Crisis

The appeal of dictatorship would seem to be a response in tragic circumstances to a natural instinct of self-preservation. Overwhelmed by events, a government falters. People lose confidence in government, in democracy, and even in themselves. There is a sense of national despair and of individual uselessness, heightened in the minds of the lower-middle class, so long the conservative bulwark of democracy, by the fear that big business on the one side and the trade unions on the other will together squeeze out the small businessman and white-collar worker. In these conditions the man with a message is listened to with attention. Thus Huey Long capitalized on the fragmented emotions of Louisiana's poor whites, while William Aberhart could persuade the not normally credulous people of Alberta that by a policy of social credit (that is, twenty-five dollars monthly free to every citizen), the Canadian province could spend its way to prosperity. Everywhere, it would seem, there is the danger that in adversity recourse will be had to the Man on Horseback or, in these days, the man whose intuition can tell him that his opponents are traitors who carry Communist party membership cards.

Nation-building

There is more in the appeal of dictatorship than a response to crisis. A key factor in any country's development is that of nation-building, yet the early liberal writers in Britain, the United States, and France overlooked this element because they took it for granted. Hegel, by contrast, was highly aware of it, as he saw his divided Germany devastated by the armies of Napoleon. For the British, highly organized socially and politically, liberalism has been an attractive counterbalance to conservatism. In Germany and Italy, according to both Hitler and Mussolini, liberalism merely worsened a tendency toward atomization. Their dictatorships offered an alternative political pattern to democracy and communism—national unity based on a sense of service to the state and willingness to accept the state and its leader as the director of all social, economic, and political life. The term used to describe this system was "totalitarian." Today many new countries have an even harder task of nation-building than did Germany and Italy. To them a dictatorship seems a way of overcoming paralyzing dissent, repairing the body politic, mobilizing the people, and making the most of scarce resources. Liberal democracy has seemed to fail many countries in these respects.

Where national tragedy has been profound, where the problems seem insurmountable, any critical inquiry into the nature of the good life tends to take second place to the hard task of putting things right. Dictators replace democratic theory and communist ideology with a pseudoideology, the expression of which, instead of being a series of (apparently) consistent propositions invented by that remarkable intellectual, Marx, is a jumbled number of peremptory commands. Hence Mussolini's admonition: "Believe! Obey! Fight!" Hitler's favorite expression, found by the invading Allied armies scrawled on the walls, was: *"Ein Volk, ein Reich, ein Führer."* If ever there was an era of salvation through incantation it was the 1930's.

The fascist dictatorships were different from all other forms of government. They were not of course based on rational discourse of the type found in the United States Congress and British House of Commons. Instead they worshipped the irrational and for a while created the impression, contrary to Hegel, that only the irrational was real. Not surprisingly, Europe awakened after 1945 like a man emerging from a nightmare. For one feature of dictatorship is that blame for failures cannot be taken by the dictator *or* put upon those who are being dictated to. Responsibility must therefore be placed on the shoulders of foreign countries or upon minorities within the boundaries of the state.

The Organic Theory

There is a side to dictatorship that is sometimes neglected and yet is worth respect, particularly in fascist Italy where the *Duce* was more intellectual than most dictators. This is the attempt to provide a credible theoretical alternative to atomized liberalism and to the class struggle of communism (for dictatorships are usually the recourse of those who would stand to lose if the proletariat seized power). This alternative is the organic theory, the notion of the "corporate state," developed in Italy and exemplified today in Spain. Instead of the body politic becoming a battleground of particular interests or a classless society, why not, so it is argued, view the state as an organism in which every person and every institution has its role to play? Legislatures can be remodeled to represent business and professional associations instead of the people directly. In Italy Mussolini created such a body, nominated by the Fascist party, while in Spain the Cortes remains such a legislature. Ordinary men participate in the political process only indirectly through their occupational associations;

brooding over all the associations and unions is the party and the leader.

It is an attractive theory, as old as Saint Paul ("We are all members of one body"), meditated on by a succession of puzzled popes saddened by the turmoil surrounding them in Italy despite the unification of 1861, and finally promised by Mussolini to the Italians in 1934. Liberals laugh at it, but many hallowed institutions in liberal democracies, from universities to business corporations, operate on much the same principle. However, in the liberal democratic state as such it just does not work because while the organic theory stresses fraternity, it really has little place for liberty and even less for equality. It is all very well to make the obvious statement that all men are not equal, but it is difficult to know how one can operate on any other assumption than that men are equal unless someone is given authority to determine the nature of the inequality. If we are all members of the body politic, who is our head and who is to determine which of us are minor members? In practice it is the leader, supported by the party he controls. No opposition is allowed.

This attempt to unite warring economic and social interests failed in fascist Italy, but it is an interesting theory and perhaps deserves more attention than it usually gets. For if anything explains the stability of the Anglo-American world it is the partial acceptance of such a doctrine. Men are not atomized individuals in the older liberal tradition, nor are they part of a class struggle. They *are* members of a body politic to which they give allegiance and that persuades them—unlike communism and fascism—to obey the rules of the game.

Many of the new countries may find the organic theory worth further study. It is frequently argued that small nations are not viable economically and that they must come to terms with their neighbors in larger unions. Yet many large federal states such as Nigeria and India have had to face the problem of hostility between different ethnic and religious groups. They require a unifying political theory that teaches men that they belong to a single body politic within which everyone has a function to perform. The organic theory, suitably modified, may prove serviceable.

It perhaps should be added that the Anglo-Americans have been less successful in unifying disparate elements than they sometimes claim. The English failed to assimilate the Irish, the English-Canadians the French-Canadians, or the English-South

Africans the Afrikaners. The Americans with their acceptance of the melting pot image came closest to success but only as far as people of Caucasian origin were concerned. The Negro riots in the 1960's have underlined the limitations of that particular ideal. Nor is it certain that the communist countries have overcome the problem of racial and ethnic tensions. They have tried to make the Communist party a unifying force, but their success remains to be seen.

Dictatorial Economies

The position of dictatorial economies is far from clear. One thing is certain: they have never been socialist. The dependence of most dictators on the upper classes of society, especially the business interests, has meant that capitalism cannot be dismantled, even if this is desired. Few dictators, old or new style, have bothered much with economic reorganization for its own sake; most have been concerned with purely political matters like bread and circuses for the populace or a powerful posture in foreign affairs. Economics has taken second place—though often the results have been quite startling. Trujillo left behind him not only monuments but thirty modern hospitals, a network of clinics and dispensaries, schools, roads and port facilities, pure water and sanitation—making the Dominican Republic one of the most advanced Latin American states in public works and health. In some ways he *was* benefactor of the nation—and this may explain why he survived for over thirty years as ruler of his country.

If dictators do not socialize the economy, what do they do? Some, as we have suggested, do nothing. Others, like Hitler, Mussolini, and Perón, had strong views on the need to make their countries powerful, Mussolini even hopefully planting trees on the Apennines to bring snow and with this a hardening of Italian manhood. These dictators therefore controlled production in the interests of a war economy. As Hitler said so bluntly to the Germans, guns come before butter. It so happened that Hitler attracted to his service some of the ablest men in Germany, including the famous Schacht as minister of economy until he resigned. (Christened Hjalmar Horace Greeley Schacht, he encouraged German trade with eastern Europe: "Go East, young man, go East.") Mussolini and Perón were less successful, and by and large none of the three dictators really knew what economics was about—in marked contrast to the communist leaders of the U.S.S.R.

In retrospect, however, the attempts of the dictators to stimulate the economies of their countries must be considered as part of the general twentieth-century pattern of economic behavior— the need to encourage economic growth. The Russians boldly set about completely planning their economy in 1928. Liberal democracies shortly afterward underwent a severe depression and emerged from it convinced of the need for tighter monetary control and for unemployment policies. Today no government would stand aside, so we hope, and let depression take its course. But business itself, except for nationalization of certain industries, remains in private hands in the liberal democracies. There are controls by government, but only in wartime is there the sort of control commonplace in the U.S.S.R. In Italy and Germany "wartime" began when the dictators began to prepare for war. Hence the control of the economy in both countries before 1939.

Dictators in the developing areas are in a very different position from Hitler. Instead of taking up the slack of an industrial economy they have to create an industrial base. This requires either the exploitation of their people in order to build for the future, or the injection of foreign capital. The latter is the safer course, the less painful, and the one more likely to bring swift results. But it does mean that the dictator's position is weakened. Instead of depending on the support of a disciplined totalitarian party he has to satisfy foreign creditors. Thus Fidel Castro has to become a debtor to either the Americans or the Russians, and to satisfy the Russians he becomes a communist. Dictators like Kwame Nkrumah and Achmed Sukarno are suspected of being in the pay of the communists; when they are overthrown it is assumed by many observers that the new regime has obtained promises of financial support from capitalist countries. Unless they are very astute, the dictators in developing countries often find themselves puppets of foreign powers.

The Urge for Aggression

It is the very weakness of dictators that often makes them bombastic and willing to undertake the hazard of war. In this way they can give release to the tensions that have built up in their tightly controlled systems. Or they may gamble on a successful war to relieve them from their financial problems or at least provide a convenient excuse for them. It is arguable that all nations, given the chance, are aggressive toward other countries. Despite their protestations of liberal democracy, the British, the French, and the Americans have fought many wars even in the twentieth century. (The Americans closed their frontier by about 1890 and have fought five wars in the Pacific and Far East since then.) Communist states such as the Soviet Union in 1945, China on the Indian border, and even Yugoslavia with its proposal to absorb Albania have not hesitated to extend their boundaries where this is possible. But dictatorships more than any other form of government seem to lend themselves to uninhibited conquest. They symbolize the urge of their people at a particular point in time to dominate others. The letters of soldiers in Napoleon's *Grande Armée* and Hitler's *Wehrmacht* convey the exhilaration that ordinary Frenchmen and Germans experienced when they were given the order to march. There was comparable excitement in Cairo in June 1967 when the Egyptians hoped that at long last the tables were turned and they would become conquerors.

A glance at maps of the world over the centuries indicates all too clearly how different peoples at different times have emerged from their native land and subdued their neighbors. There is no reason to believe that this process has come to an end, and the history of mankind suggests that the most common form of government such a people will produce at such a time is dictatorship. The glory of war can present an irresistible temptation to leaders of new countries, faced with the awful complexities of the problems associated with economic growth.

Communism

Rapid Economic Growth

The most obvious appeal of communism lies in its undoubted capacity to promote economic growth and to transform a society in the space of a single generation. It used to be thought that communism merely signified the seizure of power by a militant minority, which then imposed totalitarian controls on the hapless majority. Nowadays it is recognized that a certain degree of popular acquiescence usually accompanies the seizure of government. The Communist party may indeed be the vehicle used by a nation at a particular stage in its history when it is about to change its nature completely.

Today the dynamic personalities who want industrialization and are determined to get it are often to be found in politics, clustered around the government. The modern entrepreneur may be a civil servant or an economist, possibly on the staff of a U.N. agency assisting a country's development. A great change has come over the relation of the political system and the economy in most countries. Until fairly recently politics was considered separately and almost autonomously from economics. This is reflected in the teaching of economics and political science to this day, the study of constitutions, elections, government, and administration touching only incidentally on the main issues of economics. Many political theorists have been more concerned with the ends of human existence—for example, the freedom of the individual—than with the more mundane but vital issues of poverty and economic growth and the need for governmental intervention in the economy.

The underdeveloped areas of the world appear to be challenging these assumptions with a vengeance. They are primarily concerned with their economic growth and view the political system as the machine through which maximum growth can be obtained. They are less interested in political philosophy or even in the nature of government and the political process than in capital development and their next five-year plan. A liberal democrat may declare that a basic characteristic of democratic capitalist economies is that they are governed by the free and widely diversified choices of individual citizens to which entrepreneurs must necessarily adjust. But in announcing its third five-year plan the Indian government bluntly stated that a small increase in consumption "would be allowed" during the period and declared that heavy taxation would help to promote long-term investment by the state.

India owes far more to the United States than to the U.S.S.R. in the amount of assistance received in grain and equipment to make its development possible. It owes even more to the private investors of the United States. But in the technique India is using to expand production as rapidly as possible it also owes a great deal to the experience of the U.S.S.R. and China. In all three countries it is the government that determines economic trends. It is true that the communists have made a number of serious errors in their planning, but then not even a communist is infallible. At all events, the productive capacity of the U.S.S.R.— despite two world wars, civil war, famine, invasions, and purges —has risen very considerably, and the progress of China, despite setbacks and false propaganda claims, is remarkable.

Some observers think that the test of liberal democracy in India will be its capacity to expand its economy at a pace comparable to its two great neighbors. It is to be hoped not, for it looks as though the economic race with China is already lost. India's third five-year plan ended in 1965–66. Preliminary indications are that little advance was made during those five years in coal and steel production. Food production, intended to rise to 100 million tons of grain, actually declined from 79 million tons in 1961 to 72 million in 1965.[3] Yet foreign aid during the five-year plan totalled 5,400 million dollars.

The communists have not always been as successful as their propaganda would claim. The Russians were so successful in repairing the ravages of the ruthless German occupation and in putting satellites into space that they were tempted at the end of the 1950's to announce that they would overtake the Americans in their standard of living. Yet by 1960 their gross national product was still only 40 percent of the American and after 1961 the country fell behind the United States in growth performance.[4] In 1966 the United Nations Economic Commission for Europe reported a high growth rate once more in the Soviet Union, but in October 1967 the International Bank for Reconstruction and Development stated that the gross national product per capita of Americans was more than 50 percent higher than their nearest rivals, the Swedes and the Canadians. It was more than three times the income of the Russians—and almost thirty-eight times

---

[3] One hundred million tons was expected to be attained in 1967.

[4] U.S. Congress Joint Economic Committee, *Current Economic Indicators for the U.S.S.R.* (Washington, D.C.: U.S. Government Printing Office, 1965), p. 11.

the income of the Chinese.[5] Whether in the foreseeable future the Soviet Union will have the capacity to challenge the United States on equal terms in economic competition seems unlikely unless intensification of the Vietnam war abroad and Negro riots at home seriously disrupts the American economy.

As the Soviet Union passes its half-century, interest in what communism has to offer has extended from the short term to the long haul. The Soviet economy, it is now realized, may not be an adequate model for developing countries. Before 1917 the capitalist Russian economy was already well-developed, whatever the communists may say, and its rate of growth was probably faster than that of western Europe. Even in 1900 the Russians were producing 37 percent of the world's oil and selling much of it abroad. Like the United States, Russia had plenty of land per head of population and was able to export ten million tons of grain in 1913 (though to judge by the general low standard of living, this was hardly an agricultural surplus). Stalin was much more concerned about the collection of grain than its production. Even the urbanization of the U.S.S.R. was not accompanied by a population explosion. In eastern Asia, by contrast, population is rising rapidly, there is need to increase agricultural production even more urgently than steel, oil, and coal, and the economy of most of the countries is far more primitive than was that of Russia in 1917. Africa and Latin America each have their own peculiar problems. It is arguable that the U.S.S.R. has failed to evolve any policies for the different situations of newly emerging nations.

But this is surely going too far. The question is not whether the example of Soviet communism is one to be slavishly imitated but whether in the competition of communism and capitalism the former has produced any new techniques for the encouragement of economic growth. It has been suggested that the Soviet Union is not a model for Asia unless what is envisaged is total mobiliza-

---

[5] The actual figures were as follows:

GNP PER CAPITA IN U.S. DOLLARS

United States	3,240
Sweden	2,130
France	1,620
Great Britain	1,550
Soviet Union	1,000
China	85

tion of the population for economic objectives, the extraction of food from a poor peasantry to provide the necessary accumulation of capital, and the use of force where opposition appears. But this is just what many Asian and African leaders *do* apparently envisage, contrary though it is to the modern consumer-based economies of western Europe and North America. Their problem is how to pass through the earlier stages of an industrial revolution without exploiting the workers. In an age when the people have votes and public opinion is sovereign the traditional autonomy of capitalism is impossible. Communism provides a method of political organization as harsh and ruthless as laissez faire capitalism but one that persuades the electorate by propaganda that the sacrifice is in the general interest and not that of a particular class.

The very weaknesses of communist totalitarianism may even be assets. Its demand for sacrifice and a lowered standard of living in order that future generations shall prosper may exhilarate rather than intimidate. The tendency for communism to destroy traditional values may attract those who discover opposition to economic development among the conservative or tribal elements of the population. Its contempt for parliamentary government and a multiparty system may seem justified because parliamentarism presupposes consensus and a willingness to compromise. Where no compromise is possible, because the old and the new societies are irreconcilable, then parliamentary government may be unworkable. The liberal democrat believes that all men are equal and that every man should think for himself. The totalitarian in an underdeveloped country is a man with supreme self-confidence in his own capacity to lead and in the correctness of his (and his party's) appraisal of the country's needs. In a society where his opponents, far from being democrats by conviction, may be the jaded and corrupted relics of colonialism, it is he and not they who gains at least the passive acquiescence of the people and especially of the all-important intelligentsia.

Each underdeveloped country has to decide how far it is prepared to go in order to raise its standard of living. In much of the underdeveloped "free world" there is a startling contrast between rich sheiks, maharajahs, and merchants on the one hand and poverty-stricken *fellahin*, coolies, and peasants on the other. Foreign aid too easily goes into the pockets of the former when it is intended to help the latter.

Important though it is to be aware of the rapid economic growth of the communist world and of its challenge to liberal democracies in the economic sphere, there is no reason to believe that the Russians will soon outstrip the West. Unlike the United States the U.S.S.R. suffers from a serious manpower shortage, the extent of which has only recently become apparent. Of the 28.4 million children in the 10–15 age group in 1939 only nineteen million were alive in 1959. In that year nearly two out of every three persons in the U.S.S.R. over the age of thirty-two were women. So great were the wartime losses that the number of college-age persons (20–24 years of age) is estimated to have dropped from nearly twenty-two million in 1961 to under twelve million in 1967. The number in this age group is not expected to reach the 1961 figure again until 1975.[6] The American population is rapidly reaching the U.S.S.R.'s level. That the Russians have managed to keep such large armed forces in the field, expand industry so rapidly, and place considerable emphasis on social welfare is indeed a triumph. Stalin's postwar centralization may have been necessary owing to the shortage of able men to plan production. As the number of teenagers declines it is, however, not surprising that numbers of them will be expected to work as well as study, that the armed forces are being reduced, and that there is a heavy emphasis on automation in industry and mechanization of agriculture. The manpower shortage, together with the absence of individual liberty as it is understood in liberal democracies, means that in both the economic and political spheres the Soviet Union still remains inferior to the United States.

It should be kept in mind that political eras last longer than the half-century during which communism has been in existence—and fascism has come and gone. The advanced liberal democracies trace their gradual development over centuries and think of the present and future in far greater perspective than a five- or even ten-year plan. The test of a political system involves more than measuring the rate at which industry is presently expanding.

Transformation of the Social Structure

At first sight the communist revolution has brought about not only economic upheaval but a transformed class structure. The

---

[6] *Current Economic Indicators for the U.S.S.R.*, p. 24.

notion of the class struggle may seem a little old-fashioned in liberal democracies, but it has meaning in those places where the few are still joyfully exploiting the many. The workers of these parts of the world would be wise to unite. Yet the victory of the proletariat, and with it the end of the class war, seems curiously illogical, assuming that the Marxist dialectic has any logic at all. There is no evidence that the class structure has stopped changing. The growth of a large well-educated class—not a bourgeoisie—in so many countries is not a phenomenon that can be ignored, whatever the communists may say (or not say). No amount of semantic argument can convince noncommunists that the "new middle class" does not, in a very real sense, present the world with a new class of which Marx knew nothing. It would be helpful if the distinction between workers and intellectuals could be obliterated, but the very differences in their work, environment, and interests prevent them from becoming identical. And do we really want their substitution by a new "Soviet man"? It is surely the insistence on uniformity that has deadened the cultural life of the Soviet Union. In science and technology they have many achievements to their credit, but the world hardly turns to the communist states for inspiration in art, architecture, or even literature and theater as it does to the United States and western Europe. There was no mistaking the revival of the liberal arts when for a while communist pressure relaxed from Warsaw to Peking in 1956.

It is easy to detect the weaknesses of communism in its more dogmatic aspects. It is more difficult to criticize its racial (and ethnic) policies. If ethnic and racial tensions are the most difficult problem of the present age, then many communist states can fairly claim to have at least made an attempt to solve them—even if the alternative, the "international proletarian dictatorship," is not to everyone's liking. After all, it is the communists' record in this field, more than anything else, except possibly the planned economy, that has made it difficult for so many colored peoples to appreciate the more unpleasant aspects of the system.

Another feature of communism that deserves more consideration than it usually gets is its advanced system of social welfare. Working class Germans have a far greater chance of attending a university in East Germany than in affluent West Germany. It has been said that western Europe before 1914 helped the working man directly by introducing social insurance whereas the United

States went in for mass higher education and mass production of automobiles and household appliances.[7] The communists seem to have followed in the footsteps of both the western Europeans and the Americans, developing the social welfare policies of the former and the mass education of the latter. In the process they have foregone, until recently, automobiles, appliances, and supermarkets. But unlike the western Europeans and the Americans, the communists have made their decisions without allowing the electors, or the consumers, the opportunity to make the choice themselves.

Implications of Polycentrism

What are the implications of the rise of polycentrism, the failure of the Soviet Union to retain its ideological leadership in the communist world? At one time it seemed to many observers that communism was the wave of the future that in time would engulf much of the remainder of the world. It is still true that no communist government has been overthrown. But the divisions within the communist world and the changes that have taken place in communist countries as their standard of living has risen make it less likely that communism as a monolithic creed will retain its attraction.

The communists in the Soviet Union appear to have made three great mistakes. First, they abandoned their revolutionary doctrine in favor of "socialism in one country." Trotsky (who favored world revolution) was right in principle. Stalin may have been sensible in practice. For communism to succeed a secure base was necessary, and the Soviet Union comprised no less than one-sixth of the world's surface. Moreover, Stalin did not wholly abandon Trotsky's global outlook. Moscow was very definitely the center of world communism, and the Soviet party was generally acknowledged as the leading Communist party in the world. Until 1945 this thesis was unchallenged: there was only one road to communism.

Second, Stalin was unwise enough to agree to national communist governments in eastern Europe. Although it is true that

---

[7] W. W. Rostow, *The Stages of Economic Growth* (Cambridge, Eng.: Cambridge University Press, 1960).

at times he opposed Tito and even Mao, he tended to do so on personal or national grounds, for neither Stalin as a person nor the Soviet Union as a country wanted a rival. Stalin thus did not oppose national communism on the ideological ground that world communism must be one and indivisible. Eastern European states were set up with communist governments as buffer states in the event of a resurgent and hostile Germany. Perhaps no alternative was possible (it certainly was impossible to control Yugoslavia and China). After all, the British—past masters in the art of political manipulation—had failed to keep the dominions and colonies in one empire. Nevertheless, only a single government could control the communist world and keep it united. The Americans for their part have always recognized the necessity of the principle of "one and indivisible." Territories either become part of the United States, like Hawaii, or they are given independence, like the Philippines. Once they become states any revolt against federal authority is crushed. The South was defeated by war. Troops are even now sent into states severely affected by racial disturbance. It is true that the Russians have acted in a similar manner by sending troops into Hungary, but they are reluctant to repeat this performance because the states of eastern Europe, unlike the states of the Union, are nationally independent.

And so, while both the Americans and the Russians have succeeded in preserving the integrity of their own territories, neither is able to control its allies. Such is the price paid for liberal democracy, but differences between communist states have no place in the Marxist-Leninist canon.

The third mistake seems to have been Khrushchev's secret speech in 1956 on Stalin. As the Chinese were quick to realize, this step was the first acknowledgment of error. Henceforth unquestioning acceptance of communist ideology could no longer be taken for granted. The monolith was shattered.

Even so, these mistakes may ultimately do communism more good than harm, for the destruction of the legend of communist infallibility has lessened the fear of communism and has diminished the arrogance of communists. It is now possible to respect the many achievements of communist regimes in a way that was almost impossible at the height of the Cold War. And at the same time the many virtues of liberal democracy can be seen by all in clearer perspective.

Liberal Democracy

Long-term Political Growth

At first sight the experiences of liberal democracies seem very far removed from the problems facing new states. The democracies are generally old and well-established; they are rich and getting richer; they are white (though they are not getting any whiter), and some have a record of colonial exploitation; and, as the Chinese have noted, they are like cities, whereas Asia and Africa are the rural overpopulated areas of today's world.

Yet such a view overlooks the fact that above all the liberal democracies have valued freedom. They achieved this value before economic growth became the touchstone for success, and in some instances freedom and democracy came before the industrial revolution. Criticism of urban societies also happens to be remarkably shortsighted. Even the most rural states are becoming urbanized, and China itself probably has 100 million people living in cities. One reason cities are expanding so rapidly is that urban complexes everywhere have a much higher standard of living than the countryside. This difference in standards of living could cause war not between West and East but within a country like China itself (and may already have done so). When the current economic privations of the developing areas are overcome, what will communism have to offer? At the take-off stage, the example of the liberal democracies is not too relevant, for it is the communists who have pioneered long-term planning, industrialization, social mobilization, and public investment on a vast scale. Yet as the examples of the Soviet Union and Yugoslavia have shown, the basic transformation of an economy may take less than a generation to achieve. At this point political freedom takes on a new significance. Communism, unlike liberal democracy, seems to suffer from a built-in obsolescence.

The liberal democracies would appear to have at least three advantageous features to offer to new states as they look ahead over the next few decades. The first is the immense variety of the experience of the liberal democracies. Some, like the United States and France, have their basis in revolution and ringing declarations of independence and the rights of man. Others, like Britain and Sweden, have so stressed their evolutionary character that at first sight they seem to still be *ancien régimes* governed by sovereigns whose assent to every bill is required. There are parliamentary democracies that practice collective responsibility, and there are presidential systems that give executive authority to a single person. Most countries have remained attached to one form of government or the other, but the French have shifted from presidential to parliamentary and back for nearly 180 years. There are two-party systems and multiparty systems, and in many local jurisdictions there is effectively only one party. In Sweden and Scandinavia generally the multiparty system has not brought instability. Pressure groups vary in strength. For a while, as in nineteenth-century France, they may be outlawed. Or they may be an integral part of the public decision-making process as in twentieth-century Britain and Sweden.

In the second place, liberal democracies have not only a variety of institutions but a broad spectrum of ideas and policies, many of which are comparable to those devised by the communists. This is not surprising because the Communist party has long been powerful in states like France and Italy in western Europe. In countries like Britain and Sweden, where the Communist party is weak, its place has been taken by labor or social democratic parties that favor some of the same programs in social welfare, nationalization, and planning. Until the 1917 revolution socialists and communists shared the same intellectual heritage more than either would care to admit today.

The notion that a people must choose between Soviet communism and American capitalism is absurd. Western Europe belongs to neither form. The history of Britain and Sweden demonstrates that established nations can be transformed into social democracies if the electorate so desires. And France today represents the possibility of central direction under a powerful presidential regime—again based on the consent of the people. It is also a gross oversimplification to consider the United States a capitalist country, just as it is misleading to consider the Soviet Union communist in the strict sense of the word. Both terms are easy—perhaps too easy—shorthand expressions.

The most important feature of liberal democracies is neither the variety of their institutions nor the breadth of their political spectrum of ideas and policies. It is what they have in common—a liberality of spirit that those who have never lived under censorship or military rule too easily take for granted. We know, despite the efforts of the Kremlinologists, little more of what goes on in the heart of the Soviet government than the population of old Constantinople did of what went on in the sultan's harem. A once-powerful figure exiled to Outer Mongolia, a body in a sack in the Bosporus—these are evidence of friction, but of what friction? The secrecy of a dictatorial system may extend too far down. No one, not even the head of the apparatus, may know what is going on. His collaborators may be afraid to tell him.

Probably the strongest barrier to communism and a thousand times more formidable than the childish panics over propaganda literature or teachers with dangerous thoughts (or any thoughts) are the tremendous emotional forces that move men—especially the great force of nationalism. We should remember that today as in the past, our

> friends are exultations, agonies,
> And love, and man's unconquerable mind.

Contrary to Marx and contrary to Mao, the main effort of the Russians has been directed not to things of the spirit but to increasing the material strength of the Soviet Union.

The Weaknesses of Liberal Democracy

The disadvantages of communism and dictatorship are obvious. The weaknesses of liberal democracy are less tangible. As a political system it may take liberalism for granted and encourage complacency. If a liberal democracy exaggerates the role of mere opulence, it will go down before a state that prefers power (other things being equal, and they are nearly equal). Politicians reluctant to impose burdens (such as conscription in Britain) or to divert some of the national resources into public fields because taxpayers prefer two cars to good schools make a mockery of democracy. As G. K. Chesterton once said, "The world will never be made safe for democracy; it is a dangerous trade."

How Political Systems Should Be Judged

There is a widespread assumption that a political system must be judged by its results and in particular by its economic achievements. This is not satisfactory. Politically, if not economically, there is something else to discuss besides the relative merits of the *sovkhoz* and the *kolkhoz*, of capital versus consumption goods, and even of the various forms of education and social welfare. There is the whole question of freedom of thought and discussion that can no longer be neglected once the people are fed. This is the peculiar province of the educated, of the intelligentsia— who cannot be dismissed as an appendage of a materially minded proletariat. It is at this point, above all, that the weakness of communism shows.

One can sympathize with the distaste that the editors of the literary journal *Novy Mir* ("New World") felt for *Doctor Zhivago* with its implicit and sometimes explicit condemnation of the spiritual consequences of the Soviet regime. One can admire the care and restraint with which they analyzed Pasternak's masterpiece. But the chasm that separates totalitarianism from the truly free world is apparent from the simple sentence that they included near the end of their letter rejecting the manuscript: "As people whose standpoint is diametrically opposite yours, we, naturally, believe that the publication of your novel in the columns of the magazine *Novy Mir* is out of the question."

Many, many people—teachers, students, working mothers, scientists, and others—have reason to be grateful to the governments of the Soviet Union and the other communist countries for their efforts on their behalf. It is petty to deny the great material advances made in the communist bloc. But the loss of liberty that has accompanied material advancement cannot be ignored. In 1956, when the hundred flowers bloomed briefly in China[8] and the thaw began in the U.S.S.R., the outside world became aware of a deep longing for freedom. But whereas there is widespread publication of the figures of increased production taking place in the communist bloc, there is no way of measuring the number of Pasternaks who are murmuring unheard or the many more who must believe that politics and the political system involve ends to be discussed and who do not think that politics is solely the means to yet greater economic development. But it is doubtful whether Svetlana Alliluyeva and other Soviet critics are in such a minority as the Soviet government would have everyone believe. It is to be hoped that as the U.S.S.R. leaves its fifty-odd years of war, chaos, and forced industrial expansion behind there will be less concern with Kuibishev generators and virgin lands, and a deepening aware-

---

[8] In encouraging freedom of expression, Mao Tse-tung said, "Let a hundred flowers bloom."

ness of the spiritual sacrifice that communism has demanded. This sacrifice is the Marxist ideology's own internal contradiction.

The ultimate test of a political system is whether it is good enough to last. Fascism, as we have seen, cannot outlive its progenitor whether he be a Mussolini, a Hitler, or a Perón. Restricted democracy such as that permitted by de Gaulle seems destined to last only so long as he dominates the scene in France. True, the communist regime of the U.S.S.R. has survived the death of Stalin and the dismissal of Khrushchev—but from all accounts it was subject to much stress and strain during their lifetimes.

The contrast with the stable liberal democracies is startling. The Swedes have reelected the same party to power since the year before Hitler became chancellor of Germany, and they trace their constitution back to 1809. The Americans find their constitution of 1787 still a workable legal framework, and few basic changes in the form of government have been necessary. The British system, it goes without saying, has been working for centuries.

There are those who question the value of the example of these liberal democratic systems for the solution of the immediate pressing problems of developing countries. It may well be that these countries, like liberal democracies in wartime, temporarily have to modify their systems of government in order that the economic resources of their countries may be fully and quickly exploited. But the art of politics involves more than the day-to-day manipulation of the public through the mass media and more than the year-by-year, or even five-year, stimulation and direction of the economy. It requires above all a sense of historical perspective and an ability to detect what are the foundations on which a permanent political system can be built. The institutions that new nations build may be very different from those of the older European and American states, but they require the same solid base. The words of Burke, written at the time of the French Revolution, are as inspiring today as they were then. A state, he argued, is not merely a trading agreement in "pepper or coffee, calico or tobacco or some such low concern." Rather it is

> a partnership in all science; a partnership in all art; a partnership in every virtue and in all perfection. As the ends of such a partnership cannot be obtained in many generations, it becomes a partnership not only between those who are living, but between those who are living, those who are dead, and those who are to be born.

TABLES

THE UNITED STATES[1]

Presidents

1932–45	F. D. Roosevelt	Democrat
1945–52	H. S. Truman	Democrat
1952–60	D. D. Eisenhower	Republican
1960–63	J. F. Kennedy	Democrat
1963–	L. B. Johnson	Democrat

Party Strengths in Congress

SENATE		90TH CONGRESS, 1967	
Democrats have been the majority party since 1932 except in 1947, 1948, 1953, and 1954.		Democrats	64
		Republicans	36
			100

HOUSE OF REPRESENTATIVES			
Democrats have been the majority party since 1930 except in 1947, 1948, 1953, and 1954.		Democrats	248
		Republicans	187
			435

Presidential Elections

POPULAR VOTE	1960		1964	
Democrats	34,221,349		43,128,956	
Republicans	34,108,546	(R. M. Nixon)	27,177,873	(B. Goldwater)
Other	503		337	

ELECTORAL VOTE		
Democrats	303	486
Republicans	219	52
Other	15	0

[1] For details see Congressional Quarterly Service, *Politics in America, 1945–1964* (Washington, D.C.: Congressional Quarterly, 1965).

GREAT BRITAIN[2]

Prime Ministers

1935–37	S. Baldwin	Conservative
1937–40	N. Chamberlain	Conservative
1940–45	W. Churchill	Conservative
1945–51	C. Attlee	Labour
1951–55	W. Churchill	Conservative
1955–57	A. Eden	Conservative
1957–63	H. Macmillan	Conservative
1963–64	A. Douglas-Home	Conservative
1964–	H. Wilson	Labour

Party Strengths in the House of Commons

The Conservative party has been in the majority since the 1922 separation with Ireland except in 1924, 1929–31, 1945–51, and 1964 when the Labour party was in office.

	1959	1964	1966
Conservatives	365	303	253
Labour	258	317	363
Liberals	6	9	12
Republican Labourites	0	0	1
Speaker[3]	1	1	1
	630	630	630

General Elections

	1959	1964	1966
Conservatives	13,750,935	11,971,345	11,418,433
Labour	12,216,166	12,176,314	13,064,951
Liberals	1,640,761	3,061,843	2,327,533
Other	254,846	349,415	452,689

[2] For details up to 1960 see D. F. Butler and Jennie Freeman, *British Political Facts 1900–1960* (New York: St. Martin's Press, 1963). For details since 1960 consult *Keesing's Contemporary Archives* (London: Keesing's Publications, weekly with index).

[3] The speaker of the House of Commons renounces party affiliation for the duration of his office.

FRANCE[4]

President and Premiers (Fifth Republic)

PRESIDENT		PREMIERS[5]	
1959–	C. de Gaulle	1959–62	M. Debré
		1962–	G. Pompidou

Party Strengths in the Senate and National Assembly

	BEFORE 1967 ELECTION		1967	
	Senate	Assembly	Senate	Assembly
Gaullists and allies	119	287	109	244
Center and allies	34	56	38	42
Noncommunist left	100	98	102	126
Communists	14	41	14	73
Senate Independents	7	0	11	0
	274	482	274	485

Elections

	NATIONAL ASSEMBLY, 1967		
	First Ballot	Second Ballot	
Gaullists and allies	35.32%	42.60%	7,972,777
Center and allies	12.76	7.10	1,238,777
Noncommunist left	19.94	24.08	4,505,329
Communists	23.08	21.37	3,998,790
Other	8.90	4.81	904,255

	PRESIDENCY, 1965	
	First Ballot	Second Ballot
C. de Gaulle	10,828,523	13,083,699
F. Mitterrand (Socialist)	7,694,003	10,619,735
J. Lecanuet (Center)	3,777,119	
J.-L. Tixier-Vignancour (Right Conservative)	1,260,208	
P. Marcilhacy (Right Liberal)	415,018	
M. Barbu (no affiliation)	279,683	

---

[4] During the Third Republic (1875–1940) there were one hundred governments. Between 1944 and May 1958 there were twenty-five governments.
French figures must be treated as approximate because of the shifting nature
of party affiliations. For further details see Keesing's Contemporary Archives.
[5] Under the Fifth Republic the premier is, strictly speaking, prime minister.
Premier has been used to avert confusion with the British prime minister.

SWEDEN[6]

Prime Minister

1946–	T. Erlander	Social Democrat

Party Strengths in the Riksdag

	UPPER CHAMBER	SECOND CHAMBER	
	1965	1960	1964
Social Democrats	78	114	113
Liberals	26	40	42
Conservatives	26	39	32
Center (Agrarian)	19	34	35
Communists	2	5	8
Citizens' Front	0	0	3
	151	232	233

Second Chamber Elections[7]

	1960	1964
Social Democrats	2,032,937	2,006,921
Liberals	744,097	723,986
Conservatives	704,412	582,609
Center (Agrarian)	579,006	570,017
Communists	190,559	221,769
Christian Democratic Union	0	75,337
Citizens' Front	0	64,782

[6] For further details see *Keesing's Contemporary Archives*.
[7] In 1967 the parties agreed to the establishment of a unicameral system to be introduced in the 1970 elections.

THE SOVIET UNION[8]

Party Secretaries

1922–53	J. V. Stalin	General Secretary
1953–64	N. S. Khrushchev	First Secretary
1964–66	L. I. Brezhnev	First Secretary
1966–	L. I. Brezhnev	General Secretary

Prime Ministers (Chairmen of Council of Ministers)[9]

1930–41	V. M. Molotov
1941–53	J. V. Stalin
1953–55	G. M. Malenkov
1955–58	N. A. Bulganin
1958–64	N. S. Khrushchev
1964–	A. N. Kosygin

Presidents (Chairmen of Presidium of the U.S.S.R. Supreme Soviet)

1936–46	M. I. Kalinin
1946–53	N. M. Shvernik
1953–60	K. Y. Voroshilov
1960–64	L. I. Brezhnev
1964–65	A. I. Mikoyan
1965–	N. V. Podgorny

[8] For further details see Michael T. Florinsky, ed., *Encyclopedia of Russia and the Soviet Union* (New York: McGraw-Hill, 1961); Robert Maxwell, ed., *Information U.S.S.R.* (New York: Pergamon, 1962); and *International Who's Who* (London: Europa, annually).
[9] Until 1946 ministers were called commissars.

THE SOVIET UNION (cont.)

Party Congresses

First	1898	Minsk
Second	1903	Brussels
Third	1905	London
Fourth	1906	Stockholm
Fifth	1907	London
Sixth	1917	Petrograd
Seventh–Fourteenth	1918–25	Moscow
Fifteenth	1927	
Sixteenth	1930	
Seventeenth	1934	
Eighteenth	1939	
Nineteenth	1952	
Twentieth	1956	
Twenty-first	1959	
Twenty-second	1961	
Twenty-third	1966	

Supreme Soviet[10]

SOVIET OF NATIONALITIES	Deputies		Total
15 union republics	32 each	480	
20 autonomous republics	11 each	220	
8 autonomous regions	5 each	40	
10 national areas	1 each	10	
			750
SOVIET OF THE UNION			
Total from all districts			
of 300,000 inhabitants			767
			1,517

[10] The elections are held every four years. In 1966 over 143,000,000 people (over 99 percent of the registered electorate) voted. Over 99 percent of the votes cast were for the candidates nominated.

YUGOSLAVIA[11]

President and Vice-Presidents[12]

	PRESIDENT	VICE-PRESIDENTS	
1953–	Tito (Josip Broz)	1953–63	E. Kardelj
		1953–66	A. Rankovic
		1966	K. Popovic

Presidents of the Federal Assembly[13]

1963–67	E. Kardelj
1967–	M. Popovic

Presidents of the Federal Executive Council (Prime Ministers)

1963–67	P. Stambolic
1967–	M. Spiljak

[11] Frequent changes in the organization of Yugoslavia's political institutions including the Communist party, make adequate tabular analysis difficult. For example, Marshal Tito became prime minister in 1945 and president in 1953. The office of prime minister was abolished in 1953 and then restored in 1963 with the additional title of president of the Federal Executive Council but without its original prestige. The data here, gleaned from a variety of sources, is incomplete and an oversimplification of a complex polity.

[12] The president is elected by the Federal Assembly. The office of vice-president was abolished by the Federal Assembly in 1966.

[13] The holder of this office was made deputy to the president by the Federal Assembly in 1966.

YUGOSLAVIA (cont.)

Federal Assembly[14]

FIVE CHAMBERS	
Federal	190 members including 120 elected from communes
Chamber of Nationalities[15]	70 members delegated by the 6 republican and 2 provincial assemblies
Economic Education and Culture Social Welfare and Health Organizational-Political	} 120 members each from communes

League of Communists[16]

President	Tito
Presidium of the Central Committee	35 veteran party leaders[17]
Executive Committee of the Central Committee	11 members, none holding government offices (Secretary: M. Todorovic)[18]

Party Congresses

First	1919	Belgrade
Second	1920	Vukovar
Third	1926	Vienna
Fourth	1928	Dresden
Fifth	1948	Belgrade
Sixth	1952	Zagreb
Seventh	1958	Ljubljana
Eighth	1964	Belgrade
Ninth	1968	

[14] Reorganized in 1963. The Federal Assembly is elected for a four-year term, half of the members being elected every two years. No member is eligible for a second consecutive term in the same chamber.

[15] Deputies to the Chamber of Nationalities are full members of the Federal Chamber but in addition meet separately in cases prescribed by the constitution.

[16] Reorganized in 1966 after a forty-man commission under the chairmanship of M. Todorovic was appointed by the Central Committee to conduct an inquiry.

[17] Including E. Kardelj, K. Popovic, M. Popovic, and P. Stambolic.

[18] The secretaries of the Executive Committees of the League of Communists in the six Republics to be included.

CHINA

The Central Committee of the Chinese Communist Party

CHAIRMAN		SECRETARY-GENERAL	
1943–	Mao Tse-tung	1954–	Teng Hsiao-ping[19]

Chairmen of the People's Republic of China

1949–58	Mao Tse-tung
1959–	Lio Shao-chi[19]

Chairman of the Council of Ministers (Prime Minister)

1949–	Chou En-lai

National People's Congresses

First	1954
Second	1959
Third	1964

CHAIRMEN (SPEAKERS)
OF THE STANDING COMMITTEE

1954–59	Liu Shao-chi
1959–	Chu Teh

[19] Severely criticized by the Red Guards during the Great Proletarian Revolution of 1966–67.

CHINA (cont.)

1964 National People's Congress

1	deputy for every 400,000 inhabitants in provinces and autonomous regions (a minimum of ten deputies from each)
1	deputy for every 50,000 inhabitants in large cities
300	deputies elected by national minorities
120	deputies elected by the armed forces
30	deputies elected by the overseas Chinese
3,040	deputies elected to the 1964 National People's Congress

National Party Congresses

First	1921	Shanghai
Second	1922	Shanghai
Third	1923	Canton
Fourth	1925	Canton
Fifth	1927	Wuhan
Sixth	1928	Moscow
Seventh	1945	Yenan
Eighth	1956 and 1958	Peking (two sessions)

RECOMMENDED READING

In response to many requests we have compiled the following list of readings, which includes standard works, stimulating interpretations, introductions, and occasionally the only book on the subject. Many excellent works had to be excluded, particularly on topics that are well covered. We have included several of our own books not out of vanity but for the benefit of those readers who would like to examine our ideas in greater detail.

Many books are published simultaneously in several countries, but as a general rule we have listed the American publisher for the benefit of our American readers. Non-American readers should note that many of the books were initially published elsewhere and outside the United States may, owing to copyright, have to be purchased from a different publisher. In Canada, for example, a book may have to be purchased from a Canadian or British or American publisher, depending on the copyright.

Introduction: The European Heritage

An interesting interpretation of recent world history is to be found in Hugh Seton-Watson's *Neither War nor Peace* (New York: Praeger, 1960).

For examples of recent influential writings in the field of comparative politics see Frank Munger, ed., *Studies in Comparative Politics* (New York: T. Y. Crowell, 1967). For an excellent survey of theories of comparative politics see Eckstein's introduction in Harry Eckstein and David E. Apter, *Comparative Politics* (New York: Free Press, 1963). Gabriel Almond is one of the most influential writers in this field, and the most recent summary of his views is to be found in Gabriel A. Almond and G. Bingham Powell, *Comparative Politics* (Boston: Little, Brown, 1966).

Earlier comparative studies are Roy Macridis, *The Study of Comparative Government* (New York: Random House, 1955); Gunnar Heckscher, *The Study of Comparative Government and Politics* (New York: Macmillan, 1958); and Douglas V. Verney, *The Analysis of Political Systems* (New York: Free Press, 1960).

PART ONE
THE LIBERAL DEMOCRATIC PATTERN

1 Principles

THE UNITED STATES

A good theoretical approach is Louis Hartz, *The Liberal Tradition in America* (New York: Harcourt, Brace & World, 1955). An interesting recent history is Frank Thistlethwaite, *The Great Experiment* (London: Cambridge University Press, 1955). See also D. W. Brogan, *Politics in America* (New York: Harper & Row, 1954).

GREAT BRITAIN

There is a stimulating discussion of British political ideas in Samuel H. Beer, *British Politics in the Collectivist Age* (New York: Knopf, 1965).

For a brief discussion of political principles see Douglas V. Verney, *British Government and Politics: Life Without a Declaration of Independence* (New York: Harper & Row, 1966). A good introduction to contemporary Britain is Anthony Sampson, *Anatomy of Britain Today* (New York: Harper & Row, 1966). For an earlier study see D. W. Brogan, *The English People* (New York: Knopf, 1943).

FRANCE

For the Third Republic see D. W. Brogan, *France Under the Republic: The Development of Modern France (1870–1939)*, rev. ed. (New York: Harper & Row, 1965). For the Fourth see Philip M. Williams, *Crisis and Compromise: Politics in the Fourth Republic*, 3rd ed. (Hamden, Conn.: Shoe String Press, 1964). A recent analysis is Stanley S. Hoffman, and others, *In Search of France* (Cambridge, Mass.: Harvard University Press, 1965).

SWEDEN

The best introduction to contemporary Swedish government is Nils Andrén, *Modern Swedish Government*, 2nd ed. (Stockholm: Almqvist and Wiksell, 1968). For an earlier appreciation see Nils Herlitz, *Sweden: A Modern Democracy on Ancient Foundations* (Minneapolis: University of Minnesota Press, 1939). There is a comparison of the Swedish, American, French, and British political systems in Douglas V. Verney, *Parliamentary Reform in Sweden 1866–1921* (Oxford: Clarendon Press, 1957), Ch. 13.

2 Political Process

Groups

The most comprehensive study is Henry W. Ehrmann, ed., *Interest Groups on Four Continents* (Pittsburgh: University of Pittsburgh Press, 1958). Other studies of general interest are Seymour M. Lipset, *Political Man: The Social Bases of Politics* (Garden City, N.Y.: Doubleday, 1959), and William Kornhauser, *The Politics of Mass Society* (New York: Free Press, 1959).

Parties

Two European classics are Maurice Duverger, *Political Parties* (New York: Wiley, 1963), and Robert Michels, *Political Parties* (New York: Free Press, 1966). The main American work is Sigmund Neumann, ed., *Modern Political Parties* (Chicago: University of Chicago Press, 1955).

Political behavior

The most ambitious comparative study is Gabriel A. Almond and Sidney Verba, *The Civic Culture: Political Attitudes and Democracy in Five Nations* (Boston: Little, Brown, 1965). Another comparative study, more limited in scope, is Robert R. Alford, *Party and Society: The Anglo-American Democracies* (Chicago: Rand McNally, 1963).

THE UNITED STATES

The best general study is probably still V. O. Key, *Politics, Parties, and Pressure Groups*, 5th ed. (New York: T. Y. Crowell, 1964). On this subject see also David B. Truman, *The Governmental Process: Political Interests and Public Opinion* (New York: Knopf, 1951). Among recent studies of groups is Harman Zeigler, *Interest Groups in American Society* (Englewood Cliffs, N.J.: Prentice-Hall, 1964). The standard work on parties is Wilfred E. Binkley, *American Political Parties* (New York: Knopf, 1962), but a more analytical approach is that contained in James MacGregor Burns, *The Deadlock of Democracy: Four-Party Politics in America* (Englewood Cliffs, N.J.: Prentice-Hall, 1963). For a scholarly analysis of American voting behavior see Angus Campbell and others, *The American Voter* (New York: Wiley, 1960). For a more popular account see Theodore H. White, *The Making of the President, 1960* (New York: Atheneum, 1961). Two influential books on American society are David Riesman, *The Lonely Crowd* (New Haven, Conn.: Yale University Press, 1950), and William H. Whyte, Jr., *The Organization Man* (New York: Simon and Schuster, 1956).

GREAT BRITAIN

Richard Rose, *Politics in England* (Boston: Little, Brown, 1964), analyzes the British political process in an American theoretical framework. For groups see S. E. Finer, *Anonymous Empire: A Study of the Lobby in Great Britain* (London: Pall Mall, 1958), and W. L. Guttsman, *The British Political Elite* (London: MacGibbon & Kee, 1963). The standard work on parties is Robert T. McKenzie, *British Political Parties*, 2nd ed. (New York: Praeger, 1963). For the Conservative party, see J. D. Hoffman, *The Conservative Party Opposition, 1945–51* (London: MacGibbon & Kee, 1964). For the Labour party see Ralph Miliband, *Parliamentary Socialism: A Study in the Politics of the Labour Party* (London: Merlin, 1964). David Butler has published books on the British general elections of 1951, 1955, 1959 (with Richard Rose), 1964 (with A. S. King), and 1966 (with A. S. King) (New York: St. Martin's Press, 1952, 1956, 1960, 1965, and 1967).

FRANCE

Herbert Luthy, *France Against Herself* (New York: Praeger, 1955) is a useful general introduction. Dorothy Pickles, *The Fifth Republic: Institutions and Politics*, 3rd ed. (New York: Praeger, 1966), stresses the political process as does Philip M. Williams, *Crisis and Compromise*, 3rd ed. (Hamden, Conn.: Shoe String Press, 1964). On interest groups see Jean Meynaud, *Les Groupes de pression en France* (Paris: Colin, 1962). There is a section on France by Georges Lavau in Henry W. Ehrmann, ed., *Interest Groups on Four Continents*. Bernard E. Brown has discussed pressure groups in the Fourth Republic in "Pressure Politics in France," *Journal of Politics*, XVIII, 4 (1956), 702–19. See also his "Pressure Politics in the Fifth Republic," *Journal of Politics*, XXV, 3 (1963), 509–25. For an exploration of French elections see Peter Campbell, *French Electoral Systems and Elections Since 1789*, 2nd ed. (London: Faber and Faber, 1965).

SWEDEN

The standard American work on the Swedish political process is Dankwart A. Rustow, *The Politics of Compromise* (Princeton, N.J.: Princeton University Press, 1955). Gunnar Heckscher describes Swedish groups in Henry W. Ehrmann, ed., *Interest Groups on Four Continents*. On Swedish political behavior see Herbert Tingsten "Stability and Vitality in Swedish Democracy," *Political Quarterly* XXVI, 2 (1955), 140–51, reprinted in Nelson W. Polsby, Robert A. Dentler, and Paul A. Smith, *Politics and Social Life* (Boston: Houghton Mifflin, 1963). Tingsten presented a pioneering study, *Political Behavior*, in 1937, reprinted in 1963 by Bedminster Press, Totowa, N.J.

3 Government

Two interesting books on the presidency are James MacGregor Burns, *Presidential Government: The Crucible of Leadership* (Boston: Houghton Mifflin, 1965), and Richard E. Neustadt, *Presidential Power: The Politics of Leadership* (New York: Wiley, 1960). On Congress there is Bertram M. Gross, *The Legislative Struggle* (New York: McGraw-Hill, 1953), and David B. Truman, ed., *The Congress and America's Future* (Englewood Cliffs, N.J.: Prentice-Hall, 1965). For a concise volume on both the executive and legislative branches of government see Nelson W. Polsby, *Congress and the Presidency* (Englewood Cliffs, N.J.: Prentice-Hall, 1964).

GREAT BRITAIN

The best introduction is Herbert Morrison, *Government and Parliament*, 3rd ed. (London: Oxford University Press, 1964). The standard works are W. I. Jennings, *Cabinet Government* (London: Cambridge University Press, 1959), and *Parliament*, 2nd ed. (London: Cambridge University Press, 1959). More recently there is John P. Mackintosh, *The British Cabinet* (London: Stevens, 1962). For criticism see Bernard Crick, *Reform of Parliament* (London: Weidenfeld & Nicolson, 1964), and Andrew Hill and Anthony Wichelow, *What's Wrong with Parliament?* (Harmondsworth, Eng.: Penguin, 1964).

FRANCE

To gain insight into contemporary France it is necessary to study de Gaulle either through his war memoirs, *The Complete War Memoirs of Charles De Gaulle* (New York: Simon and Schuster, 1967), or through biographies by writers such as Robert Aron, *An Explanation of De Gaulle* (New York: Harper & Row, 1966), or François Mauriac, *De Gaulle* (Garden City, N.Y.: Doubleday, 1966). For the Third and Fourth Republics see D. W. S. Lidderdale, *The Parliament of France* (London: Hansard, 1951), and Nathan Leites, *On the Game of Politics in France* (Stanford, Calif.: Stanford University Press, 1959).

SWEDEN

In addition to the studies already mentioned there is Elis Håstad, *The Parliament of Sweden* (London: Hansard, 1957). Many excellent scholarly works remain untranslated from the Swedish, notably a seventeen-volume work on the Swedish Parliament published to celebrate the Riksdag's quincentenary in 1935.

Note on constitutions:

The constitution is of some importance for well-established liberal democracies. A useful compendium is Amos J. Peaslee, ed., *Constitutions of the Nations*, 2nd ed. (The Hague: Nijhoff, 1956), 3 vols.

4 Social and Economic Planning

GENERAL

On social policy see T. H. Marshall, *Social Policy* (London: Hutchinson, 1965). There are several compilations of world-wide statistics of which the annual *Statistical Yearbook* (New York: United Nations Publications) is the most useful. In addition, see Bruce M. Russett and others, *World Handbook of Political and Social Indicators* (New Haven, Conn.: Yale University Press, 1964), and Arthur S. Banks and Robert B. Textor, *A Cross-Polity Survey* (Cambridge, Mass.: M.I.T. Press, 1963). For a general discussion of economic policy see Andrew Shonfield, *Modern Capitalism: The Changing Balance of Public and Private Power* (London: Oxford University Press, 1965).

THE UNITED STATES

On social policy there is Leonard H. Goodman, ed., *Economic Progress and Social Welfare* (New York: Columbia University Press, 1966). A classic on social security is Eveline M. Burns, *Social Security and Public Policy* (New York: McGraw-Hill, 1956). Two influential books are Michael Harrington, *The Other America: Poverty in the United States* (New York: Macmillan, 1962), and John K. Galbraith, *The New Industrial State* (Boston: Houghton Mifflin, 1967). On medical care there is Herman M. Somers and Anne R. Somers, *Doctors, Patients, and Health Insurance* (Washington, D.C.: Brookings Institution, 1961).

A standard work on the American economy is Merle Fainsod, Lincoln Gordon, and Joseph C. Palamountain, Jr., *Government and the American Economy*, 3rd ed. (New York: Norton, 1959). There is also Emmette S. Redford, *American Government and the Economy* (New York: Macmillan, 1965).

GREAT BRITAIN

The standard work on the social services is M. Penelope Hall, *The Social Services of Modern England*, 4th ed. (London: Routledge and Kegan Paul, 1964). A stimulating discussion of social policy is Richard M. Titmuss, *Essays on the Welfare State*, 2nd ed. (London: Allen & Unwin, 1963). Two books on the immigration problem are Paul Foot, *Immigration and Race in British Politics* (Baltimore: Penguin, 1965), and Richard Hooper, ed., *Colour in Britain* (London: British Broadcasting Corporation [Publications Management], 1965).

On the economy see J. W. Grove, *Government and Industry in Britain* (London: Longmans, Green, 1962). On nationalization there is William A. Robson, *Nationalized Industry and Public Ownership*, rev. ed. (London: Allen & Unwin, 1962), and A. H. Hanson, *Parliament and Public Ownership* (New York: Oxford University Press, 1961); 2nd ed. (London: Cassell, 1962).

FRANCE

For social policy see *Social Security in France* (Paris: Ministry of Labor and Social Security, 1965), and Wallace C. Peterson, *The Welfare State in France* (Lincoln: University of Nebraska Press, 1960).

For a description of French public policy see F. F. Ridley and Jean Blondel, *Public Administration in France* (London: Routledge and Kegan Paul, 1964). On the economy see John B. Sheahan, *Promotion and Control of Industry in Postwar France* (Cambridge, Mass.: Harvard University Press, 1963).

SWEDEN

For a discussion of the Ombudsman see Donald C. Rowat, *The Ombudsman* (London: Allen & Unwin, 1965). On the economy see Douglas V. Verney, *Public Enterprise in Sweden* (Liverpool: University Press of Liverpool, 1959). For a discussion of social policy see Swedish Social Welfare Board, *Social Sweden* (London: Allen & Unwin, 1953).

5 International Role

THE UNITED STATES

For a general survey see John W. Spanier, *American Foreign Policy Since World War II*, 2nd rev. ed. (New York: Praeger, 1965). An illuminating book is Gabriel A. Almond, *The American People and Foreign Policy* (New York: Harcourt, Brace & World, 1950). One of the most influential books has been Henry A. Kissinger, *Nuclear Weapons and Foreign Policy* (Garden City, N.Y.: Doubleday, 1958).

GREAT BRITAIN

Britain's new role is discussed in F. S. Northedge, *British Foreign Policy: The Process of Readjustment, 1945–1961* (London: Allen & Unwin, 1962). On the decline of the British empire see John Strachey, *The End of Empire* (New York: Random House, 1960). On Britain and the United States see Harry C. Allen, *The Anglo-American Pre-*

dicament (New York: St. Martin's Press, 1960), and H. G. Nicholas, *Britain and the United States* (London: Chatto & Windus, 1963). Britain and Europe are discussed in Uwe Kitzinger, *Britain, Europe and Beyond* (Leyden, Netherlands: Sythoff, 1965).

FRANCE

A general work is Alfred Grosser, *French Foreign Policy Under De Gaulle* (Boston: Little, Brown, 1967). On France and Europe see Miriam Camps, *What Kind of Europe?* (New York: Oxford University Press, 1965), and Frank R. Willis, *France, Germany, and the New Europe, 1945–1963* (Stanford, Calif.: Stanford University Press, 1965).

SWEDEN

Swedish neutrality is evident from Herbert Tingsten, *The Debate on the Foreign Policy of Sweden, 1918–1939* (London: Oxford University Press, 1950).

PART TWO
THE COMMUNIST PATTERN

6   Principles

THE SOVIET UNION

A readable introduction to Soviet communism is provided by R. N. Carew-Hunt, *The Theory and Practice of Communism* (Harmondsworth, Eng.: Penguin, 1963). A more theoretical analysis is found in John Plamenatz, *German Marxism and Russian Communism* (London: Longmans, Green, 1954). For recent developments see Robert C. Tucker, *The Soviet Political Mind* (New York: Praeger, 1963).

YUGOSLAVIA

A polemical attack on Yugoslav communism—and communism generally—is provided by Milovan Djilas, *The New Class: An Analysis of the Communist System* (New York: Praeger, 1957).

CHINA

For the principles underlying Chinese communism see John Wilson Lewis, *Major Doctrines of Communist China* (New York: Norton, 1964), and Stuart R. Schram, *The Political Thought of Mao Tse-tung* (New York: Praeger, 1963).

7 Political Process

THE SOVIET UNION

A useful series of case studies is Alexander Dallin and Alan F. Westin, eds., *Politics in the Soviet Union: 7 Cases* (New York: Harcourt, Brace & World, 1966). On an important segment of Soviet society see Richard Pipes, ed., *The Russian Intelligentsia* (New York: Columbia University Press, 1961). For a general interpretation of the Communist party see Alfred Meyer, *The Soviet Political System* (New York: Random House, 1965). A scholarly analysis of the party is provided by Leonard Schapiro, *The Communist Party of the Soviet Union* (New York: Random House, 1960). There are descriptions of life in the Soviet Union in Alex Inkeles and Raymond A. Bauer, *The Soviet Citizen* (Cambridge, Mass.: Harvard University Press, 1959), and Geoffrey Wheeler, *Racial Problems in Soviet Muslim Asia* (London: Oxford University Press, 1960).

YUGOSLAVIA

The best general work is George W. Hoffman and Fred W. Neal, *Yugoslavia and the New Communism* (New York: Twentieth Century Fund, 1962).

CHINA

The best general work is Herbert Franz Schurmann, *Ideology and Organization in Communist China* (Berkeley: University of California Press, 1966).

8 Government

THE SOVIET UNION

The standard work is Merle Fainsod, *How Russia Is Ruled*, 2nd ed. (Cambridge, Mass.: Harvard University Press, 1963). On Stalin, consult Isaac Deutscher, *Stalin: A Political Biography*, 2nd ed. (New York: Oxford University Press, 1967), and Leon Trotsky, *Stalin: An Appraisal of the Man and His Influence*, ed. and trans. Charles Malamuth (New York: Harper & Row, 1941). For Khrushchev's secret speech see Bertram D. Wolfe, *Khrushchev and Stalin's Ghost* (New York: Praeger, 1956). For the Khrushchev era see Carl A. Linden, *Khrushchev and the Soviet Leadership, 1957–1964* (Baltimore: Johns Hopkins Press, 1966).

YUGOSLAVIA

Yugoslavia is ably treated in the context of eastern Europe in

Harold Gordon Skilling, *The Governments of Communist East Europe* (New York: T. Y. Crowell, 1966).

The crucial leadership issue in China is dealt with in John Wilson Lewis, *Leadership in Communist China* (Ithaca, N.Y.: Cornell University Press, 1963).

9 Economic and Social Planning

For an introduction to Soviet economic policy see Harry G. Schwartz, *The Soviet Economy Since Stalin* (Philadelphia: Lippincott, 1965). The Soviet entrepreneur is described in David Granick, *The Red Executive* (Garden City, N.Y.: Doubleday, 1960). At a more theoretical level there is P. J. D. Wiles, *The Political Economy of Communism* (Cambridge, Mass.: Harvard University Press, 1963). On social policy see U. S. Social Security Administration, A *Report on Social Security Programs in the Soviet Union* (Washington, D.C.: U. S. Government Printing Office, 1960). For a study of Soviet policy based on captured documents see Merle Fainsod, *Smolensk Under Soviet Rule* (Cambridge, Mass.: Harvard University Press, 1958).

A useful introduction to Yugoslavia and its policies is Phyllis Auty, *Yugoslavia* (New York: Walker, 1965).

Articles from *China Quarterly* are reproduced in Roderick MacFarquhar, ed., *China Under Mao: Politics Takes Command* (Cambridge, Mass.: M.I.T. Press, 1966).

10 International Role

On the communist states generally see Harold Gordon Skilling, *Communism, National and International* (Toronto: University of Toronto Press, 1965), and Adam Bromke, ed., *The Communist States at the Crossroads* (New York: Praeger, 1965).

On foreign policy see George F. Kennan, *Russia and the West Under Lenin and Stalin* (Boston: Little, Brown, 1961); Philip E.

Mosely, ed., *The Kremlin and World Politics* (New York: Vintage, 1960); and Marshall Shulman, *Beyond the Cold War* (New Haven, Conn.: Yale University Press, 1966).

YUGOSLAVIA

A recent work is John Coert Campbell, *Tito's Separate Road: America and Yugoslavia in World Politics* (New York: Harper & Row, 1967).

CHINA

For documentation of the conflict with the Soviet Union see William E. Griffith, *The Sino-Soviet Rift* (Cambridge, Mass.: M.I.T. Press, 1964), and his *Sino-Soviet Relations, 1964–1965* (Cambridge, Mass.: M.I.T. Press, 1967). A recent biography of considerable interest is Stuart R. Schram, *Mao Tse-tung* (New York: Simon and Schuster, 1967).

THE COMMUNIST BLOC

The best study of what used to be called the Soviet bloc is Zbigniew K. Brzezinski, *The Soviet Bloc: Unity and Conflict*, rev. ed. (Cambridge, Mass.: Harvard University Press, 1967).

Conclusion: Implications for New States

On developing areas see Gabriel A. Almond and James S. Coleman, eds., *The Politics of the Developing Areas* (Princeton, N.J.: Princeton University Press, 1960), and Lucian W. Pye and Sidney Verba, *Political Culture and Political Development* (Princeton, N.J.: Princeton University Press, 1965).

Another developmental study is Joseph LaPalombara, ed., *Bureaucracy and Political Development* (Princeton, N.J.: Princeton University Press, 1965). A Soviet view is provided by Thomas Perry Thornton, ed., *The Third World in Soviet Perspective* (Princeton, N.J.: Princeton University Press, 1964).

Among other approaches that offer implications for the new states are Hannah Arendt, *The Origins of Totalitarianism*, new rev. ed. (New York: Harcourt, Brace & World, 1966); John Plamenatz, *On Alien Rule and Self-Government* (London: Longmans, Green, 1960); Ferrell Heady, *Public Administration: A Comparative Perspective* (Englewood Cliffs, N.J.: Prentice-Hall, 1966); and Zbigniew K. Brzezinski and Samuel P. Huntington, *Political Power: U.S.A./U.S.S.R.* (New York: Viking Press, 1964).

INDEX

China (*Cont.*)
istry of, 192–93; party congresses in, 259; political power in, 194–95; press in, 183–84; prime minister of, 258

Chou En-lai, 192

Churchill, Randolph, 75

Churchill, Winston, 66, 73–74, 75

Civil service, 91–96; in France, 59, 94–95; in Great Britain, 92–93; in India, 92; in Sweden, 95–96; in totalitarian systems, 94; in United States, 93–94

Class structure. See Social structure

Class struggle, 144, 196

Cold War, 11, 223, 244

Collective bargaining, 33, 125

Collective farms, 163, 205–06

Collectivization: in Poland, 165; in Soviet Union, 164, 204–07; in Yugoslavia, 167, 212

Comecon, 224, 226

Cominform, 151, 224

Commissariat du Plan, 122

Commissions for Foreign Affairs (U.S.S.R.), 222

Common Market. See European Economic Community

Commonwealth Immigrants Act, 13

Communes: in China, 167–68; in Soviet Union, 206

Communism, 129, 143–55, 229; in China, 151, 152–54; and economic growth, 236–41; establishment of, 149–54; and government, 186–200; ideology of, 148–49; and intelligentsia, 168–73; international aspects of, 154–55, 220–27; and peasants, 162–68; and revolution, 143–48; and social groups, 156–73, 242–44; and socialization, 201–04; stability of, 146–48, 197–200; weaknesses of, 239–40, 242; and welfare state, 214–19; and working class, 160–62; in Yugoslavia, 151–52

Communist party: of China, 176; and democratic centralism, 177–79; and elections, 180–82; of France, 47–48, 59; and occupational groups, 156–57; organization of, 174–77, 186–200; and peasantry, 164; policy formed by, 186–87, 194; power structure of, 191; of Soviet Union, 146–48,

156–57, 164, 173–75, 191; of Sweden, 50; of Yugoslavia, 175–76

Confederation of British Industry, 29

Congress (U.S.), 46, 47, 54, 70, 72, 195, 196, 250

Conservatism, 37, 38, 99, 101, 232

Conservative party: of France, 37, 47, 48; of Great Britain, 27–28, 42–43, 75; of Sweden, 50, 51, 52, 58

Constituent Assembly (U.S.S.R.), 163

Constitution, 88–90; of China, 157, 178; of Communist party, 168; of France, 63, 64, 83, 85, 86, 87; of Great Britain, 77; of Soviet Union, 145, 148, 157, 164, 173, 187; of Sweden, 64, 68; of United States, 63

Constitutional Court (France), 87

Constitutional Democratic party (U.S.S.R.), 150

Constitutional monarchies, 22, 62–63, 88–89

Continental Congress, 21, 63

Cortes, 232

Council of Economic Advisers (U.S.), 120

Council of Ministers: in China, 192; in Soviet Union, 190–91, 194

Council of Nationalities (Yugoslavia), 188, 199

Council of Producers (Yugoslavia), 152, 188

Council of the Republic (France), 85

Council of State (France), 95

Crimean War, 147

Cripps, Stafford, 74

Cromwell, Oliver, 36

Cross-voting, 54

Crown: dissolution power of, 61; and foreign affairs, 138; sovereignty of, 62–65

Cuba, 14, 224

Curia, 158

Curzon, George, 78

Czechoslovakia, 10, 151

Darwin, Charles, 102

Declaration of Independence, 23

Declaration of the Rights of Man, 23

D 1
E 2
F 3
G 4
H 5
I 6
J 7